Typographic Design:
Form and Communication

Second Edition

P9-CLS-610

"The whole duty of typography,
 as with calligraphy,
 is to communicate to the imagination,
 without loss by the way,
 the thought or image
 intended to be communicated
 by the Author."

Thomas James Cobden-Sanderson

St. Barbara. Polychromed
walnut sculpture, Fifteenth-
century German or French,
The Virginia Museum of
Fine Arts

Typographic Design:
Form and Communication

Second Edition

Rob Carter

Ben Day

Philip Meggs

VNR
Van Nostrand Reinhold
New York

Copyright © 1993 by Van Nostrand Reinhold

Library of Congress Catalog Card Number 92-21405
ISBN 0-442-00759-0

All rights reserved. No part of this work covered by the copyright hereon may be reproduced or used in any form or by any means—graphic, electronic, or mechanical, including photocopying, recording, taping, or information storage and retrieval systems—without the written permission of the publisher.

I⟨T⟩P Van Nostrand Reinhold is an International Thomson Publishing company.
       ITP logo is a trademark under license.

Printed in the United States of America

Van Nostrand Reinhold
115 Fifth Avenue
New York, NY 10003

International Thomson Publishing GmbH
Königswinterer Str. 418
53227 Bonn
Germany

International Thomson Publishing
Berkshire House,168-173
High Holborn, London WC1V 7AA
England

International Thomson Publishing Asia
221 Henderson Bldg. #05-10
Singapore 0315

Thomas Nelson Australia
102 Dodds Street
South Melbourne 3205
Victoria, Australia

International Thomson Publishing Japan
Kyowa Building, 3F
2-2-1 Hirakawacho
Chiyoda-Ku, Tokyo 102
Japan

Nelson Canada
1120 Birchmount Road
Scarborough, Ontario
M1K 5G4, Canada

COUWF 16 15 14 13 12 11 10 9 8 7 6 5 4 3

Library of Congress Cataloging-in-Publication Data
Carter, Rob.
    Typographic design: Form and communication / Rob Carter,
Ben Day, Philip Meggs.—2nd ed.
        p.   cm.
    Includes bibliography (p.   ) and index.
    ISBN 0-442-00759-0
    1. Printing, Practical—Style manuals. 2. Printing, Practical
Layout. I. Day, Ben. II. Meggs, Philip B. III. Title.
Z253.C32   1993
686.2'24—dc20   92-21405
                                            CIP

For Sally, Melanie, and Libby

Introduction

While typography has changed and expanded during the past two decades, the resource materials available today do not reflect the nature and scope of typographic design in our times. It is the authors' intention to provide a concise, yet comprehensive overview of the fundamental information necessary for effective typographic-design practice. A knowledge of form and communication encompasses a range of subjects, including our typographic heritage, letterform anatomy, visual organization, and the interface between form and meaning.

In addition to these fundamentals, this volume presents other topics critical to informed design practice. Recent research provides the designer with an expanded awareness of legibility factors, enabling increased communicative clarity. Technological complexity requires comprehension of earlier and current typesetting processes, for both affect the language of typography. Theoretical and structural problem-solving approaches, evolved by design educators, reveal underlying concepts. Case studies in applied problem solving demonstrate a knowledge of typographic form and communication. An understanding of typographic classification and form subtlety is gained from the study of type specimens.

Through the seven chapters of this book, the authors share a compilation of information and examples with practitioners and students. It yields both insights and inspiration, bringing order to the complex and diversified subject of typographic design.

Contents

Typography is an intensely visual form of communication. Because this visible language communicates thoughts and information through human sight, its history is presented here in chronological visual form on four timelines. This evolution is shown in the context of world events, architectural development, and art history.

The first timeline predates typography. It begins with the invention of writing over five thousand years ago and ends with the invention of movable type in Europe during the middle of the fifteenth century. The second timeline covers the long era of the handpress and handset metal types. This period, from Gutenberg's invention of movable type to the end of the eighteenth century, lasted about three hundred and fifty years. In the third timeline, the Industrial Revolution and nineteenth century are revealed as an era of technological innovation accompanied by an outpouring of new typographic forms. The fourth timeline begins with the year 1900 and continues until the present. The aesthetic concerns of modernism, the need for functional communication, and technical progress have shaped twentieth-century typographic design.

From the origins of writing to Gutenberg's invention of movable type: 3150 B.C.–A.D. 1450

Note: Picture credits and further descriptive information for timeline illustrations start on page 271.

1.
c. 3150 B.C.: The earliest written documents are impressed clay tablets from Sumer. The signs represent clay tokens, which were used for record keeping before the invention of writing.

2.
c. 3000 B.C.: Cuneiform, the earliest writing system, consisting of wedge-shaped marks on clay tablets, was invented by the Sumerians.

2500 B.C.: Egyptians begin to make papyrus, a new writing material derived from the stems of the papyrus plant.

3.
c. 2600 B.C.: Completion of the pyramids at Giza, Egypt.

4.
c. 2400 B.C.: False-door stele inscribed with hieroglyphic writing, from Old Kingdom Egypt.

5.
c. 2100 B.C.: Cuneiform tablet listing expenditures of grain and animals.

6.
c. 1800–1400 B.C.: Stonehenge, a megalithic monument of thirty-foot-tall stones set into circular patterns.

7.
c. 1570–1349 B.C.: Polychromed wood sculpture from New Kingdom Egypt, with hieroglyphic inscriptions.

8.
c. 1450 B.C.: Detail, *The Book of the Dead* of Tuthmosis III, hieroglyphic writing on papyrus.

c. 3150 B.C.

1.

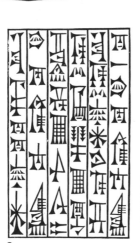

2.

5.

7.

3.

4.

6.

2

9.
c. 1500 B.C.: The twenty-two characters of the Phoenician alphabet.

c. 800 B.C.: Homer writes the *Iliad* and *Odyssey*.

540 B.C.: The first public library is established in Athens, Greece.

10.
389 B.C.: Inscription in the Phoenician alphabet on a fragment of a marble bowl.

11.
Fourth Century B.C.: Greek manuscript writing.

12.
448–432 B.C.: The Parthenon, temple of the goddess Athena, on the Acropolis in Athens, Greece.

13.
414–413 B.C.: Fragment of a Greek record of sale, carved on stone.

c. 160 B.C.: Parchment, a new writing material made from animal skins, is developed in the Greek state of Pergamum.

44 B.C.: Julius Caesar is murdered.

14.
c. 50 B.C.–A.D. 500: Roman square capitals (*capitalis quadrata*) were carefully written with a flat pen.

c. A.D. 33: Crucifixion of Christ.

15.
c. 79: Brush writing from a wall at Pompeii, preserved by the volcanic eruption of Vesuvius.

105: Ts'ai Lun invents paper in China.

16.
150: The Roman codex, with folded pages, begins to be used alongside the rolled scroll.

16.
c. 100–600: Roman rustic writing (*capitalis rustica*) conserved space by using more condensed letters written with a flat pen held in an almost vertical position.

c. 1500 B.C.

8.

9.

11.

12.

13.

MARTISQ·DOLO

14.

15.

CONNERTANTPRIA
SINMANIBUSUESTRI
VLTROASIAMMAGNO

16.

10.

17.

118–25: The Pantheon, Rome.

18.

Undated: The fluid gestural quality, harmonious proportions, and beautiful forms of Roman writing are effectively translated into the permanent stone carving of monumental capitals (*capitalis monumentalis*).

19.

312–315: Arch of Constantine, Rome. Carved into marble, monumental Roman capitals survived the thousand-year Dark Ages.

325: Emperor Constantine adopts Christianity as the state religion of the Roman Empire.

c. 400–1400: During the thousand-year medieval era, knowledge and learning are kept alive in the Christian monastery, where manuscript books are lettered in the scriptoria.

452: Attila the Hun invades and ravages northern Italy.

476: Emperor Romulus Augustulus, last ruler of the western Roman Empire, is deposed by the Ostrogoths.

20.

533–49: Church of Sant' Apollinare in Classe, Ravenna.

21.

Third–Sixth Centuries: Uncials are rounded, freely drawn majuscule letters, first used by the Greeks as early as the third century B.C.

22.

Third–Ninth Centuries: Half-uncials, a lettering style of the Christian Church, introduces pronounced ascenders and descenders.

23.

Sixth–Ninth Centuries: Insular majuscules, a formal style with exaggerated serifs, was developed by Irish monks from the half-uncials.

A.D. 118

17.

19.

18.

20.

musadquequamuisconsci
mitatisnostraetrepidatio
murtamenfideinestuincit
21.

montuautscm
22.

magnum quoderit
23.

efc quiauremfuperp
27.

732: The Battle of Tours ends the Muslim advance into Europe.

800: Charlemagne is crowned emperor of the Holy Roman Empire by Pope Leo III.

24.

c. 800: Portrait of Christ from *The Book of Kells,* a Celtic manuscript.

868: The earliest extant printed manuscript, the *Diamond Sutra,* is printed in China.

25.

Tenth Century: High Cross at Kells, Meath County, Ireland.

26.

c. Eleventh Century: Round tower on the Rock of Cashel, Tipperary County, Ireland, a lookout and refuge against Viking invaders.

27.

Eighth–Twelfth Centuries: Caroline minuscules became the standard throughout Europe after Charlemagne issued his reform decree of 796, calling for a uniform writing style.

1034: Pi Sheng invents movable type in the Orient.

1096–1099: The First Crusade.

28.

1163–1250: Construction of Notre Dame Cathedral, Paris.

29.

Eleventh–Twelfth Centuries: Early Gothic lettering, a transitional style between Caroline minuscules and Textura, has an increased vertical emphasis.

30.

Twelfth Century: Bronze and copper crucifix from northern Italy.

1215: The Magna Carta grants constitutional liberties in England.

31.

Thirteenth–Fifteenth Centuries: Gothic Textura Quadrata, or Textura, the late Gothic style with rigorous verticality and compressed forms.

1347–1351: First wave of the Black Death, a plague that decimates the European population.

32.

Thirteenth Century: Byzantine School, *Madonna and Child on a Curved Throne.*

A.D. 732

32.

25.

26.

noftro qui feder super thronum et agno. Et omnes angli ftabant i circuitu throni z ceciderunt z adora uerunt deum dicentes. amen. Bñ dictio z claritas z sapientia z gra rum actio. honor z uirtus z fortitu do deo nro in fecla feclorum. amen

31.

early gothic

29.

24.

28.

30.

33.

Thirteenth–Fifteenth Centuries: Rotunda, a more rounded Gothic letter, flourished in southern Europe.

34.

Fourteenth Century: Lippo Memmi, *Saint John the Baptist*.

35.

1420–36: Filippo Brunelleschi, Dome of Florence Cathedral.

1431: Jeanne d'Arc is burned at the stake.

36.

Fifteenth Century: First page of a block-book, *Apocalypse*. Woodblock printing probably appeared in Europe before 1400.

37.

1440–45: Fra Filippo Lippi, *Madonna and Child*.

c. 1450: Johann Gutenberg invents movable type in Mainz, Germany.

38.

c. 1450–55: Page from Gutenberg's 42–line Bible, the first European typographic book.

39.

Woodblock print of the hand-printing press, with compositors setting type from a type-case in the background.

40.

The cathedral in the medieval city of Mainz, Germany

c. 1200

34.

37.

35.

33.

36.

38.

39.

40.

Typography from Gutenberg to the nineteenth century: A.D.1450–1800

The humanist philosophy that flowered during the Renaissance embraced the study of classical literature, a belief in human dignity and worth, a spirit of individualism, and a shift from religious to secular concerns.

1450–1500: Books printed in the first half century of typographic printing are called Incunabula.

41.
1465: Sweynheym and Pannartz, the first type designed in Italy. It had some Roman features.

42.
1467: Sweynheym and Pannartz, the first roman-style type, influenced by Roman inscriptional capitals and manuscripts written in Caroline minuscules.

43.
1470: Nicolas Jenson, early Venetian roman typeface.

44.
1475: William Caxton, typography from the first book printed in the English language.

45.
c. 1485: Filippino Lippi, *Portrait of a Youth*.

46.
1486: Erhard Ratdolt, the earliest known specimen sheet of printing types.

1492: Christopher Columbus lands in America.

47.
c. 1494: Scholar and printer Aldus Manutius established the Aldine Press in Venice to publish works by the great Greek and Roman thinkers.

48.
1495: Francesco Griffo (punch cutter for Aldus Manutius), roman type first used in *De aetna* by Pietro Bembo.

1450

bat ille ihesus: q quom pmū auses uocareꞇ moises figurā psentiens tussit eū ihesum uocari: ut dux militie delectus esset aduersus amalech qui oppugnabant filios israhel: et aduersariū debellaret p nois figuram: et populū m

41.

esse sensum semitas queritur. tanꞇ illi ad cogitandum rheda & quadrigis opus eēt. Democritus quasi in puteo quodam sic alto ut fundus sit nullus: ueritatem iacere demersam nimirum stulte

42.

ab omnipotenti deo missus deus uerbum quasi lucis isi cunctis annūciat. Non hinc aut alrunde: sed undiꝗ cun ad deum uerum: græcos simul et barbaros omnem sexū

43.

In the tyme of pͤ troublous worldꝛ and of the sions beyng andꝛ regnyng as well in the top englondꝛ andꝛ fraunce as in all other places vn

44.

45.

47.

lud admirari ,quod uulgus solet:magnu esse scilicet tantas flammas ,tam immen sos ignes post hominum memoriam sem

48.

46.

49.

1501: Francesco Griffo, the first italic typeface, based on chancery script handwriting.

50.

Home of Albrecht Dürer, Nuremberg, Germany.

51.

Woodblock initial by Geoffroy Tory, who returned to France from study in Italy in 1505, inspired by roman letterforms and Renaissance design ideals.

52.

1523: Lodovico Arrighi, an Italian writing master, introduces his formal chancery italic type.

53.

1517: Martin Luther posts his ninety-five theses on the door of Wittenberg Palace Church, launching the Reformation.

54.

1525: Albrecht Dürer, construction of the letter *B*.

55.

1529: Geoffroy Tory, construction of the letter *B*.

56.

1519–47: Pierre Nepveu, Chateau of Chambord, France.

c. 1480–1561: Claude Garamond, outstanding designer of Old Style typefaces during the French Renaissance.

1501

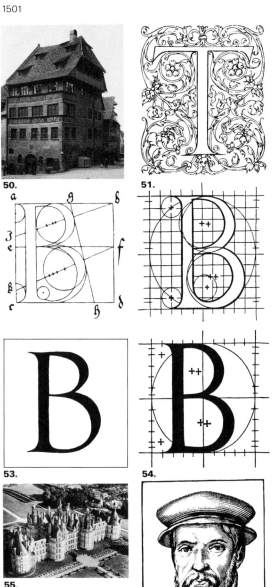

50.

51.

53.

54.

55.

56.

49.

52.

57.

c. 1540: Titian, *Portrait of Cardinal Pietro Bembo.*

1543: Copernicus publishes his theory of the heliocentric solar system.

58.

1544: Simone de Colines, title page with woodcut border.

59.

1546: Jacque Kerver, typography, illustration, and decorative initials which were combined into a rare elegance during the French Renaissance.

60.

after l577: El Greco, *Saint Martin and the Beggar.*

1582: Pope Gregory XIII initiates the Gregorian Calendar, which is still in use.

1584: Sir Walter Raleigh discovers and annexes Virginia.

61.

1595: Johann Theodor de Bry, illustrative initial *E.*

1603: Shakespeare writes *Hamlet.*

62.

1607: Carlo Maderna, facade of St. Peter's, the Vatican.

1609: Regular weekly newspapers appear in Strasbourg, Germany.

63.

1621: Jean Jannon, typefaces upon which twentieth-century Garamonds are based.

64.

1628: The Vatican Press, specimen of roman capitals.

c. 1540

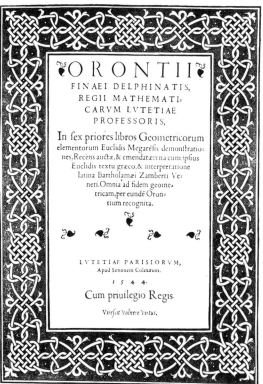

58.

FRANCISCVS

64.

61.

57.

60.

59.

62.

63.

65.
1632–43: The Taj Mahal, India.
66.
c. 1630: Sir Anthony van Dyck, portrait of *Henri II de Lorraine*.

1639: The first printing press in the British Colonies is established in Massachusetts.

1657: First fountain pen is manufactured, in Paris.
67.
c. 1664: Jan Vermeer, *Woman Holding a Balance*.

1666: The great fire of London.

1667: Milton writes *Paradise Lost*.

68.
c. 1670: Christoffel van Dyck, Dutch Old Style type.

1686: Sir Isaac Newton sets forth his law of gravity.
69.
1675–1710: Sir Christopher Wren, St. Paul's Cathedral, London.

During the eighteenth century, type design went through a gradual transition from Old Style to Modern Style fonts designed late in the century.

1700: The emergence of the Rococo Style.
70.
1702: Philippe Grandjean (punch cutter), Romain du Roi, the first transitional face.

71.
1709: Matthaus Poppelmann, Zwinger Palace, Dresden.

1709: England adopts the first modern copyright law.
72.
1720: William Caslon, Caslon Old Style types which from this date were used throughout the British Empire.

1632

Ad me profectam esse aiebant. D. quid
Quæso, igitur commorabare, ubi id
68.

65.

67.   **69.**

66.   **73.**

72.

sa doctrine et de ses lois. Après, il nous fait voir tous les hommes renfermés en un seul homme, et sa femme même tirée de lui ; la concorde des mariages et la
70.

lumes in-4° sur papier-vélin de la fabrique de messieurs Matthieu Johannot pere et fils, d'Annonai, premiers fabricants de cette sorte de papiers en
81.

71.

73.

1722: Castletown, near Dublin, Ireland.

1738: First spinning machines are patented in England.

74.

1744: Benjamin Franklin, title page using Caslon type.

75.

1750: François Boucher, *The Love Letter* (detail).

76.

1750s: John Baskerville creates extraordinary transitional typefaces.

77.

1765: Thomas Cottrell introduces display types two inches tall (shown actual size).

78.

1768: Pierre Simon Fournier le Jeune, ornamented types.

79.

1773: Johann David Steingruber, letter *A* from *Architectonishes Alphabet.*

80.

1774: John Holt, broadside of the American revolutionary era, using Caslon type.

81.

1784: François Ambroise Didot, the first true Modern Style typeface.

1789: The fall of the Bastille launches the French Revolution.

82.

1791: Giambattista Bodoni, Modern Style typefaces of geometric construction, with hairline serifs.

1775: James Watt constructs the first efficient steam engine.

1776: American Declaration of Independence is signed.

1791: American Bill of Rights guarantees freedoms of religion, speech, and the press.

1793: French King Louis XVI and Marie Antoinette are sent to the guillotine.

1796: Aloys Senefelder invents lithography.

1799: Nicolas-Louis Robert invents the papermaking machine.

1722

M. T. CICERO's
CATO MAJOR,
OR HIS
DISCOURSE
OF
OLD-AGE:

With Explanatory NOTES.

PHILADELPHIA:
Printed and Sold by B. FRANKLIN,
MDCCXLIV.

74.

LA
DIVINA
COMMEDIA
DI
DANTE ALIGHIERI
CON
ILLUSTRAZIONI

TOMO I.

PISA
DALLA TIPOGRAFIA
DELLA SOCIETÀ LETTERARIA
MDCCCIV.

82.

76.

75.

77.

To the PUBLICK.

NEW-YORK, October 3, 1774.

80.

HISTOIRE
DE
LOUIS DE BOURBON,
SECOND DU NOM,
*PRINCE
DE CONDÉ,*
PREMIER PRINCE DU SANG,
Surnommé *LE GRAND.*

LIVRE PREMIER.
1611-1643.

LOUIS DE BOURBON, second du nom , naquit à Paris 1621. le 7 Septembre 1621 ; il fut titré *Duc d'Enguien* , nom heureux qui rappelloit la mémoire du vain-

78.

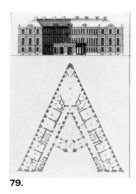

79.

The nineteenth century and the Industrial Revolution: A.D. 1800–1899

The Industrial Revolution had a dramatic impact upon typography and the graphic arts. New technology radically altered printing, and designers responded with an outpouring of new forms and images.

83.
c. 1803: Robert Thorne designs the first Fat Face.

1804: Napoleon Bonaparte crowned Emperor of France.

1808: Beethoven composes his Fifth Symphony.
84.
1812: Jacques-Louis David, *Napoleon in his Study.*

1814: Friedrich Koenig invents the steam-powered printing press.

85.
1815: Vincent Figgins shows the first Egyptian (slab-serif) typefaces.
86.
1815: Vincent Figgins shows the earliest shaded type.

87.
1816: William Caslon IV introduces the first sans serif type.
88.
1818: Page from *Manuale Tipographico,* which presented the lifework of Giambattista Bodoni.
89.
1821: Robert Thorne, Tuscan styles with splayed serifs.

1800

R. THORNE

85.
ABCDEFGHIJK

86.
ABCDEFGHIKM

87.
LETTERFOUNDER

89.
Manchester

PARANGONE

Quousque tandem abutère, Catilina, patientiâ nostrâ? quamdiu etiam furor iste tuus nos eludet? quem ad finem sese effrenata jactabit audacia? nihilne te nocturnum præsidium Palatii, nihil urbis vigiliæ, nihil timor populi, nihil concursus bonorum omnium, nihil hic munitissimus habendi se-
MARCUS TULL. CICERO
ORATOR ATQUE PHILOSOPHUS.

CHERASCO

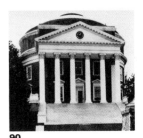

83.   84.   88.   90.

90.

1822: Thomas Jefferson, Rotunda of the University of Virginia in the neoclassical style based on Greek and Roman architecture.

1822: Joseph Niepce produces the first photographic printing plate.

91.

c. 1826: Bower, Bacon and Bower, early reversed-type entitled White.

1826: Joseph Niepce takes the first photograph from nature.

92.

1827: Darius Wells invents the mechanical router, making the manufacture of large display wood types possible.

93.

1833: Vincent Figgins introduces outline types.

94.

1836: Davy and Berry, poster printed with wood type.

1830s–80s: Wood-type posters and broadsides flourished in America and Europe.

95.

1836: Vincent Figgins, perspective type.

96.

1837: Handbill set in Fat Face.

1837: Victoria crowned Queen of England.

1822

THEATRE-ROYAL, NORWICH.

FOR THE BENEFIT OF

R. Battley,

FRUITERER.

On THURSDAY, 12th May, 1836,

Will be performed the POPULAR PLAY, of The

CASTLE SPECTRE.

Earl Osmond....Mr. MADDOCKS
Reginald ....Mr. HAMERTON | Kenric....Mr. G. SMITH
Earl Percy....Mr. NICHOLS | Saib....Mr. HARRISON
Father Philip..Mr. GRAY | Muley....Mr. BRYAN
Motley ......Mr. GILL | Hassan....Mr. NANTZ.

Angela ....Mrs. G. SMITH
Alice.... Mrs. WATKINSON | Evelina ....Miss HONEY.

END OF THE PLAY,

A COMIC SONG

BY MR. MARTIN.

To conclude with the NAUTICAL DRAMA, of The

PILOT,

OR, A

STORM AT SEA!

The Pilot, Mr. MADDOCKS
Barnstable, Mr. G. SMITH—Captain Boroughcliffe, (a regular Yankee), Mr. GILL
Long Tom Coffin, Mr. NANTZ
Captain of the Alacrity, Mr. HAMERTON—Colonel Howard Mr. GRAY
Lieutenant Griffith, Mr. TAYLOR—Serjeant Drill, Mr. NICHOLS.
Sailors, Soldiers, &c.
Kate Plowden, Mrs. PLUMER—Cecilia, Miss HONEY
Irish Woman, Mrs. WATKINSON

DAVY & BERRY, PRINTERS, ALBION OFFICE.

94.

HOUSEHOLD FURNITURE, PLATE, CHINA-WARE, JEWELS, WATCHES

93.

DARIUS WELLS.

92.

95.

96.

Working Men, Attention!!

Globe Office
Saturday, November 20. 1837

It is your imperious duty to drop your *Hammers and Sledges*! one and all, to your post repair, *THIS AFTERNOON*, at *FIVE* o'clock P. M. and attend the

GREAT MEETING

called by the papers of this morning, to be held at the CITY HALL, then and there to co-operate with such as have the GREAT GOOD OF ALL THEIR *FELLOW CITIZENS* at Heart. Your liberty! yea, your *LABOUR!!* is the subject of the call: who that values the services of HEROES of the *Revolution* whose blood achieved our Independence as a Nation, will for a moment doubt he owes a few hours this afternoon to his wife and children?

HANCOCK.

91.

STOCKS

97.

c. 1840–52: Sir Charles Barry and A. W. N. Pugin, Houses of Parliament, inspiration for the Gothic Revival.

98.

c. 1841: Wood and Sharwoods, ornamental type.

During the 1840s, ornamented type becomes increasingly important.

99.

1845: Robert Besley, the first Clarendon style.

1848: The California gold rush begins.

1851: Joseph Paxton designs the Crystal Palace.

100.

1853: Handbill combining Egyptian, outline, and decorative types.

101.

1854: Broadside using elongated Fat Face fonts.

1854: The United States makes its first treaty with Japan.

1856: Sir Henry Bessemer develops process for converting iron to steel.

102.

1859: William H. Page and Company, Ornamented Clarendons.

1859: Charles Darwin publishes *Origin of Species by Means of Natural Selection*.

103.

1860: *Charleston Mercury*, broadsheet announcing the dissolution of the Union.

c. 1840

97.

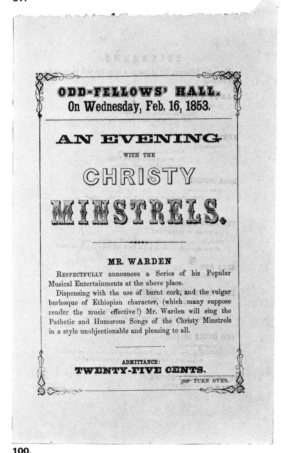

100.

PRES'T. MADISON'S LIBRARY, AT AUCTION.

AT Orange Court House Virginia, on Tuesday the 27th day of June, prox., being the day after the County Court of Orange in that month; I shall sell at public auction, to the highest bidder, that part of the Library of the late James Madison, which, in a recent division of his books with the University of Virginia, fell to the share of my testator; and at the same time I will sell other books, the property of my said testator. In all there are some

SEVEN OR EIGHT HUNDRED VOLUMES,

among which are many very rare and desirable works, some in Greek, some in Latin, numerous others in French, and yet more in English, in almost all the departments of Literature; not a few of them being in this manner exposed to sale only because the University possessed already copies of the same editions. The sale beginning on the day above mentioned, will be continued from day to day till all the books shall have been sold, on the following terms:

Cash will be required of each purchaser whose aggregate purchases shall amount to no more than Five dollars; those whose purchases shall exceed that amount, will have the privilege either to pay the cash or to give bond with approved security, bearing interest from the date, and payable six months thereafter.

ELHANON ROW, Administrator, with the will annexed of John P. Todd, dec'd.

May 30, 1854.

101.

98.

MAVERICK & WISSINGER
ENGRAVERS,
LITHOGRAPHERS & PRINTERS,
BLANK BOOKS & STATIONERY,
176 FULTON STREET.
Opposite St. Pauls Chapel.
NEW YORK.
BONDS, CERTIFICATES OF STOCK, CHECKS, DRAFTS, NOTES, DIPLOMAS, &c.
B. MAVERICK.
J. G. WISSINGER.
OVER

108.

audacia tua? nihilne te nocturnum præsidium palatii, nihil urbis vigiliæ, nihil timor

99.

1861–65: American Civil War.

1863: Abraham Lincoln signs the Emancipation Proclamation.

104.

c. 1865: Honoré Daumier: *The Third-Class Carriage.*

1866: The first successful transatlantic cable is laid.

1867: Alfred Nobel invents dynamite.

1867: Christopher Sholes constructs the first practical typewriter.

105.

1868: Currier and Ives, *American Homestead Winter.*

106.

c. 1875: J. Ottmann, chromolithographic card for Mrs. Winslow's Soothing Syrup.

1876: Alexander Graham Bell invents the telephone.

1877: Thomas Edison invents the phonograph.

1879: Thomas Edison invents the electric lightbulb.

107.

1883: The Brooklyn Bridge is opened to traffic.

1883: William Jenney designs the first skyscraper, a ten-story metal frame building in Chicago.

108.

c. 1885: Maverick and Wissinger, engraved business card.

109.

c. 1880s: Lettering printed by chromolithography.

110.

1886: Ottmar Mergenthaler invents the Linotype, the first keyboard typesetting machine.

1861

104.

105.

106.

102.

109.

107.

103.

110.

111.
1887: Advertisement for Estey Organs.

1887: Tolbert Lanston invents the monotype.

112.
1889: Alexandre Gustave Eiffel, the Eiffel Tower.

113.
c. 1890s: Coca-Cola syrup jug.

114.
1892: Paul Gauguin, *By the Sea.*

115.
William Morris' typeface designs: 1890, Golden; 1892, Troy; 1893, Chaucer.

116.
1891–98: William Morris' Kelmscott Press launches a revival of printing and typography.

117.
1892: William Morris, page from *News from Nowhere.*

1887

111.

112.

114.

This is the Golden type.

This is the Troy type.

This is the Chaucer type.

115.

Kelmscott
William Morris

116.

Afloat again CHAPTER XXIV. UP THE THAMES. THE SECOND DAY.

HEY were not slow to take my hint; & indeed, as to the mere time of day, it was best for us to be off, as it was past seven o'clock, & the day promised to be very hot. So we got up and went down to our boat; Ellen thoughtful and abstracted; the old man very kind and courteous, as if to make up for his crabbedness of opinion. Clara was cheerful & natural, but a little subdued, I thought; and she at least was not sorry to be gone, and often looked shyly and timidly at Ellen and her strange wild beauty. So we got into the boat, Dick saying as he took his place, "Well, it is a fine day!" and the old man answering "What! you like that, do you?" once more; and presently Dick was sending the bows swiftly through the slow weed-checked stream. I turned round as we got into mid-stream, and waving my hand to our hosts, saw Ellen leaning on the old man's shoulder, and caressing his healthy apple-red cheek, and quite a keen pang smote me as I thought how I should never see the beautiful girl again. Presently I insisted on taking the sculls, and I rowed a good deal that day; which no doubt accounts for the fact that we got very late
230

117.

118.

1893: Henri van de Velde, title page for *Van Nu en Straks.*

1895: The Lumière brothers give the first motion-picture presentation.

119.

1897: Edmond Deman, title page in the curvilinear Art Nouveau style.

120.

1890s–1940s: Inspired by Kelmscott, Americans Frederick Goudy and Bruce Rogers bring renewed excellence to book and type-face design.

121.

1897: Will Bradley, title page in his "Chap Book" style, reviving Caslon type and colonial woodcut techniques.

1898: Zeppelin invents his air-ship.

122.

1899: Josef Hoffmann, catalogue cover for a Vienna Secession exhibition.

123.

1898–1902: Hector Guimard, entrance to Paris Metro Station.

1893

118.

122.

120.

119.

121.

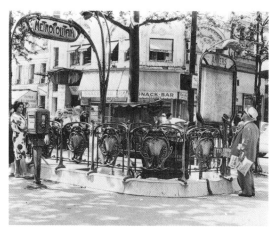

123.

Typography in the twentieth century: 1900–present.

The twentieth century has been a period of incredible ferment and change. Unprecedented advances in science and technology and revolutionary developments in art and design have left their marks on typography.

124.
1900: Peter Behrens, dedication page from *Feste des Lebens und der Künst.*

1903: The Wright brothers succeed in the first powered flight.

1905: Einstein proposes his theory of relativity.

125.
1909: Filippo Marinetti founds Futurism, experimentation with typographic form and syntax.

126.
c. 1910: German sans-serif "block style."

127.
1913: Wassily Kandinsky, *Improvisation 31 (Sea Battle).*

1914–18: World War I.

c. 1915: Kasimir Malevich, Suprematist painting shown at the *0.10* group exhibition launching Suprematism.

128.
c. 1916: Bert Thomas, British war bonds poster.

1917–22: The Dada movement protests the war and conventional art.

129.
1917: John Heartfield, Dadaist advertisement.

130.
1917: Vilmos Huszar, De Stijl magazine cover.

1918: Czar Nicholas II and his family are executed.

131.
1919: Raoul Hausmann, Dada poem.

1900

124.

125.

126.

127.

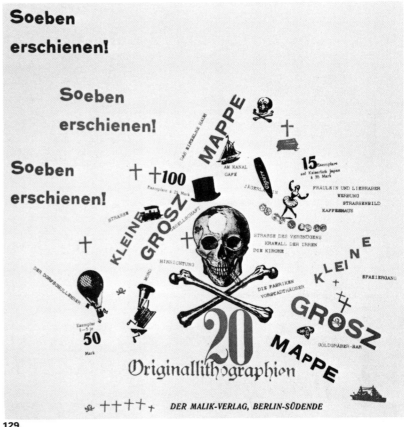

129.

128.

130.

131.

1920: Women's suffrage is granted in the United States.

1920: Bolsheviks triumph in the Russian Revolution.

132.
1921–25: Piet Mondrian, *Diamond Painting in Red, Yellow, and Blue.*

133.
c. 1923: Alexander Rodchenko, Russian Constructivist poster.

1924: Surrealist manifesto.

134.
1924: Gerrit Rietveld, Schroeder house.

135.
1925: El Lissitzky, title page.

136.
1925: Herbert Bayer, universal alphabet.

137.
1925: Constantin Brancusi, *Bird in Space.*

138.
1925: Jan Tschichold, title page for his article "Elementary Typography."

139.
1926: Piet Zwart, advertisement.

1927: Charles Lindbergh makes the first solo Atlantic flight.

140.
1928: Piet Zwart, advertisement.

1920

132.

134.

133.

135.

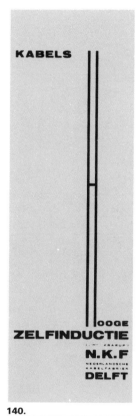

137.

140.

138.

136.

139.

bauhaus

136.

19

1929: The New York Stock Market collapses, and the Great Depression begins.

141.
1930: Paul Renner, prospectus for Futura.

142.
1930: Chrysler Building, an example of Art Deco decorative geometric style.

143.
1931: Max Bill, exhibition poster.

144.
c. 1932: Alexey Brodovitch, exhibition poster.

1933: Adolf Hitler becomes chancellor of Germany.

145.
1936: Walker Evans, family of sharecroppers.

1939: Germany invades Poland; World War II begins.

146.
1942: Jean Carlu, advertisement.

147.
1944: Max Bill, exhibition poster.

1945: Atomic bombs destroy Hiroshima and Nagasaki; World War II ends.

148.
1948: Paul Rand, title page.

1929

141.

147.

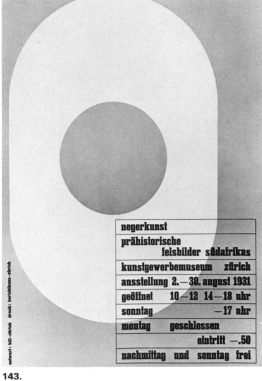

143.

144.

145.

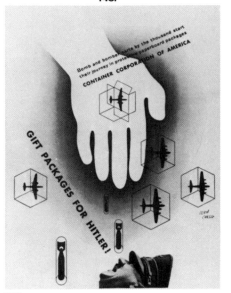

146.

142.

148.

20

149.
1948: Willem de Kooning: *Painting.*

150.
1950: Ladislav Sutner, book cover.

1950: North Korea invades South Korea.

151.
1950–55: Le Corbusier, Notre Dame de Haut.

1952: School segregation is declared unconstitutional by the Supreme Court.

152.
1952: Henri Matisse, *Woman with Amphora and Pomegranates.*

153.
1955: Josef Müller-Brockmann, concert poster.

154.
1956: Saul Bass, advertisement.

155.
1956: Willem Sandberg, book cover.

1957: Russia launches Sputnik I, the first earth satellite.

156.
1959: Saul Bass, film title.

157.
1959: Frank Lloyd Wright, the Guggenheim Museum, New York.

158.
1958: Carlo L. Vivarelli, magazine cover.

1948

149.

152.

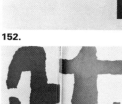

155.

150.

158.

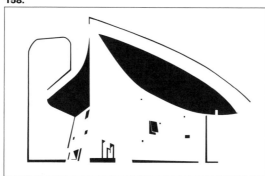

151.

157.

153.

154.

156.

159.
1959: Henry Wolf, magazine cover.
160.
c. 1959: Gerald Holton, "peace symbol."

161.
1959: Otto Storch, figurative typography.
162.
1960: Karl Gerstner, advertisement.
163.
c. 1960: Herb Lubalin, advertisement.

164.
c. 1961: George Lois, pharmaceutical advertisement.
165.
1962: Eero Saarinen, Dulles International Airport.

1963: President John F. Kennedy is assassinated.
166.
1965: Seymour Chwast and Milton Glaser, poster.

1965: The U.S. Marines land in force in Vietnam.
167.
1966: George Lois, magazine cover.

1959

159.

160.

DIVINE TO EAT, EASY TO MAKE, AND BEAUTIFUL TO LOOK ON: ELEGANT PARFAITS. THERE ARE TWO TYPES: THE FRENCH, WHICH IS A CREAMY, DELICATE, COOL (BUT NOT ICY) MIXTURE WITH A BASE OF SUGAR, EGGS, CREAM, FRUIT AND/OR FLAVORINGS; AND THE AMERICAN, MADE WITH COMMERCIAL ICE CREAMS OR SHERBETS OR BOTH WITH A SURPRISE INGREDIENT, SUCH AS FRUITS, CORDIALS, COGNAC, NUTS, SAUCES (SEE McCALL'S FINE SAUCE RECIPES ON PAGE 00). WITH AMERICAN PARFAITS, YOUR IMAGINATION CAN HAVE FREE REIN. WITH THE FRENCH, HOWEVER, YOU MUST FOLLOW RECIPE DIRECTIONS TO THE LETTER. PARFAIT MEANS, OF COURSE, PERFECT, AND WE CAN IMAGINE FEW MORE PERFECT DESSERTS, ESPECIALLY IF YOU WANT TO SHOW OFF. FOR THESE ARE TRULY SHOW-OFF RECIPES! FROM THE COOK'S STANDPOINT, THERE IS A REAL ADVANTAGE IN SERVING FROZEN DESSERTS. FOR THE OBVIOUS REASON, THEY MUST BE MADE WELL AHEAD AND REFRIGERATED. THUS, THE BIG DESSERT PROBLEM IS OUT OF THE WAY WHEN IT'S TIME TO PREPARE THE MAIN PART OF THE MEAL. AT FAR RIGHT, YOU SEE AN AMERICAN PARFAIT, VANILLA ICE CREAM LAYERED WITH PISTACHIO AND TOPPED WITH WALNUTS AND WHIPPED CREAM. THE STRAWBERRY AND APRICOT PARFAITS ARE BOTH CLASSIC FRENCH. FOR THE RECIPES, TURN TO PAGE 00, WHERE YOU WILL FIND THE FRENCH AS WELL AS GOOD VARIATIONS OF THE QUICK AND POPULAR AMERICAN PARFAITS. THEN, PLAN A PARTY.

161.

163.

164.

The true story of M Company. From Fort Dix to Vietnam.

167.

165.

162.

166.

168.
c. 1968: Seymour Chwast and Milton Glaser, poster.

169.
1968: R. Buckminster Fuller, American Pavilion, Montreal World's Fair.

170.
c. 1967: Symbol for the environmental movement.

171.
1969: First moon walk.

172.
1972: Wolfgang Weingart, typographic interpretation of a poem.

173.
1974: Herb Lubalin, newspaper cover.

174.
1974: Cook and Shanosky, standard symbol signs.

175.
1975: The Vietnam War ends.

175.
1976: American Bicentennial. Symbol design by Bruce Blackburn.

1968

168.

169.

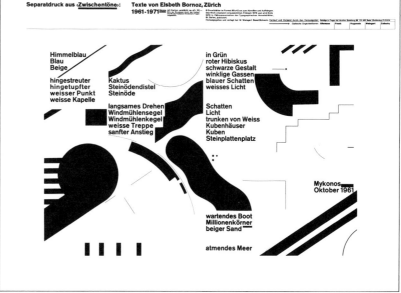

172.

170.

173.

174.

175.

171.

176.
1977: Pompidou National Center of Arts and Culture, Paris.
177.
1977: Bill Bonnell, RyderTypes trademark.

178.
1978: Willi Kunz, poster design.
179.
1979: Richard Greenberg, film titles.

1979: Soviet troops invade Afganistan.

1980s: Digital typography and computer technology impact typographic design, leading to electronic page design by the end of the decade.
180.
1983: Michael Graves, Portland, Oregon, city hall.

181.
1984: Warren Lehrer, page from *French Fries*.
182.
1991: Ted Mader + Associates, book jacket.

1991: The Soviet Union dissolves.

1977

181.

178.

176.

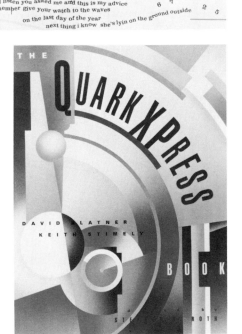

177.

180.

179.

182.

Typographic design is a complex area of human activity, requiring a broad background for informed practice. This chapter explores the basic language of typography. Letterforms, the fundamental components of all typographic communications, are carefully examined. Nomenclature, measurement, and the nature of the typographic font and family are presented.

The alphabet is a series of elemental visual signs in a fixed sequence, representing spoken sounds. Each letter signifies only one thing: its elementary sound or name. The twenty-six characters of the alphabet can be combined into thousands of words, creating a visual record of the spoken language. This is the magic of writing and typography, which have been called "thoughts-made-visible" and "frozen sounds."

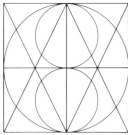

1.
Strokes written with the reed
pen (top), and brush (middle),
and carved with a chisel
(bottom).

2.

3.
Capital and lowercase letterform construction.

The four timelines in chapter one graphically present the evolution of letterforms and typographic
design from the beginning of writing to the present. Our contemporary typographic forms have
been forged by this historical evolution. Typography evolved from handwriting, which is created
by making a series of marks by hand; therefore, the
fundamental element constructing a letterform is
the linear stroke. Each letter of our alphabet developed as a simple mark whose visual characteristics
clearly separated it from all the others.

The marking properties of brush, reed pen, and
stone engraver's chisel influenced the early form of
the alphabet (Fig. **1**). The reed pen, used in ancient
Rome and the medieval monastery, was held at an
angle, called a cant, to the page. This produced a
pattern of thick and thin strokes. Since the time of
the ancient Greeks, capital letterforms have consisted of simple geometric forms based on the square,
circle, and triangle. The basic shape of each capital
letter can be extracted from the structure in Figure
2, which is composed of a bisected square, a circle,
a triangle, an inverted triangle, and two smaller cir-
cles.

The resulting vocabulary of forms, however, lacks
several important attributes: optically adjusted proportions, expressive design properties, and maximum legibility and readability. The transition from
rudimentary mark to letterforms with graphic clarity and precision is a matter of design.

Because early capital letters were cut into stone,
these letters developed with a minimum number of
curved lines, for curved strokes were difficult to cut
(Fig. **3**). Lowercase letters evolved as reed-pen writing. Curved strokes could be quickly written and
were used to reduce the number of strokes needed
to write many characters.

The parts of letterforms
Over the centuries, a nomenclature has evolved
that identifies the various components of individual
letterforms. By learning this vocabulary, designers
and typographers can develop a greater understanding and sensitivity to the visual harmony and
complexity of the alphabet. The following list (Fig. **4**)

identifies the major components of letterform construction. In medieval times, horizontal guidelines
were drawn to contain and align each line of lettering. Today, letterforms and their parts are drawn
on imaginary guidelines to bring uniformity to
typography.

Baseline: An imaginary line upon which the base of
each capital rests.

Capline: An imaginary line that runs along the tops
of the capital letters.

Meanline: An imaginary line that establishes the
height of the body of lowercase letters.

x-height: The distance from the baseline to the
meanline. Typically, this is the height of lowercase
letters and is most easily measured on the lowercase *x.*

All characters align *optically* on the baseline. The
body height of lowercase characters align optically
at the x-height, and the tops of capitals align optically along the capline. To achieve precise alignments, the typeface designer makes optical adjustments.

Apex: The peak of the triangle of an uppercase *A.*

Arm: A projecting horizontal stroke that is
unattached on one or both ends, as in the letters *T*
and *E.*

Ascender: A stroke on a lowercase letter that rises
above the meanline.

Bowl: A curved stroke enclosing the counterform of
a letter. An exception is the bottom form of the
lowercase roman *g,* which is called a loop.

Counter: The negative space that is fully or partially
enclosed by a letterform.

Crossbar: The horizontal stroke connecting two
sides of the letterform (as in *e, A,* and *H*) or bisect-
ing the main stroke (as in *f* and *t*).

Capline

Meanline

x-height

Baseline

Descender: A stroke on a lowercase letterform that falls below the baseline.

Ear: A small stroke that projects from the upper right side of the bowl of the lowercase roman *g.*

Eye: The enclosed part of the lowercase *e.*

Fillet: The contoured edge that connects the serif and stem in bracketed serifs. (Bracketed serifs are connected to the main stroke by this curved edge; unbracketed serifs connect to the main stroke with an abrupt angle without this contoured transition.)

Hairline: The thinnest strokes within a typeface which has strokes of varying weights.

Leg: The lower diagonal stroke on the letter *k.*

Link: The stroke that connects the bowl and the loop of a lowercase roman *g.*

Loop: See *Bowl.*

Serifs: Short strokes that extend from and at an angle to the upper and lower ends of the major strokes of a letterform.

Shoulder: A curved stroke projecting from a stem.

Spine: The central curved stroke of the letter *S.*

Spur: A projection—smaller than a serif—that reinforces the point at the end of a curved stroke, as in the letter *G.*

Stem: A major vertical or diagonal stroke in the letterform.

Stroke: Any of the linear elements within a letterform; originally, any mark or dash made by the movement of a pen or brush in writing.

Tail: A diagonal stroke or loop at the end of a letter, as in *R* or *j.*

Terminal: The end of any stroke that does not terminate with a serif.

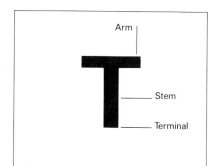

Arm — Stem — Terminal

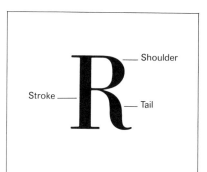

Shoulder — Stroke — Tail

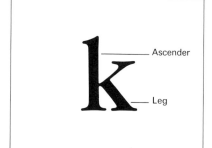

Ascender — Leg

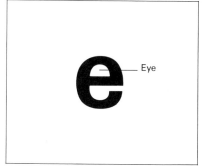

Eye

Spine

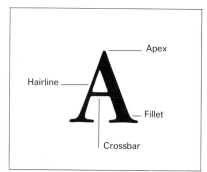

Apex — Hairline — Fillet — Crossbar

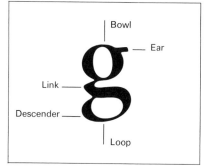

Bowl — Ear — Link — Descender — Loop

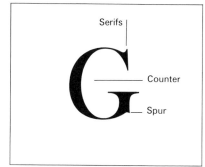

Serifs — Counter — Spur

4.

27

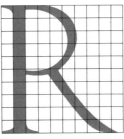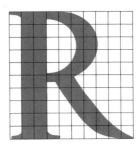

5.

1499 Old Style

1757 Baskerville

1793 Bodoni

1816 First sans serif

c. 1928 Ultra Bodoni

O

1957 Univers 55

6.

Proportions of the letterform

The proportions of the individual letterform are an important consideration in typography. Four major variables control letterform proportion and have considerable impact upon the visual appearance of a typeface: the ratio of letterform height to stroke width; the variation between the thickest and thinnest strokes of the letterform; the width of the letters; and the relationship of the x-height to the height of capitals, ascenders, and descenders.

The stroke-to-height ratio. The roman letterform, left, has the stroke-width-to-capital-height proportion found on Roman inscriptions (Fig. **5**). Superimposition on a grid demonstrates that the height of the letter is ten times the stroke width. In the adjacent rectangles, the center letter is reduced to one-half the normal stroke width, and the letter on the right has its stroke width expanded to twice the normal width. In both cases, pronounced change in the weight and appearance of the letterform occurs.

Contrast in stroke weight. A change in the contrast between thick and thin strokes can alter the optical qualities of letterforms. The series of *O*s in Figure **6**, shown with the date of each specimen, demonstrates how the development of technology and printing has enabled typeface designers to make thinner strokes.

In the Old Style typography of the Renaissance, designers attempted to capture some of the visual properties of pen writing. Since the writing pens of the period had a flat edge, they created thick and thin strokes. *Stress* is the term to define this thickening of the strokes, which is particularly pro-

nounced on curves. Note how the placement of weight within the Old Style *O* creates a diagonal axis. As time has passed, type designers have been less influenced by writing.

By the late 1700s, the impact of writing declined, and this axis became completely vertical in many typefaces of that period. In many of the earliest sans-serif typefaces, stress disappeared completely. Some of these typefaces have a monoline stroke that is completely even in weight.

Expanded and condensed styles. The design qualities of the typographic font change dramatically when the widths of the letterforms are expanded or condensed. The word *proportion,* set in two sans-serif typefaces, demonstrates extreme expansion and condensation (Fig. **7**). In the top example, set in Aurora Condensed, the stroke-to-height ratio is one to nine. In the bottom example, set in Information, the stroke-to-height ratio is one to two. Although both words are exactly the same height, the condensed typeface takes up far less area on the page.

X-height and proportion. The proportional relationship between the x-height and capital, ascender, and descender heights influences the optical qualities of typography in a significant way. The same characters are set in seventy-two-point type using three typefaces with widely varying x-heights (Fig. **8**). This example demonstrates how these proportional relationships change the appearance of type. The impact of x-height upon legibility will be discussed in chapter four.

8.

On the same size body (72 point), the x-height variation between three typefaces—Garamond Old Style, Bodoni, and Univers—is shown. The proportion of the x-height to the point size significantly affects the appearance of type.

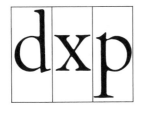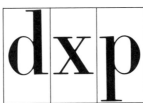

72 Points

PROPORTION PROPORTION

A font is a set of characters of the same size and style containing all the letters, numbers, and marks needed for typesetting. A typographic font exhibits structural unity when all the characters relate to one another visually. The weights of thick and thin strokes must be consistent, and the optical alignment of letterforms must appear even. The distribution of lights and darks within each character and in the spaces between characters must be carefully controlled to achieve an evenness of tone within the font.

In some display faces, the font might include only the twenty-six capital letters. In a complete font for complex typesetting, such as for textbooks, it is possible to have nearly two hundred characters. The font for Adobe Garamond (Fig. **9**) includes the following types of characters.

Capitals: The set of large letters that is used in the initial position.

Lowercase: The smaller set of letters, so named because in metal typesetting these were stored in the lower part of a type case.

Small caps: A complete set of capital letters that are the same height as the x-height of the lowercase letters. These are often used for abbreviations, cross references, and emphasis.

Lining figures: Numbers that are the same height as the capital letters and sit on the baseline.

Old Style figures: A set of numbers that are compatible with lowercase letters; *1, 2,* and *0* align with the x-height; 6 and 8 have ascenders; and *3, 4, 5, 7,* and *9* have descenders.

Superior and inferior figures: Small numbers, usually slightly smaller than the x-height, used for footnotes and fractions. Superior figures hang from the capline, and inferior figures sit on the baseline.

Fractions: Common mathematical expressions made up of a superior figure, an inferior figure, and a slash mark. These are set as a single type character.

Ligatures: Two or more characters linked together as one unit, such as *ff.* The ampersand is a ligature originating as a letter combination for the French word *et* ("and") in medieval manuscripts.

Digraphs: A ligature composed of two vowels which are used to represent a dipthong (a monosyllabic speech sound composed of two vowels).

Mathematical signs: Characters used to notate basic mathematical processes.

Punctuation: A system of standard signs used in written and printed matter to structure and separate units and to clarify meaning.

Accented characters: Characters with accents for foreign language typesetting or for indicating pronunciation.

Dingbats: Assorted signs, symbols, reference marks, and ornaments designed for use with a type font.

Monetary symbols: Logograms used to signify monetary systems (U.S. dollar and cent marks, British pound mark, and so on).

7.

abcdefghijklmnopqrstuvwxyz
ABCDEFGHIJKLMNOPQRSTUVWXYZ
ABCDEFGHIJKLMNOPQRSTUVWXYZ
1234567890& 1234567890& 1234567890&
¼½¾ ⅛⅜⅝⅞ ⅓⅔‰ 1234567890/1234567890-

fffiflffiffl ÆŒßRpæœ√π=±+÷∞°-–—
ÂÅÅÇÍÎÏØÓÒÔÚ(.,;:'"!?^‶‵‴‷¨˘¯˜‹«»)
áéíóú åäëïöüàèìòùâêîôûøÁÉÍÓÚÅÄËÏÖÜ
™©®@#$$$¢¢Đ¢£¥%^*
{}[]¡¡¢§¶•†‡

9.

15.

Optical relationships within a font

Mechanical and mathematical letterform construction can result in serious spatial problems because diverse form within an alphabet appear optically incorrect. These letterform combinations show the optical adjustment necessary to achieve visual harmony within a font.

10.

Pointed and curved letters (Fig. **10**) have little weight at the top and/or bottom guidelines; this can make them appear too short. To make them appear the same height as letters that terminate squarely with the guidelines, the apexes of pointed letters beyond the baseline and capline. Curved letterforms are drawn slightly above and below these lines to prevent them from appearing too small.

HBESKX38

11.

In two-storied capitals and figures (Fig. **11**), the top half appears too large if the form is divided in the mathematical center. To balance these letters optically, the center is slightly above the mathematical center, and the top halves are drawn slightly narrower than the bottom half.

Horizontal strokes (Fig. **12**) are drawn slightly thinner than vertical strokes in both curved and straight letterforms. Otherwise, the horizontals would appear too thick.

Tight junctions where strokes meet (Fig. **13**) are often opened slightly to prevent the appearance of thickening at the joint.

Letters combining diagonal and vertical strokes (Fig. **14**) must be designed to achieve a balance between the top and bottom counterforms. Strokes can be tapered slightly to open up the spaces, and adjustments in the amount of stroke

overlap can achieve a harmony of parts. Letters whose vertical strokes determine their height (Fig. **15**) are drawn slightly taller than letters whose height is determined by a horizontal stroke. Optically, they will appear to be the same height.

MBNB

16.

The stroke weight of compact letterforms (Fig. **16**), such as those with closed counterforms, are drawn slightly smaller than the stroke weight of letterforms having open counterforms. This optically balances the weight.

OHQ

17.

Curved strokes are usually thicker at their midsection than the vertical strokes, to achieve an even appearance (Fig. **17**).

These adjustments are very subtle and are often imperceptible to the reader. However, their overall effect is a more ordered and harmonious visual appearance.

Unity of design in the type font

Tremendous diversity of form exists in the typographic font. Twenty-six capitals, twenty-six lowercase letters, ten numerals, punctuation, and other graphic elements must be integrated into a system that can be successfully combined into innumerable words.

Letterform combinations from the Times Roman Bold font (Fig. **18**) demonstrate visual similarities that bring wholeness to typography. Letterforms share similar parts. A repetition of curves, verticals, horizontals, and serifs are combined to bring variety and unity to typographic designs using this typeface. All well-designed fonts of type display this principle of repetition with the variety that is found in Times Roman Bold.

ETO

12.

M

13.

NK

14.

DCGOQ

Curved capitals share a common round stroke.

The diagonal stokes of the *A* are repeated in *V W M*.

AVWM   jiru

Lowercase letters have common serifs.

F E B demonstrates that the more similar letters are, the more common parts they share.

FEB   mnhut

Repetition of the same stroke in *m n h u* creates unity.

Likewise, the letters *b d p q* share parts.

bdpq   SCGH

Capital serifs reoccur in similar characters.

BRKPR   atfr

ZLE   MYX

Subtle optical adjustments can be seen. For example, the bottom strokes of the capital *Z* and *L* have longer serifs than the bottom stroke of the *E*. This change in detail compensates for the larger counterform on the right side of the first two letters.

bq   bhlk   ceo

18.

An infinite variety of type styles is available today. Digital typography, with its simple and economical introduction of new typefaces, has made the entire array of typefaces developed over the centuries available for contemporary use. Numerous efforts have been made to classify typefaces, with most falling into the following major categories. Some classification systems add a decorative, stylized, or novelty category for the wide range of fanciful type styles that defy categorization.

Old Style

Old Style type began with designs of the punchcutter Francesco Griffo, who worked for the famous Venetian scholar-printer Aldus Manutius during the 1490s. Griffo's designs evolved from earlier Italian type designs. His Old Style capitals were influenced by carved Roman capitals; lowercase letters were inspired by fifteenth-century humanistic writing styles, based on the earlier Carolingian minuscules. Old Style letterforms have the weight stress of rounded forms at an angle, as in handwriting. The serifs are bracketed (that is, unified with the stroke by a tapered, curved line). Also, the top serifs on the lowercase letters are at an angle.

Italic

Italic letterforms slant to the right. Today, we use them primarily for emphasis and differentiation. When the first italic appeared in the earliest "pocket book," printed by Aldus Manutius in 1501, it was used as an independent typestyle. The first italic characters were close-set and condensed; therefore, Manutius was able to get more words on each line. Some italic styles are based on handwriting with connected strokes and are called scripts.

Transitional

During the 1700s, typestyles gradually evolved from Old Style to Modern. Typefaces from the middle of the eighteenth century, including those by John Baskerville, are called Transitional. The contrast between thick and thin strokes is greater than in Old Style faces. Lowercase serifs are more horizontal, and the stress within the rounded forms shifts to a less diagonal axis. Transitional characters are usually wider than Old Style characters.

Modern

Late in the 1700s, typefaces termed Modern evolved from Transitional styles. These typefaces have extreme contrasts between thick and thin strokes. Thin strokes are reduced to hairlines. The weight stress of rounded characters is vertical. Serifs are horizontal hairlines that join the stems at a right angle without bracketing. The uppercase width is regularized; wide letters such as *M* and *W* are condensed and other letters, including *P* and *T,* are expanded. Modern-style typefaces have a strong geometric quality projected by rigorous horizontal, vertical, and circular forms.

Egyptian

In 1815, the English typefounder Vincent Figgins introduced slab-serif typestyles under the name Antique. At the time, there was a mania for ancient Egyptian artifacts, and other typefounders adopted the name Egyptian for their slab-serif designs. These typestyles have heavy square or rectangular serifs that are usually unbracketed. The stress of curved strokes is often minimal. In some slab-serif typefaces, all strokes are the same weight.

Sans Serif

The first sans serif typestyle appeared in an 1816 specimen book of the English typefounder William Caslon IV. The most obvious characteristic of these styles is, as the name implies, the absence of serifs. In many sans serif typefaces, strokes are uniform, with little or no contrast between thick and thin strokes. Stress is almost always vertical. Many sans serif typefaces are geometric in their construction; others combine both organic and geometric qualities.

The development of photo and digital technology has stimulated the design and production of countless new typefaces whose visual characteristics defy standard classification. The visual traits of these "hybrid" forms may fall into more than one of the historical classifications presented on the preceding two pages. The following is a classification system derived from the visual features common to letters throughout the typeface kingdom. It may be used for comparative purposes to pinpoint the most dominant traits of specific typefaces. Type designers use these variations to create a family of typefaces. The type family is discussed on pages 37-39.

Serifs:

Serifs provide some of the most identifiable features of typefaces, and in some cases they reveal clues about their historical evolution. The serifs shown are those that appear most frequently in typefaces.

b	b	b	b	b	b
straight	oblique	bracketed	unbracketed	squared	rounded

b	b	b	b	b	b
wedged	concave	pointed	hairline	sans serif	hybrid stroke terminals

Weight:

This is a feature defined by the ratio between the relative width of the strokes of letterforms and their height. On the average, a letter of normal weight possesses a stroke width of approximately 15% of its height, whereas bold is 20% and light is 10%.

A	A	A	A	A	A
ultra bold	extra bold	bold	normal	light	extra light

A
ultra light

Width:

Width is an expression of the ratio between the black vertical strokes of the letterforms and the intervals of white between them. When white intervals appear larger, letters appear wider. A letter whose width is approximately 80% of its height is considered normal. A condensed letter is 60%, and an expanded letter is 100% of its height.

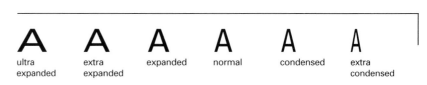

A	A	A	A	A	A
ultra expanded	extra expanded	expanded	normal	condensed	extra condensed

A
ultra condensed

Posture:

Roman letters that slant to the right but are structurally the same as upright roman letters are referred to as oblique. Italic letters, which are based on handwriting, are structurally different from roman letters of the same type family. Italic letters with connecting strokes are called scripts. The angle of posture varies from typeface to typeface; however, a slant of approximately 12% is considered to be normal.

h	h	h
italic	oblique	script

all 50's anne weight

Thick/thin contrast:

This visual feature refers to the relationship between the thinnest parts of the strokes in letters and the thickest parts. The varying ratios between these parts produce a wide range of visual textures in text type.

high contrast   medium contrast   low contrast   no contrast

x-height:

This proportional characteristic can vary immensly in different typefaces of the same size. Typically, x-heights are considered to be "tall" when they are at least two-thirds the height of capital letters. They are "short" when they measure one-half the height of capital letters.

extra tall   tall   medium   short   extra short

Ascenders/descenders:

Ascenders and descenders may appear longer in some typefaces and shorter in others, depending on the relative size of the x-height. Descenders are generally slightly longer than ascenders among letters of the same typeface.

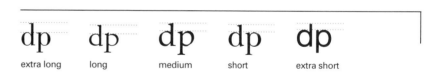

extra long   long   medium   short   extra short

Stress:

The stress of letters, which is a prominent visual axis resulting from the relationships between thick and thin strokes, may be left-angled, vertical, or right-angled in appearance.

left-angled   vertical   right-angled

Typographic measurement

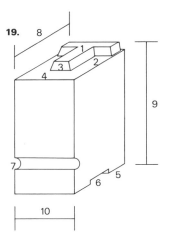

19.

1. Face (printing surface)
2. Counter
3. Beard
4. Shoulder
5. Feet
6. Groove
7. Nick

8. Point size (body size)
9. Type-high (.918'' height)
10. Set width

Our measurement system for typography was originally developed for the handset metal type invented by Johann Gutenberg around A.D. 1450. The rectangular metal block of type (Fig. **19**) has a raised letterform on top, which was inked to print the image.

Metal type measurement

The small sizes of text type necessitated the development of a measuring system with extremely fine increments. There were no standards for typographic measurements until the French type designer and founder Pierre Simon Fournier le Jeune introduced his point system of measurement in 1737. The contemporary American measurement system, which was adopted during the 1870s, has two basic units: the point and the pica (Fig. **20**). There are approximately 72 points in an inch (each point is 0.138 inches) and 12 points in a pica. There are about six picas in an inch.

Metal type exists in three dimensions, and an understanding of typographic measurement begins with this early technology. The depth of the type (Fig. **19**, caption 8) is measured in points and is called the point size or body size. All metal type must be the exact same height (Fig. **19**, caption 9), which is called typehigh (.918 inch). This uniform height enabled all types to print a uniform impression upon the paper. The width of a piece of type is called the set width (Fig. **19**, caption 10) and varies with the design of each individual letter. The letters *M* and *W* have the widest set width; *i* and *l* have the narrowest. The length of a line of type is the sum of the set width of all the characters and spaces in the line. It is measured in picas.

Before the development of the point and pica system, various sizes of type were identified by names, such as brevier, long primer, and pica; these became 8-point, 10-point, and 12-point type. The chart in Figure **21**, reproduced from a nineteenth-century printers' magazine, shows the major point sizes of type with their old names. Type that is 12 point and under is called text type

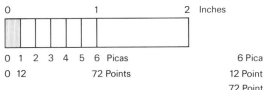

0   1   2   Inches

0 1 2 3 4 5 6 Picas   6 Picas = 1 Inch
0 12   72 Points   12 Points = 1 Pica
                             72 Points = 1 Inch

20.

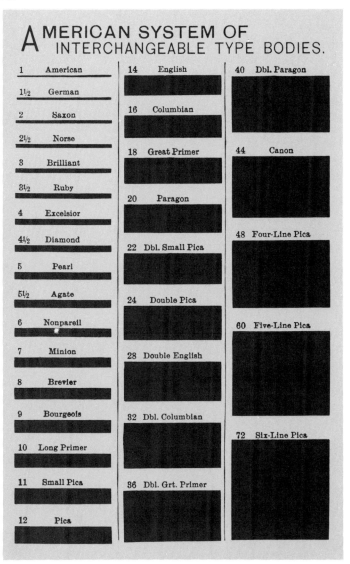

21.
Reproduced actual size from
The Inland Printer, April l885.

23.

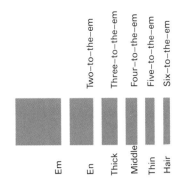

Two–to–the–em	Three–to–the–em	Four–to–the–em	Five–to–the–em	Six–to–the–em		
Em	En	Thick	Middle	Thin	Hair	

This line has word spacing with em quads.

This line has word spacing with en quads.

This line has word spacing with thick quads.

This line has word spacing with middle quads.

This line has word spacing with thin quads.

This line has word spacing with hair quads.

and is primarily used for body copy. Sizes above 12 point are called display type, and they are used for titles, headlines, signage, and the like.

Traditional metal type had a range of text and display sizes in increments from 5 point to 72 point (Fig. **22**). The measurement of point size is a measurement of the metal block of type including space above and below the letters; therefore, one cannot measure the point size from printed letters themselves. This is sometimes confusing. Refer to the labels for x-height, cap height, and point size on Figure **22** and observe that the point size includes the cap height plus a spatial interval above and below the letters.

Spatial measurement

In addition to measuring type, the designer also measures and specifies the spatial intervals between typographic elements. These intervals are: interletter spacing (traditionally called letterspacing), which is the interval between letters; interword spacing, also called wordspacing, which is the interval between words; and interline spacing, which is the interval between two lines of type. Traditionally, interline space is called leading, because thin strips of lead are placed between lines of metal type to increase the spatial interval between them.

In traditional metal typography, interline and interword spacing are achieved by inserting metal blocks called quads between the pieces of type. Because these are not as high as the type itself, they do not print. A quad that is a square of the point size is called an *em.* One that is one-half an em quad is called an *en.* In metal type, other smaller divisions of space are fractions of the em (Fig. **23**). These metal spacers are used for letter- and wordspacing, paragraph indentations, and centering or justifying lines of type.

5 Point
6 Point
7 Point
8 Point
9 Point
10 Point
11 Point
12 Point
14 Point
18 Point
24 Point
30 Point
36 Point
42 Point
48 Point
54 Point
60 Point
72 Point

Cap height

Body size

22.

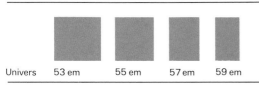

| Univers | 53 em | 55 em | 57 em | 59 em |

24.

This line is set with plus one unit of interletter spacing.

This line is set with normal, unaltered interletter spacing.

This line is set with minus one unit of interletter spacing.

This line is set with minus two units of interletter spacing.

This line is set with minus three units of interletter spacing.

26.

For design considerations, the em of a condensed typestyle can be narrower than a square, and the em of an expanded typesize can be wider than a square. This is demonstrated by the em quads from four styles in the Univers family of typefaces (Fig. **24**).

While em and en are still used as typographic terms, spacing in digital typesetting and desktop publishing is controlled by a computer, using a unit system. The *unit* is a relative measurement determined by dividing the em (that is, the square of the type size) into equal vertical divisions. Different typesetting systems use different numbers of units; sixteen, thirty-two, and sixty-four are common. Some desktop publishing software even permits adjustments as small as twenty-thousandths of an em. The width of each character (Fig. **25**) is measured by its unit value. During typesetting, the character is generated, then the typesetting machine advances the number of units assigned to that character before generating the next character. The unit value includes space on each side of the letter for normal interletter spacing. Adding or subtracting units to expand or contract the space between letters is called *tracking.* Changing the tracking changes the tone of the typography (Fig. **26**). As will be discussed later, tracking influences the aesthetics and legibility of typesetting.

Some letter combinations, such as *TA*, have awkward spatial relationships. An adjustment in the interletter space to make the interval more consistent with other letter combinations is called kerning. In metal type, kerning was achieved by sawing notches in the types. Contemporary typesetting software can contain automatic kerning pairs, and the designer can manually change the kerning between characters when these awkward combinations appear.

| 13 Units | 10 Units | 9 Units | 5 Units | 10 Units | 11 Units |

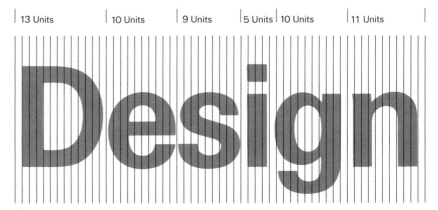

25.
The unit value of each letter
in the word *Design* is shown.

In this setting, minus one unit
is used for tighter interletter
spacing.

In this setting, minus two
units is used. The letters
almost touch.

A type family consists of a group of related type-faces, unified by a set of similar design characteristics. Each face in the family is an individual one that has been created by changing visual aspects of the parent font. Early type families consisted of three fonts: the regular roman face, a bolder version, and an italic. The roman, bold, and italic fonts of the Baskerville family (Fig. **27**) demonstrate that a change in stroke weight produces the bold version, and a change in stroke angle creates the italic. The bold font expands typographic possibilities by bringing impact to titles, headings, and display settings. Today, italics are primarily used for emphasis as a variation of roman. In addition to weight and angle changes, additional members of a type family are created by changing proportions or by design elaboration.

Weight changes. By simply changing the stroke width relative to the height of the letters, a whole series of alphabets, ranging from extremely light to very bold, can be produced. In England, a classification standard has been developed that contains eight weights: extralight, light, semilight, medium, semibold, bold, extrabold, and ultrabold. Most type families do not, however, consist of eight weights. Four weights—light, regular or book, medium, and bold—are often sufficient for most purposes. In the Avant Garde family (Fig. **28**), stroke weight is the only aspect that changes in these five fonts.

Proportion. Changing the proportions of a type-style by making letterforms wider (expanded) or narrower (condensed), as discussed earlier, is another method for adding typefaces to a type family. Terms used to express changes in proportion include: ultra-expanded, extra-expanded, expanded, regular, condensed, extra-condensed, and ultra-condensed.

Sometimes confusion results because there is no standardized terminology for discussing the variations in type families. For example, the regular face is sometimes called normal, roman, or book. Light weights are named lightline, slim, and hairline. Black, elephant, massive, heavy, and thick have been used to designate bold weights. Names given to condensed variations include narrow, contracted, elongated, and compressed. Expanded faces have been called extended, wide, and stretched.

27.

Baskerville

Baskerville

Baskerville

AVANT GARDE

AVANT GARDE

AVANT GARDE

AVANT GARDE

AVANT GARDE

28.

Futura Italic

Baskerville Italic

Bodoni Italic
29.

Angle. In our discussion about the basic classification of typefaces, italics were presented as a major independent category. They were first introduced four hundred years ago as a new style. Now italics serve as a member of type families, and they are used for contrast or emphasis. Italic fonts that retain curvilinear strokes inspired by handwriting are called cursives or scripts. In geometric typefaces constructed with drafting instruments, the italic fonts created by slanting the stroke angle are called obliques. Baskerville Italic (Fig. 29) is a cursive, demonstrating a handwriting influence; Futura Italic is an oblique face; and Bodoni Italic has both cursive and oblique qualities. Although the Bodoni family was constructed with the aid of drafting instruments, details in the italic font (for example, some of the lower serifs) evidence a definite cursive quality.

Elaboration. In design an elaboration is an added complexity, fullness of detail, or ornamentation. Design elaboration can be used to add new typefaces to a type family. These might include outline fonts, three-dimensional effects, and the application of ornaments to letterforms. Some of the variations of Helvetica (Fig. **30**) that are available from the German firm of Dr. Boger Photosatz Gmbh include outlines, inlines, perspectives, rounded terminals, and even a chipped antique effect.

While many elaborations are gaudy and interfere with the integrity and legibility of the letterforms, others can be used successfully. Goudy Handtooled (Fig. 31) is based on Goudy Bold. A white linear element is placed on each major stroke. Dimensionality is suggested, and the face alludes to incised inscriptional lettering.

Decorative and novelty typestyles should be used with great care by the graphic designer. At best, these can express a feeling appropriate to the content and can allow for unique design solutions. Unfortunately, the use of design elaboration is often a mere straining for effect.

The Cheltenham family

One of the most extensive type families is the Cheltenham series of typefaces (Fig. **32**). The first version, Cheltenham Old Style, was initially designed around the turn of the century by architect Bertram G. Goodhue in collaboration with Ingalls Kimball of the Cheltenham Press in New York City. When this typeface went into commercial production at the American Type Founders Company, designer Morris F. Benton supervised its development. Benton designed about eighteen additional typefaces for the Cheltenham family. Variations developed by other typefounders and manufacturers of typesetting equipment expanded this family to more than thirty styles. The design properties linking the Cheltenham family are short, stubby slab serifs with rounded brackets, tall ascenders and long descenders, and a moderate weight differential between thick and thin strokes.

Cheltenham
Cheltenham
Cheltenham
Cheltenham
Cheltenham
Cheltenham
Cheltenham
Cheltenham
Cheltenham
Cheltenham
Cheltenham
Cheltenham
Cheltenham
Cheltenham
Cheltenham
Cheltenham
Cheltenham
Cheltenham
Cheltenham
Cheltenham
Cheltenham

32.

Goudy Handtooled

31.

30.
Elaborations of Helvetica
Medium.

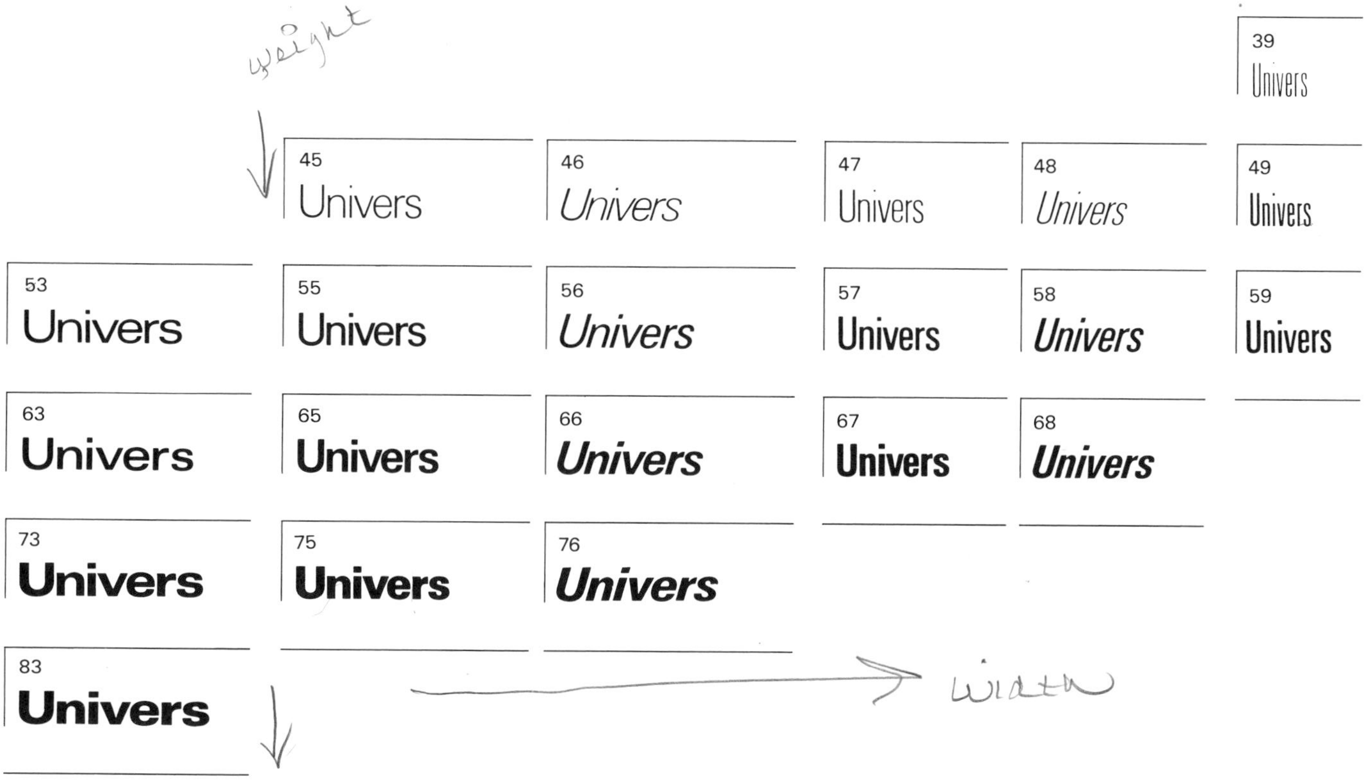

Same #s - width (handwritten)

weight (handwritten)

					39 Univers
45 Univers	46 *Univers*		47 Univers	48 *Univers*	49 Univers
53 Univers	55 Univers	56 *Univers*	57 Univers	58 *Univers*	59 Univers
63 Univers	65 Univers	66 *Univers*	67 Univers	68 *Univers*	
73 Univers	75 Univers	76 *Univers*			
83 Univers					

width (handwritten)

33.

The Univers family

A full range of typographic expression and visual contrast becomes possible when all the major characteristics—weight, proportion, and angle—are orchestrated into a unified family. An exceptional example is the Univers family (Fig. **33**). This family of twenty-one typestyles was designed by Adrian Frutiger. Instead of the usual terminology, Frutiger used numerals to designate the typefaces. Univers 55 is the "parent" face; its stroke weight and proportions are the norm from which all the other designs were developed. The black-and-white relationships and proportions of Univers 55 are ideal for text settings. Careful study of Figure **33** reveals that the first digit in each font's number indicates the stroke weight, three being the lightest and eight the heaviest. The second digit indicates expansion and contraction of the spaces within and between

the letters, which results in expanded and condensed styles. Roman fonts are designated with an odd number, and oblique fonts are designated with an even number.

In the design of Univers, Frutiger sparked a trend in type design toward a larger x-height. The lowercase letters are larger relative to ascenders, descenders, and capitals. The size and weight of capitals are closer to the size and weight of lowercase letters, creating increased harmony on the page of text. Because the twenty-one members of the Univers family share the same x-height, capital height, and ascender and descender length and are produced as a system, they can be intermixed and used together without limitation. This gives extraordinary design flexibility to the designer (Fig. **34**).

34.
Typographic interpretation of *The Bells* by Edgar Allen Poe using the Univers family. (Designer: Philip Meggs)

Hear the

sledges with the **Bells**

SILVER **Bells**- -

What a world of **merriment** their *melody* foretells!

How they *tinkle,*

tinkle,

tinkle, in the icy air of night!

While the stars that

o v e r s p r i n k l e

All the heavens seem to t w i n k l e

With a *crystalline* delight:

Keeping *time, time,* **time,**

In a sort of **R**unic rhyme,

To the **tin**tin*nab*u**la**tion that so *musically* wells

From the *bells,* bells, Bells,

Bells,

BELLS, **Bells**- -

From the *jingling* and the *tingling* of the bells.

Like the anatomy of typography, typographic syntax and communication have a language that must be learned to understand typographic design. Syntax is the connecting of typographic signs to form words and sentences on the page. The elements of design—letter, word, line, column, and margin—are made into a cohesive whole through the use of typographic space, visual hierarchy, ABA form, and grid systems. In this chapter, the relationship between form and meaning is also addressed. The imaginative designer can expand and clarify content through the communicative use of visual form.

Typographic syntax

In grammar, syntax is the manner in which words are combined to form phrases, clauses, or sentences. We define *typographic syntax* as the process of arranging elements into a cohesive whole. The study of typographic syntax begins with its basic unit, the letter, and progresses to word, line, column, and margin.

1.

This composition demonstrates contrasting visual characteristics of three letterforms. (Designer: Robert Boyle)

2.

Through precise letterform drawing and carefully considered form-to-counterform interaction, two dissimilar letters form a cohesive sign. (Designer: Gail Collins)

3.

Two letterforms are each broken into two geometric shapes of varying size and density, and the four resulting forms are combined into a delicate, asymmetrically balanced symbol. (Designer: Frank Armstrong)

1.

2.

The letter

Our initial discussion of typographic syntax addresses the intrinsic character of the individual letter. This well-drawn form, exhibiting subtlety and precision, is the unit that distinguishes one family of type from another. It exists in various weights, sizes, and shapes (Fig. **1**).

Although the letter typically functions as part of a word, individual letters are frequently combined into new configurations. As shown in Figures **2** and **3**, combinations of letters *A* and *g* and *P* and *Q* reveal a stable gestalt. In the illustrated examples, there is an expressiveness and boldness to the individual letters. The syntax displayed here is an example of letter combinations acting as signs, extracted from a larger system of signs.

A typographic sign is visually dynamic because of its interaction with the surrounding white space or void—the white of the paper. This form-to-void relationship is inherent in the totality of typographic expression. The repetition of the letter *T* in Figure **4** is balanced and complemented by its white space. In the title page for Hans Arp's book *On My Way,* the visual interplay between the three letterforms animates the page (Fig. **5**). This equilibrium and spatial interaction and the manner in which it is achieved will be discussed further in our study of typographic space.

Contemplating this ability of space to define form, Amos Chang observed, ". . . it is the existence of intangible elements, the negative, in architectonic forms which makes them come alive, become human, naturally harmonize with one another, and enable us to experience them with human sensibility."

4.

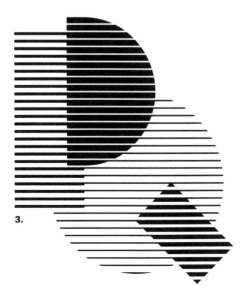

3.

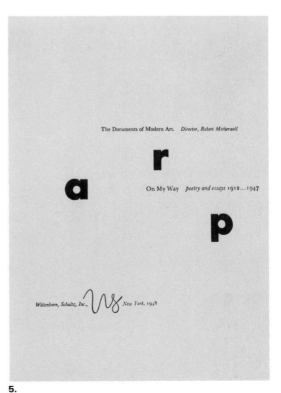

5.

4.
It is the figure/ground reversal in the repetition of the letter *T* that creates a balanced and expressive poster. (Designer: Willi Kunz)

5.
A dynamic composition is formed by the precise spatial location of the letterforms *a, r,* and *p,* which also spell the author's name. (Designer: Paul Rand)

6.

A star, a glass, and a word contribute to form a sign for joy. The word's meaning is expressed visually and poetically. (Designer: Frank Armstrong)

8.

This dissection of the word *Camerata* displays the letterform combinations and the relationships between consonants and their connecting vowels. Contrast and repetition create lateral movement within a word, and the overall arrangement relates to the word's meaning. (Designer: Sergio de Jesus)

6.

8.

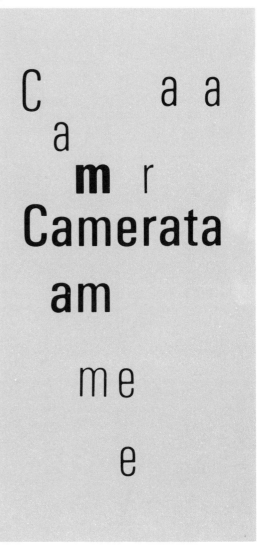

7.

Word-to-word interaction exhibits rhythmic recurrences of form and counterform. Individual letterforms are paired and the their corresponding interior counters are related here. (Designer: John Rodgers)

The word

By definition, a word has the potential to express an idea (Fig. **6**), object, or event. Word signs are independent of the things they represent, yet by design they can be made to signify and reveal their meaning.

Form and counterform relationships, found within individual letterforms, also exist within individual words. Speaking on the structural consideration of form and counterform and the designing of typefaces, Adrian Frutiger stated: "The material of typography is the black, and it is the designer's task with the help of this black to capture space, to create harmonious whites inside the letters as well as between them."

By observing this principle and by combining form and counterform into word units, the designer discovers subtle typographic connections and rhythms (Fig. **7**). The word unit is a constellation of individual letterforms, suggesting a union and forming a cohesive whole. Optically adjusted spaces and consistent counterform relationships assure the overall clarity of this union.

Discussing interletter spacing, the painter and graphic artist Ben Shahn tells about his training as an apprentice who lettered on lithographic stones in 1913. The shop foreman explained, "Imagine you have in your hand a glass that will hold only so much water. Now you must provide space between your letters—whatever their slants and curves may be—to hold just that much water, no more or less." The universal principle for spacing letters is this: the typographer, calligrapher, or designer attempts to make the interletter space between each pair of letters appear equal to the space between every other pair of letters. Because these counterform spaces have such different configurations, this spacing must be achieved through optical balance, rather than through measurement.

Figure **8** shows a dissection of the word *Camerata,* displaying various interletter relationships, including both geometric and organic features. In this example, the word's internal pattern is created by the visual properties of the individual letterforms and their various juxtapositions. This arrangement displays the nature of the internal pattern. *Camerata* is an Italian word meaning "a room full of people"; this meaning supplies yet another interpretation of the overall pattern. Such form-to-content relationships will be discussed later in this chapter.

A concern for form and counterform is evident in the equilibrium that is established among the letterforms comprising the word *Camerata.* It is extremely important to see the interior rhythms of a single word. In the example shown, the letters *C, m, r,* and *t* function as elements of contrast, while the three *a*s and the *e* act as the unifying elements. A similar use of contrast and repetition is demonstrated by the progression of letterforms within the corporate logotype for Olivetti (Fig. **9**).

Obviously, not all words offer the potential for such a rich typographic internal pattern. The complex and lively forms reproduced here clearly show the variety and fullness of form that exists in some deceptively simple word units.

In the Olivetti logo, the x-height establishes continuity, and the five ascending vertical forms create a horizontal rhythm. The repetition of rounded forms (*o* and *e*) and the "echo effect" of a rounded form followed by vertical strokes create a lively unity; the angled strokes of the letter *v* introduce an element of contrast. (Designer: Walter Ballmer)

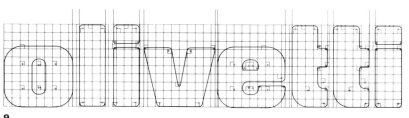

9.

*Of all the achievements
of the human mind, the birth of the alphabet
is the most momentous.*

10.

Symmetrical placement
produces a quiet, balanced
configuration.

11.

Asymmetrical placement
achieves a dynamic division
of space on the page.
(Designer: Ivy Li)

The line

Words are joined to form verbal sentences and
typographic lines. The configuration and
placement of lines of type are significant structural
concerns. In its most basic form, a line of type
consists of a single point size and a single weight
extended horizontally over a specific line width.

Lines of type can be arranged symmetrically (Fig.
10), or asymmetrically (Fig. **11**). The viewer/reader
must sense a clearly established relationship
between individual lines of type and the
surrounding space (Fig. **12**).

The smallest change in point size, weight, or line
length controls the overall emphasis given to a line
of type. The designer or typographer must determine when the overall effect is balanced and fully
integrated. All design considerations—typeface
selection, alignments, and spacing—should
display connections that are apparent and distinct
(Fig. **13**). Jan Tschichold states, "The relationship
of the sizes must in any case be clearly visible, its
effect must be lively, and it must always follow the
sense of the text exactly."

The length of a group of lines of type can be equal
(justified) or unequal (flush left/ragged right,
ragged left/flush right, or centered). The examples
in this section illustrate various typographic
alignments. Typographic form becomes lively and
harmonious through these alignments, which
enhance individual lines of type and activate the
surrounding space (Figs. **14** and **15**).

The placement of punctuation marks is of special
significance to these alignments. In Figure **16**
punctuation marks extend into the margin. Slight
adjustments and subtle refinements heighten the
degree of unity.

Typographic rules are used in conjunction with
type and separate one line of type from another or
one group of typographic lines from another as in
Figure **12**, or in footnotes. Rules are found in a
variety of forms (Fig. **17**) and numerous sizes and
weights. (The use of visual punctuation, including
typographic rules, is detailed in *Visual Hierarchy.*)

Earlier, we discussed kerning and the optical
spacing of letterforms. Control of these factors
makes possible a judicious use of letterspacing in a
line of type. The orientation of lines raises a
multiplicity of other spacing concerns; for example,
interword spacing, interline spacing, and line-to-
page relationships, as well as the establishment of
columns and margins.

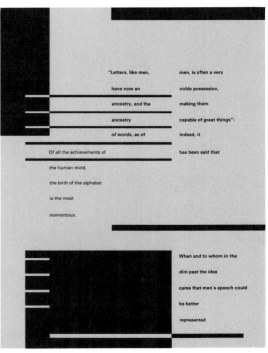

12.

Type and rules combine to
bring a sense of unity to the
page. Note the recurrence of
similar space intervals and
the attention given to individual line breaks (the rhythmic
pattern of line endings). (Designer: Cheryl Van Arnam)

13.

This multiple-line composition contains varying line
weights, yet expresses
wholeness through the careful placement of all elements.
It displays the diversity possible in the spacing of lines of
type. (Designer: Wolfgang
Weingart)

12.

"Bauhaus Masters"
Marcel Breuer
Paul Klee
Herbert Bayer

"Bauhaus Masters"
Marcel Breuer
Paul Klee
Herbert Bayer
16.

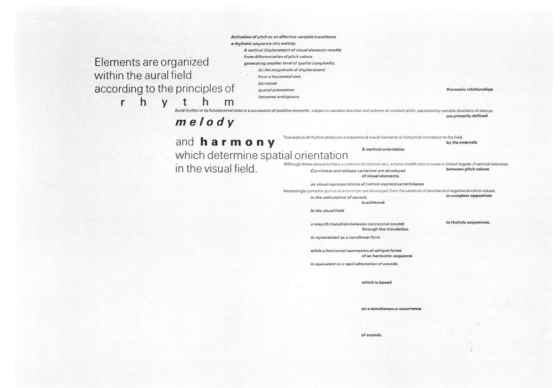

14.

14.

Complex and subtle relationships in interline spacing are
achieved here by varying
type size, weight, and spatial
interval which separate the
statements for the reader.
The overall effect is rhythmic
and expressive. (Designer:
Frank Armstrong)

15.

In this conversation, the
placement of lines and
intervals reflects the dialogue.
(Designer: Warren Lehrer)

16.

In the *top* setting the lines are
flush left, but the edge
appears uneven because of
the punctuation. In the bottom version, "hanging" the
punctuation into the margin
is an adjustment resulting in
an optically aligned edge.

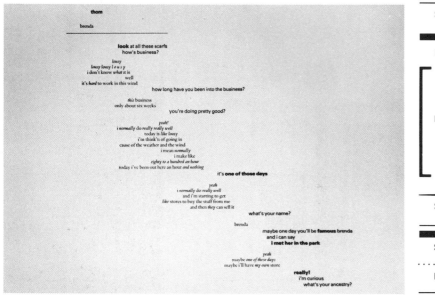

15.

Straight-line rule

Bar rule

Bracket rule

Swelled rule

Scotch rule

Leader

17.

18.

Six columns of type are arranged horizontally, allow-ing ample breathing space for the photographic image. Varying column depths make possible a clear integration of typographic and pictorial form. (Art Director: Bart Crosby; Designer: Carl Wohlt)

19.

Three columns of type create a vertical movement. Their uneven depths serve to bal-ance other elements. The use of rules and bold headings breaks the overall grayness of the text. (Art Directors: Bart Crosby and Carl Wohlt)

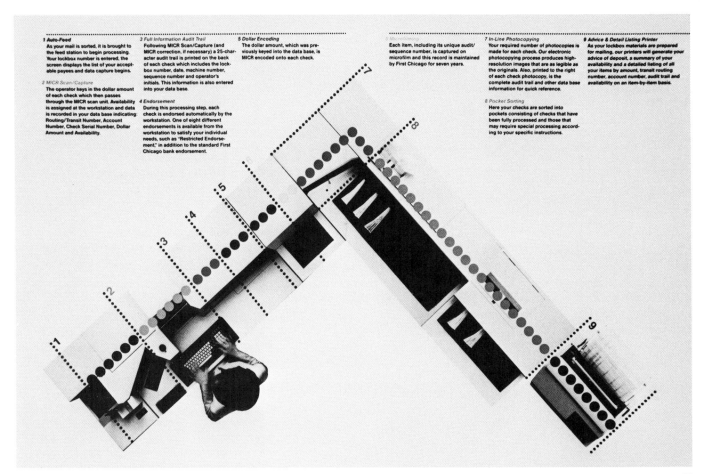

18.

19.

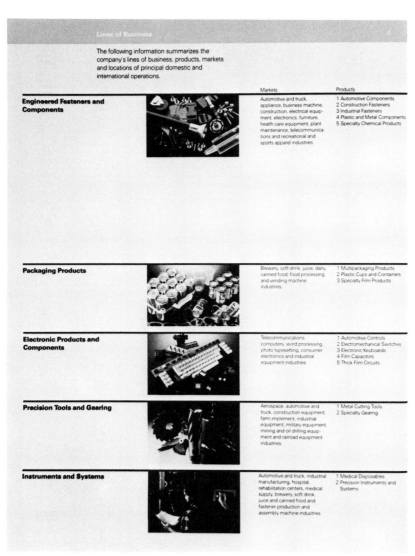

The following information summarizes the company's lines of business, products, markets and locations of principal domestic and international operations.

	Markets	Products
Engineered Fasteners and Components	Automotive and truck, appliance, business machine, construction, electrical equipment, electronics, furniture, health care equipment, plant maintenance, telecommunications and recreational and sports apparel industries.	1 Automotive Components 2 Construction Fasteners 3 Industrial Fasteners 4 Plastic and Metal Components 5 Specialty Chemical Products
Packaging Products	Brewery, soft drink, juice, dairy, canned food, food processing and vending machine industries.	1 Multipackaging Products 2 Plastic Cups and Containers 3 Specialty Film Products
Electronic Products and Components	Telecommunications, computers, word processing, photo typesetting, consumer electronics and industrial equipment industries.	1 Automotive Controls 2 Electromechanical Switches 3 Electronic Keyboards 4 Film Capacitors 5 Thick Film Circuits
Precision Tools and Gearing	Aerospace, automotive and truck, construction equipment, farm implement, industrial equipment, military equipment, mining and oil drilling equipment and railroad equipment industries.	1 Metal Cutting Tools 2 Specialty Gearing
Instruments and Systems	Automotive and truck, industrial manufacturing, hospital, rehabilitation centers, medical supply, brewery, soft drink, juice and canned food and fastener production and assembly machine industries.	1 Medical Disposables 2 Precision Instruments and Systems

20.

20.

Columns and margins are carefully balanced through the use of contrasting type sizes and weights and of two rule weights. (Art Director: Bart Crosby; Designer: Carl Wohlt)

Column and margin

As an extension of the spatial qualities inherent in single letters, pages also possess form and counterform relationships due to the interaction of columns and their surrounding spaces. Functional clarity and visual beauty are established in the harmonious relationships of these spaces.

Three specific variables related to columns govern these relationships: the proportion of column height to width, texture (the tactile appearance of the type), and tone (the lightness and darkness of type). It is through the manipulation of these contrasting variables that pages are spatially activated, optically balanced, and hierarchically ordered. Additionally, the height and width of columns (and their adjoining space intervals) should be carefully examined to ensure adequate legibility (for further discussion, see Chapter 4).

When organizing text columns, either horizontal or vertical movements may be emphasized. One will often dominate, as shown in Figures **18** and **19**. Eye movement across the page (side to side and top to bottom) is controlled by column rhythms, typographic weights, and rules functioning as visual punctuation. By the manipulation of these elements, the designer groups information according to its role in a given layout, and guides the eye methodically through the space of the page. Each of the vertical columns in Figure **20**, for example, separates specific categories of information to make them easier to find. The first column, with bold-weight type, contains general information and is dominant; the two right-hand columns, with lightweight type, contain secondary information and are subordinate.

21.

In this annual report there are subtle spatial relationships. These include the form/counterform of the column to the margin; the placement of the heading and subheading, which extend into the margin for emphasis; and the column mass to rules, photograph, and caption. (Designer: Frank Armstrong)

22.

This magazine page exhibits the needed contrast between text and caption elements. The column width of the text is double the column width of the caption. (Art Director: Ben Day; Designer: Anne Stewart)

The one- and two-column arrangements shown in Figures **21** and **22** illustrate some of the possibilities for text-column placement. In the two-column arrangement, the column depths are equal. Vitality and contrast are achieved by the placement of the adjacent photograph, its caption, and the bar rule containing the title. In both examples, the caption-column width and the text-column width are of different lengths, providing sufficient contrast to indicate to the reader that the caption is not part of the text. Such contrasts in column size, shape, texture, and tone are used to distinguish between different kinds of information and to provide visually luminescent pages.

Figure **23** is another example of how columns contrast one with another. Differences in the columns are produced by changing the interline spacing and the size and weight of the text type. Relative to one another, the columns can be seen as open or closed, light or dark.

The difference in tonality, which is an important design consideration, hierarchically leads the eye from one element to the next, and finally into the white of the page (for further discussion, see *Visual Hierarchy*). The critically determined spatial intervals create an engaging visual rhythm.

The size of type may vary from column to column (Fig. **24**) or within a column (Fig. **25**). As indicated in the latter diagram, type that is larger or heavier in weight appears more dense and is therefore emphasized on the page. Changes in density provide a kind of contrast that makes it possible to balance various typographic elements and add rhythmic qualities to the page.

The scale and proportion of columns, intervals between columns, and margins and their relationships to one another must be carefully adjusted as determined by the kinds of information they support. In Figure **21**, generous, unequal margins frame a single column of quiet text type for a hospital's annual report, while in Figure **19**, narrow margins surround quickly read narrow columns for an efficient-looking publication about computers. Margins not only frame parts within

1982: Highlights

The Bridgeport Hospital family, 4,367 members strong, is a special and meaningful community. Our goals blend the values of fine health care and human compassion with a balanced regard for technology and the demands of cost containment. Our mission is health care; the time clock of our Hospital community is idiosyncratic and without regard for "appropriate hours of rest." Every person in this community values, and is valued for, his and her role in the complex process of healing. The photographs and essay on these pages bring to your attention some of the highlights of fiscal year 1982.

The state Commission on Hospitals and Health Care (CHHC) approved three certificate of need applications from Bridgeport Hospital in 1982: *a linear accelerator*, whose high energy X-ray and electron beams destroy cancer cells in the treatment of patients with cancer: *a full body CAT-Scanner*, a computerized diagnostic tool that produces X-ray pictures of thin sections of the entire human body: and *a new, state-of-the-art, cardiovascular laboratory*, and *a special radiologic procedures lab* for the diagnoses of cardiovascular disease and peripheral vascular diseases.

Historically, patients undergoing surgery spend a fair amount of time in the hospital for pre-operative testing and post-operative recuperation. In an attempt to realistically assess and better meet the needs of patients as well as to improve operating room utilization, Dr. Claude Duval, chairman of the department of Anesthesiology, in conjunction with assistant administrator Erica Pifer, began work on modifying our existing one-day surgery center project. On April 20, the facility expanded its operation with a dedicated team of nurses in a new area constructed by plant operations.

New Faces Highlight the Year

Dennis Wasson, M.D., an attending surgeon, served as president of the Bridgeport Hospital attending staff in 1981 and was re-elected in 1982 to serve as president of the 478 active and courtesy physicians. At the annual meeting of the medical staff in 1983, Anthony Musto, M.D., an attending physician in Ophthalmology, was named president of the Bridgeport Hospital attending staff for 1983 and Dr. Wasson was named Chief of Staff and chairman of the attending staff executive committee. Howard L. Taubin, M.D., an attending physician in the section of Gastroenterology, was chairman of the executive committee and Chief of Staff in 1982. Some of the other personnel changes during the year include the naming of Robert M. Daly, M.D., as chairman of the newly created department of Psychiatry; and the appointment of Wesley D. Simmons to the newly created post, vice president of finance.

Two new sections of the department of Surgery were established during 1982. Glenn W. Sandberg, M.D., was named chief of the new section of Cardiothoracic Surgery and Stuart A. Levinson, M.D., was named chief of the new section of Vascular Surgery.

Wilbur Stratton
pharmacist
Department of Pharmacy

21.

23.

This experimental text composition reveals various combinations of typographic texture and tone.

24.

Variation in size, column to column.

25.

Variation in size within a column.

25.

24.

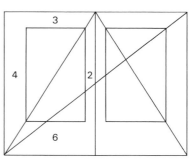

by Joseph Dyer

For centuries the mainstay of music and art in the Western world was a system of patronage sustained by the twin pillars of court and church. Musicians, if not entirely comfortable with the arrangement, adjusted to the demands of their princely or ecclesiastical employers. Haydn's international fame eventually freed him from the constraints of court service. Mozart chafed under the yoke of subordination forced upon him at Salzburg, until in desperation he threw it off for a freelance career. Beethoven broke completely with the old system. His genius was such that, despite the coarseness of his manners and sometimes insolent behavior, patrons and would-be recipients of dedications paid court to him.

With a change in the social climate and the development of a large middle-class audience founded on the new mercantile and industrial wealth, composers became less dependent on direct subsidy. Profits from publication further strengthened their independence. Patronage, however, continues to be an important factor even in its modern form, institutionalized by governments and foundations.

The works on Handel & Haydn's February program represent different facets of this historical phenomenon. For Mozart the delightful "Epistle" Sonata, K. 244, constituted little more than the fulfillment of an obligation connected with his duties as a cathedral musician. Haydn's *Theresienmesse* and the Poulenc Organ Concerto owe their existence to special relationships between their composers and two princess-patrons.

When Haydn returned from his second trip to England in 1795, he had a new master, Nicolaus II Esterházy, grandson of the prince for whom he had created so many masterpieces between 1762 and 1790. Haydn was no longer willing to accept the servant-master relationship which had prevailed in the past. Princess Marie

took a series of lovers, and poured out her dismay in lacrymose poetry. Notwithstanding his divided loyalties, her husband saw to it that her name day in September was celebrated in a manner befitting the consort of a Hungarian potentate. The festivities—concerts, theatrical events, fireworks, hunting parties—occupied several weeks. Yearly, between 1796 and 1802 (with the exception of 1802) a new Mass by Haydn was sung in the Bergkirche at Eisenstadt as the centerpiece of the religious observances.

The prince was not a man of cultivated musical tastes, and his favorite church music tended to the conservative side. According to one of Haydn's pupils, Johann Nepomuk Hummel, the six late Masses of his teacher reflect the taste of the princess, "for whom a Mass in an attractive elegant style would have more value than a learned or more serious work." (I bue to a misunderstanding, the Mass in B flat of 1799 was assumed to have been written for Marie Therese, wife of Emperor Francis II, hence the name *Theresienmesse.*)

Marie Hermenegild expressed her affection for Haydn's devoted service in many touching ways. She commiserated with the sufferings caused by the agonizing decline in his physical condition. With accustomed thoughtfulness she sought to soften the blow of his brother Johann's death in 1805 by bringing the news to him personally. A year later, learning that Haydn's pension was insufficient for his living expenses, she appealed to her husband. Prince Nicolaus wrote to Haydn immediately, expressing his "esteem and friendship" for him and increasing his retirement income by a generous amount.

The princess paid Haydn many visits at his house in Gumpendorf, where he lived as a semi-invalid. Her solicitude also assured a steady supply of special wine from the princely cellars. The famous depiction of a performance of

Haydn, Poulenc and the Princesses

Hermenegild helped to smooth over the dissimilar expectations of her haughty husband and his famous *Kapellmeister.* Haydn knew how to play the diplomat as well, and the two men soon established an understanding based on mutual respect.

Prince Nicolaus II had a particular interest in church music, an unusual passion for one of Vienna's most notorious débauchés. He established his paramours in houses of their own, where (in the words of an English observer) "they share his favours and diminish his faculties." The princess resigned herself to these indignities,

Haydn's Creation in the great hall of the old University of Vienna shows her presenting her shawl to Haydn as protection against the chill—a heartfelt expression of her tender concern for the genius who honored her with so many masterpieces.

The Princess Edmond de Polignac (1865-1943), led a nearly legendary existence, immersed in all the leading literary, artistic and musical currents which had Paris as their center. She was born Winnaretta Singer, eighteenth child of Isaac Merritt Singer (of sewing machine fame). When she was two years of age, the family moved to

22.

The whole duty of typography, as of calligraphy, is to communicate to the imagination, without loss by the way, the thought or image intended to be communicated by the Author. And the whole duty of beautiful typography is not to substitute for the beauty or interest of the thing thought and intended to be conveyed by the symbol, a beauty or interest of its own, but, on the one hand, to win

The whole duty of typography, as of calligraphy, is to communicate to the imagination, without loss by the way, the thought or image intended to be communicated by the Author. And the whole duty of beautiful typography is not to substitute for the beauty or interest of the thing thought and intended to be conveyed by the symbol, a beauty or interest of its own, but, on the one hand, to win access for that communication by the clearness and beauty of the

The whole duty of typography, as of calligraphy, is to communicate to the imagination, without loss by the way, the thought or image intended to be communicated by the Author.

23.

---

pages, they also contain supportive elements (marginalia) such as running heads, folios, and captions.

The elegant margins shown in Figure **26** have proportions identical to the page. The margin ratio is two margin units to three to four to six, as indicated. In other words, the bottom margin is twice as high as the top margin. Jan Tschichold has pointed out that this complex series of column-to-margin ratios, based on the golden section, is found in numerous medieval manuscripts. (For further discussion about margins, see *The Typographic grid,* page 68).

Paragraph breaks within a column greatly influence the relationship between a column of text and its surrounding margins. A break may be introduced as an indention, as a space interval, or as a combination of both. Designers have also developed their own ways to indicate paragraphs (Fig. **27**). The overall page organization will determine the most suitable method.

When columns, margins, and their interrelationships are clear and appropriate to content, the result is a printed page of distinction. Every problem demands a fresh approach, yet an ordered unity that is responsive to the meaningful blend of form and counterform is always the goal.

---

independence in the student.
"Accordingly, handicraft in the workshops was right from the start, not an end in itself, but laboratory experiment preparatory to industrial production. If the initial products of the Bauhaus looked like individual craft products, this was a necessary detour for the groping student whom we avoided to prod with a foregone conclusion."

We salvaged the best of experimental education and added to it a carefully constructed program of information-based design that produced noncommercial products that worked. It was a different school with different people with different goals in a different time. Our aim was to produce designers who had the will, the ability, and the ethical base to change American production for the better.

I was somewhat concerned that this might be a middle-of-the-road

27.

Placement of a bullet (a typographic dot used for emphasis) upon intercolumn rules designates new paragraphs in this booklet design. (Designer: Jeff Barnes)

26.

28.
Spatial elements are balanced through the principle of visual compensation, achieving equilibrium and tension. Elements form relationships with other elements through carefully planned juxtapositions and alignments.

Tension exists between the edge of the composition and adjacent elements. These basic forces affect typographic organization and help achieve dynamic, asymmetrical composition. (Designer: JeanBrueggenjohn)

"Speech proceeds in time and writing proceeds in space." Applying Karl Gerstner's statement to typographic design, typographic space is the rhythmic and dimensional field in which typographic communication exists. This field consists of positive form (the typographic elements) and void (the spatial ground) upon which the elements are arranged. Unity within the space is achieved by visual compensation; that is, the spatial balance and arrangement of typographic elements. Amos Chang, discussing the relationship between compensation and visual dynamics, wrote, "this process of growth from deficiency to compensation brings inherent movement to physical form . . . we may borrow an important rule of balance from the anatomy of a zoological being, man in particular . . . man's body is in a state of balance when his arms and legs are in a position to be moved effectively to compensate for position changes of the body."

Visual compensation is achieved by balancing elements against each other, adjusting their sizes, weights, spatial intervals, and other visual properties until unity and equilibrium are achieved (Figs. **28-30**). In Figure **3**, two contrasting letterform pairs are balanced. The letterform pair *fj* suggests contraction and consonance, while *gv* expresses expansion and dissonance. Consonance is a harmonious relationship between similar or corresponding elements, while dissonance is a discordant relationship between dissimilar elements. In Figure **32**, dissonant elements are combined with consonant form-to-void relationships, resulting in a state of visual balance and unity.

29.
Pictorial and typographic elements are placed in asymmetrical balance. Two pointed arches balance three rounded arches, and the ruled line moving into the margin corresponds to the letterspaced word, *Messiah*.

30

This dynamic poster combines both large three-dimensional letterforms and a complex arrangement of two-dimensional elements. From the arrangement emerges a spatial wholeness: the overlapping of elements is precise and expressive. Compensation is achieved through careful placement, with attention given to the surrounding void. (Designer: Frank Armstrong)

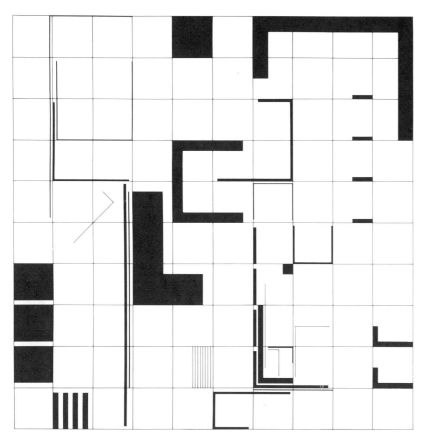

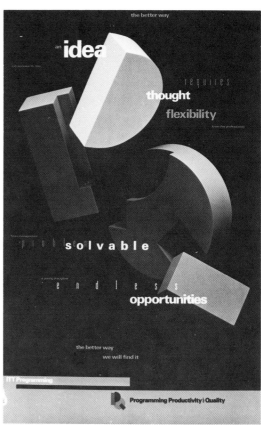

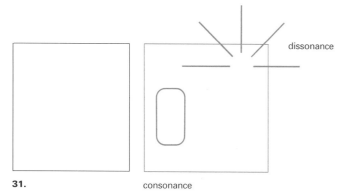

31.
(Designer: Lark Pfleegor)

32.

The contrast between geometric and gestural letterforms is dissonant. Unity is achieved by carefully planned shape correspondences and form-to-void relationships.

33.
Alignments create visual relationships between forms in space. (Designer: Jennifer Mugford Wieland)

34.
In this asymmetrically balanced composition, the edge of the type column aligns with the central axis of the circle. (Designer: Sergio de Jesus)

The structure of typographic space can be defined by alignments (Figs. **33-35**) and form-to-void relationships that establish a composition's underlying spatial order. This substructure is developed and enhanced through optical adjustment (Fig. **36**). Often inconspicuous, optical adjustment is the precise visual alignment of typographic elements in space based, not on mathematical, but perceptual alignment. The designer's understanding and use of optical adjustment is necessary for visual clarity.

Visual compensation and optical adjustment within the typographic space link printed elements and the spatial ground. This structural integration is not an end in itself; its order, simple or elaborate, acts as a stimulus, controlling the visual dynamics of the message transmission and response.

Nathan Knobler's observation in *The Visual Dialog* that "psychologists tell us that the need to understand, to find meaning in the world around us, is coupled with the need for stimulation and involvement" applies to design. To communicate with clarity and exactitude, the designer must be aware of the need to stimulate and involve the viewer. In typographic problem solving, the designer creates complex, highly interactive spatial environments (Fig. **37**) that establish coherence between the viewing experience and typographic form, between the verbal statement and written language.

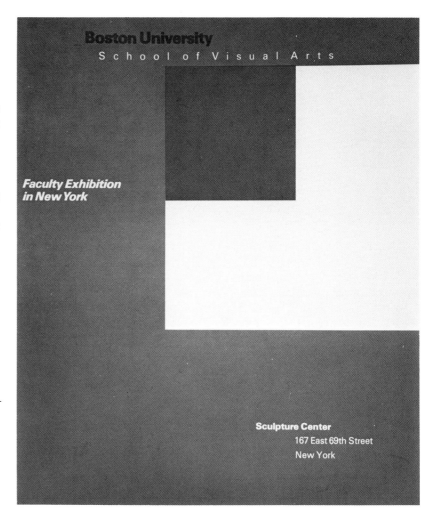

35.
Typographic elements are aligned with the horizontal and vertical edges of the geometric configuration.

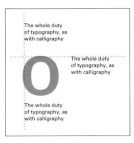

36.

Dotted lines indicate the use of alignments to relate forms to each other. Note the optical adjustment in relating the large *O* to the text type.

37.

In this exhibition catalog cover, horizontal and vertical alignment of elements bring order to a dynamic, asymmetrical design. Texture and tone create a vibrant luminosity. (Designer: Wolfgang Weingart)

Visual Hierarchy

38.
Type style, size, color, weight, and spacing are consistent, resulting in an even texture and tone. Visual hierarchy is almost nonexistent in this arrangement.

39.
A spatial interval equal to one line space separates the title from the other information, giving it prominence in the composition.

40.
Setting the title in bolder type further separates it from the overall tone and texture, increasing the hierarchical contrast.

A visual hierarchy is an arrangement of elements in a graduated series, from the most prominent to the least prominent, in an area of typographic space. When establishing a visual hierarchy, a designer carefully considers the relative importance of each element in the message, the nature of the reader, the environment where the communication will be read, and the need to create a cohesive arrangement of forms within the typographic space.

The study of visual hierarchy is the study of the relationships of each part to the other parts and the whole. When elements have similar characteristics, they have equality in the visual hierarchy, but when they have contrasting characterisitcs, their differences enable them to take dominant and subordinate positions in the composition.

Contrast between elements within the space is achieved by carefully considering their visual properties. Important contrasts used to create hierarchical arrangements include size, weight, color, and spatial interval. The location of an element within the space plays an important role in establishing a visual hierarchy. The spatial relationships with other elements can also influence an element's relative importance in the arrangement.

Principles used to achieve visual hierarchy through careful contrast between the elements are demonstrated by the nine small diagrams on this page (Figs. **38-46**). The nine typographic designs on the opposite page (Figs. **38a-46a**) correspond to these diagrams.

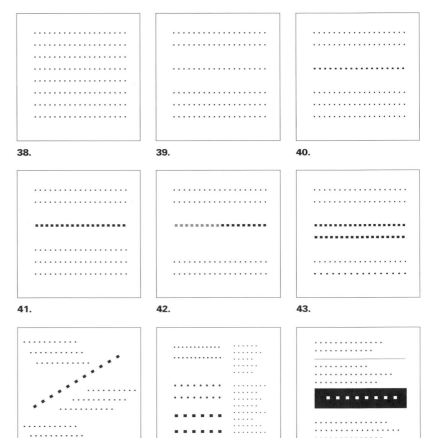

38.   39.   40.

41.   42.   43.

44.   45.   46.

41.
Changing the size and weight of the title makes it even more prominent in the visual hierarchy.

44.
The diagonal position of the title increases its prominence in the space. The smaller type elements align with the diagonals of the title's baseline and posture, unifying the composition.

42.
Color or value can create another level of contrast that can be controlled by the designer to create hierarchy.

45.
This composition demonstrates how extreme contrasts of type size and weight increase visual hierarchy and legibility from a distance.

43.
Two sizes and three weights of type are used to create subtlety and variety within the composition.

46.
Reversing the title from a black rectangle heightens contrast and increases the visual hierarchy. A ruled line separates the secondary type into two zones of information.

The Modern Literature
Society presents a lecture
by Raoul Ramirez,
Professor of Literature,
Santaneo State University
Modern Hispanic Poetry
7:30 p.m. March 23
The Humanities Center Auditorium
Admission is free

38a.

The Modern Literature
Society presents a lecture
by Raoul Ramirez,
Professor of Literature,
Santaneo State University

Modern Hispanic Poetry

7:30 p.m. March 23
The Humanities Center Auditorium
Admission is free

39a.

The Modern Literature
Society presents a lecture
by Raoul Ramirez,
Professor of Literature,
Santaneo State University

Modern Hispanic Poetry

7:30 p.m. March 23
The Humanities Center Auditorium
Admission is free

40a.

The Modern Literature
Society presents a lecture
by Raoul Ramirez,
Professor of Literature,
Santaneo State University

Modern Hispanic Poetry

7:30 p.m. March 23
The Humanities Center Auditorium
Admission is free

41a.

The Modern Literature
Society presents a lecture
by Raoul Ramirez,
Professor of Literature,
Santaneo State University

Modern Hispanic Poetry

7:30 p.m. March 23
The Humanities Center Auditorium
Admission is free

42a.

The Modern Literature Society
presents a lecture

Santaneo State University
Professor of Literature

Raoul Ramirez
Modern Hispanic Poetry

7:30 p.m. March 23
The Humanities Center Auditorium
Admission is free

43a.

The Modern Literature
Society presents
a lecture
Modern Hispanic Poetry

by Raoul Ramirez,
Professor of Literature,
Santaneo State University

7:30 p.m. March 23
The Humanities Center Auditorium
Admission is free

44a.

Santaneo State University
Professor of Literature

Raoul Ramirez

Modern Hispanic Poetry

The Modern
Literature
Society
presents
a lecture

7:30 p.m.
March 23
The
Humanities
Center
Auditorium
Admission
is free

45a.

The Modern Literature
Society presents a lecture

by Raoul Ramirez,
Professor of Literature,
Santaneo State University

Modern Hispanic Poetry

7:30 p.m. March 23
The Humanities Center Auditorium
Admission is free

46a.

47.
The letters *f* and *j* are
typographic counterparts
because their forms correspond. Integration and
equilibrium are achieved.
(Designer: Lark Pfleegor.)

When creating a visual hierarchy in typographic space, a designer balances the need for harmony, which unifies a design, with the need for contrast, which lends vitality and emphasis. As in music, elements can have a counterpart or a counterpoint relationship. Typographic counterparts are elements with similar qualities that bring harmony to their spatial relationship (Figs. **47** and **48**). Elements have a counterpoint relationship when they have contrasting characteristics, such as size, weight, color, tone, or texture. Counterpoint relationships bring opposition and dissonance to the design (Fig. **49**).

Typographic elements can have both counterpart and counterpoint relationships. In Figure **50**, extreme scale contrasts create a counterpoint relationship, while the modular letters, constructed from parallel horizontal and vertical elements, become typographic counterparts. Because the forms correspond, the *A*s (Fig. **41**) are counterparts, but their extreme scale contrast permits them to have a dissonant counterpoint relationship in the space. When organizing typographic elements into a visual hierarchy, it is useful to consider counterpart and counterpoint relationships.

48.
In this diagram, forms in the photograph and the letter *s* correspond. This counterpart relationship creates unity between these unlike elements. (Designer: Ivy Li)

49.
In these arrangements, the dominant elements (addition and multiplication signs) have a counterpoint relationship to the text blocks due to contrasts of scale and weight. Because the text blocks echo the structure of the addition and multiplication signs, and the elements have a balanced arrangement in the space, unity is achieved. (Designer: Lark Pfleegor)

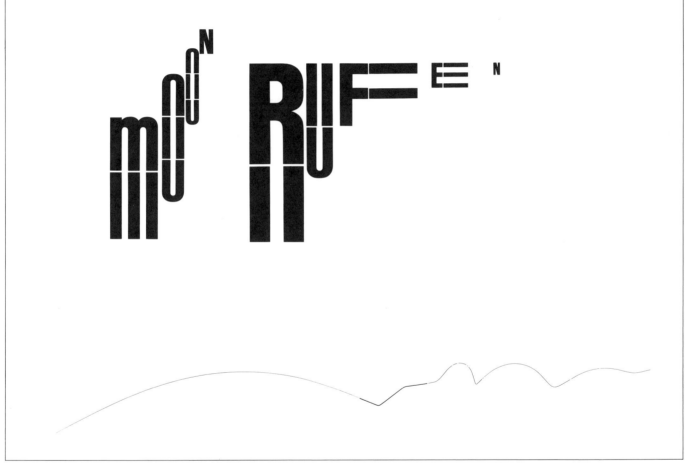

50.
A hierarchy of size gains unity and rhythm through the modular construction of letterforms. "Moon rufen" translates as "moon howling"; the type expresses the sound of a lone wolf howling at the moon. (Designer: Wolfgang Weingart)

51.
The repetition of the letter *A* in two different point sizes creates a dynamic hierarchical structure. (Designer: Paul Rand)

53.

In these typographic exercises, rules and space intervals are used as visual punctuation. (Designers: Bryan
Leister and Rebecca Lantz)

 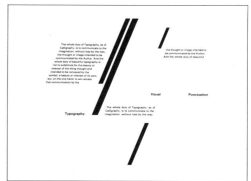

53.

52.

The word *sassafras* calls for
a response and the phrase *a
flavoring agent* provides the
reply. (Designer: Ivy Li)

Often, typographic elements in a visual hierarchy can be designated as questioning forms and answering forms (Fig. **52**). The typographic unit assigned the questioning role invites or calls for an answer. In a sense, the answering form has a counterpart relationship to the questioning form because it completes the communication. The most prominent visual element of a typographic hierarchy is frequently a questioning form. Consider the role of both typographic form and pictorial form: do individual components of a composition suggest a question or an answer? The questioning component expresses dissonance (unrelieved tension), while the answering component expresses consonance (relieved tension).

A typographic arrangement is partly governed by visual punctuation. As a writer uses standard punctuation marks to separate words and clarify meaning, a designer introduces visual punctuation (space intervals, rules, or pictorial elements) to separate, group, or emphasize words or lines. Visual punctuation (Figs. **53** and **54**) clarifies the reader/viewer's understanding of the content and structure of a typographic arrangement. Visual punctuation helps to clarify the meaning of the typographic message, while visual emphasis or accentuation is used to make one element more important. Emphasis is relative to the contrasting properties of elements; for example, in Figure **54** the word *collage* is dominant in the visual hierarchy due to its scale, weight, and position.

Visual accentuation is giving emphasis or stress to properties (round and straight, thick and thin, geometric and organic, etc.) of typographic and pictorial signs, usually through contrast with dissimilar elements. The bold and compelling mark combining the letter *A* and the scroll of a violin in Figure **45** is an example of visual accentuation through contrast. The geometric properties of the letter *A* are accentuated in opposition to the organic properties of the musical instrument. In this example, details in both the letter and pictorial form are accentuated or deleted, yet the legibility of the original letter and object has been retained. The letter *A* and the violin are incomplete, yet each retains its essence.

Typographic joinery is the visual linking and connecting of elements in a typographic composition through structural relationships and form repetition. The assembly of separate typographic elements to form a unified sign is seen in the logotype for the American Broadcasting Corporation (Fig. **56**). The pronounced geometry and emphasis given to the circular forms joins the forms through the use of the repetition. The shape of the circle is common to every part of this mark. The three letterforms and their circular container are blended to become one sign.

Some typographic designs are seen from different distances (far, middle, close). The viewer's perceptions are greatly influenced by shifts in the viewing experience. Attention to visual hierarchy and the perceptual environment is vital in graphic media (signage, posters, and exhibitions) where the viewing experience is in constant flux (Fig. **57**).

Typography's hierarchical order derives from the basic process of pattern-forming found in nature, in verbal and written language, the arts, and computer technology. This is aptly described by Gyorgy Doczi, speaking of his research on proportional harmonies in art and design, "The rhythms of writing are created by the same pattern-forming process of sharing that creates rhythms of dance, music and speech. Movements shared make dance, patterns shared make music and speech."

The shared patterns of typography find expression through visual dynamics that enable it to function as both a message-carrier and a rhythmic, visual structure. The typographic message, with all its limitless thought and diversity of form, is shaped by this subtle and meaningful hierarchical language.

ABC abc abc abc

56.

As typographic joinery becomes more developed, the unity of a mark is enhanced dramatically. (ABC logo, designer: Paul Rand)

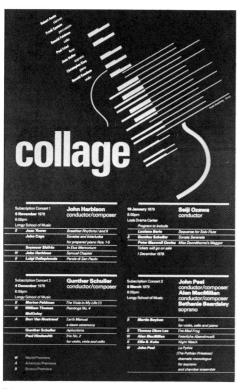

54.

55.

54.

In this poster, a complex system of rules separates, connects, and emphasizes the names of composers, conductors, and other information about numerous events. In the top area of the poster, ruled lines perform a different function: they combine to create a rhythmic visual sign for music. (Designer: Frank Armstrong)

55.

Visual accentuation is demonstrated by this symbol. Striking visual contrast is achieved through the opposition of straight and curved edges and shapes. (Designer: Nick Schrenk)

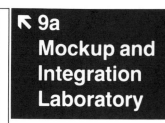

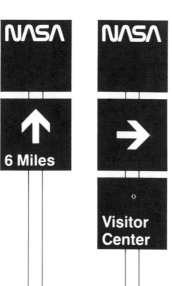

57.

In this signage for NASA, viewing context determines the visual hierarchy. For example, the size and position of the arrow in the interior directional signage are quite different from the size and position of the roadside signage. (Designer: Danne and Blackburn)

57.

ABA form

59.
Even though the functions of the small text block and the photograph are unrelated, these elements correspond to one another because of their similar sizes.

60.
Letters, when combined together as text, provide a treasury of textural contrasts. Corresponding textures reveal visual links between elements.

61.
When typographic elements possess contrasting tonal qualities, the eye perceives an implied three-dimensionality.

In typographic communication, visual relationships are established through an active dialogue between two fundamental design principles: repetition and contrast. It is through these principles that the typographic designer imbues messages with visual order and rhythmic variety.

Music structure is also based upon repetition and contrast, and because it is linear in nature, a quality that is common also to typography, it provides an excellent model for understanding basic typographic structure. The primary structural pattern of music is the three-part form of statement-depar-ture-re-turn (ABA). The unifying components (the two *A*s) function as repetition, while the middle component (the *B*) functions as contrast. Arnold Schoenberg observed that "the principle function of form is to advance our understanding. It is the organization of a piece which helps the listener to keep the idea in mind, to follow its development, its growth, its elab-oration, its fate." This quote also clarifies the mis-sion of typographic form, where relationships between visible typographic elements are guided by the dynamics of ABA form.

The viewer of typographic communication per-ceives form relationships as being either in opposi-tion or correspondence. This principle suggests that a fully integrated typographic composition depends upon the successful blending of elements of con-trast and repetition. The viewer seeks a variety that stimulates both eye and mind, while structuring the communications experience. This is the dual basis of ABA form.

ABA form in typography, as in music, is based upon a fundamental three-part structure where two *repeating* parts are in correspondence, and a third

58.

A	B	A	B

59.

A	B	A	B

60.

A	B	A	B

61.

contrasting part stands in opposition (Fig. **58**). This fundamental structure, however, may be found in abundant variation. This is true because contrasting and repeating typographic elements within a composition are governed by the dynamic principles of proportion and rhythm. It is via these principles that ABA form grows in complexity and diversity. By definition, proportion in ABA form is the ratio determined by the quantity, size, weight, texture, tone, shape, color (or other syntactic quality) of similar and dissimilar typographic elements (A**A**BA**A**BA**A**). Rhythm is established in the intervals of space separating these elements (A**A** . B . A**A** . B . A**A**). The following examples illustrate this idea:

When typographic elements are similar in size to one another, an immediate correspondence between these elements is established (Fig. **59**). This correspondence is heightened because the tonality of the photograph and small text block is darker than the tone of the larger text block. In the middle diagram, the correspondence between the smaller text blocks is also magnified (Fig. **60**). A third variation is created by altering the tone of the elements: a bold typeface is introduced in the smaller text blocks, linking them together. Here, the factors of both scale and tone establish a distinct pattern of repetition and contrast (Fig. **61**). In an applied example—the design of a concert poster—the recurrence and contrast of typographic tone and texture are demonstrated (Fig. **62**).

Further variations in ABA form are discovered when elaborations (ABa, ABAb or AbAc) of corresponding elements occur to establish subtle contrasts (Fig. **63**), or when primary and secondary relationships occur in compositions simultaneously (Fig. **64**). The foregoing examples show the influence of

62.

This poster is zoned into three spatial corridors: two columns of text, finely textured and light in tonal value, flank a dynamic arrangement of music-related visual signs, coarser in texture and darker in tone.

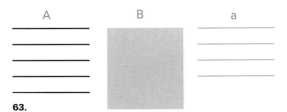

63.

proportion upon the relationships between typographic elements. The rhythmic patterns in each of these examples are identical, with equal or nearly equal intervals of space separating the elements. In a detail of the concert poster (Fig. **65**), a distinct rhythm composed of unequal spatial intervals between typographic elements can be observed. This rhythmic pattern may be viewed on two levels: the major group (A . BA), and the minor group (**a** . bb . . **a** . b . . **a** . bb . . **a**, etc.). The intervals between these elements facilitate the functional grouping of the parts of the message: the "instruments" are separated from the "performers" by a "1X" interval of space, and each of these groupings is separated one from another by a "2X" interval of space. Other syntactic traits bind and isolate the parts: the "instruments" are bold in typographic weight, linking them together, while the "performers" are light in weight. At the same time, all these typographic elements share the same type size to distinguish them from the location of the event, which is presented in a larger, italic, all-capitals typeface.

In this example, it is also possible to observe a phenomenon that appears at first as a contradiction in terms, but nonetheless is a condition in typographic design: perceiving typographic forms that are *simultaneously* in correspondence and opposition. This is a concept that is linked to a fundamental design notion: achieving unity within diversity (Fig. **66**). ABA form variations are capable of unifying diverse forms through visual correspondence, while at the same time bringing variety to similar forms through opposition. The skilled designer manipulates typographic elements to achieve this essential balance.

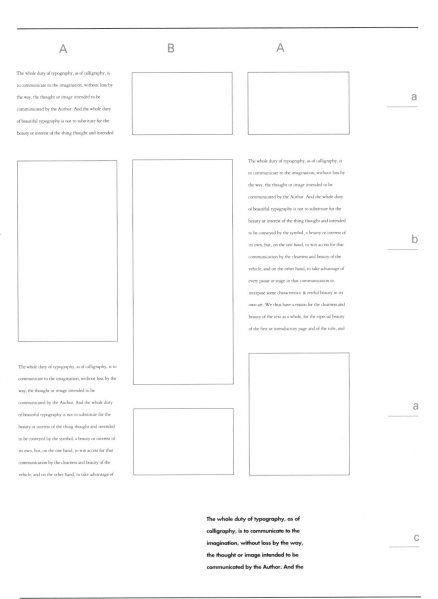

64.
The relationships established by the three vertical columns of equal width (ABA) achieve visual dominance over the three horizontal bands (aba). The small column of text (c), which departs from the visual pattern of the main unit in position and type weight, provides an additional variation.

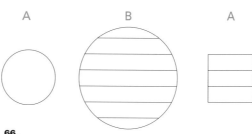

A B A

66.
Shape relates the first and middle forms; texture relates the middle and right forms; and size relates the left and right forms.

ABA form is comprised of both simple and complex patterns that give order and emphasis to the visual linking of typographic elements. These are not fixed systems but are a way of understanding the inter-relationships of typographic form. About music Joseph Machlis stated, "the forms . . . are not fixed molds into which the composer pours his material. What gives a piece of music its aliveness is the fact that it adapts a general plan to its own requirements."

a **Bass**

b Thomas Coleman
b Anthony Beadle

a **Flute**

b Elinor Preble

a **Oboe**

b Peggy Pearson
b Raymond Toubman

a **Clarinet**

a

S Y M P H O N Y

H A L L

b

a **Bassoon**

b Francis Nizzari
b Ronald Haroutunian

a **French Horn**

b Oaneka Oaujub

a

65.

67

The typographic grid

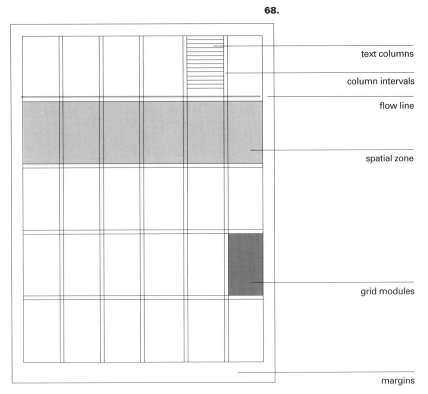

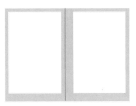

An elemental grid is based upon a "Cartesian" co-ordinate system of intersecting, perpendicular axes. It consists of rectangular modules defined by a network of horizontal and vertical lines (Fig. **67**). The typographic grid, which is an adaptation of this basic structure, possesses unique anatomical characteristics. These include margins that provide boundaries for typographic elements and define the "active" space of the page; grid modules that provide a framework for the designer in placing type and image; columns and the intervals of space between them that accommodate text settings; spatial zones that provide a means of organizing the various parts of information; and flow lines that establish a dominant flow of elements through alignment (Fig. **68**). The proportional relationships of these features, as well as the number of modules incorporated in a grid are influenced by the specific nature of the content, legibility considerations (see Chapter 4), and desired visual effect. Each of these considerations should be given the utmost attention by the designer.

An important consideration in determining an appropriate grid is that of margins. Regardless of the typographic application, these spatial zones, which surround the type area, can provide a sense of spatial stability if sensitively proportioned. For proportional harmony, margins should be at least as wide as the intervals of space between columns. Narrow margins create compositional tension as typographic elements interact dynamically with the edges of the page, whereas wide margins provide a sense of calm (Fig. **69**). No rules govern the use of margins; however, when margin intervals are unequal, the resulting visual tension can provide a pleasing asymmetrical appearance. In publications involving spreads, the gutter margins should take into account the amount of space needed for binding. Text columns should not appear as though they are being swallowed by the gutter. Also, margins should be generous enough to prevent printed elements from being improperly trimmed during the printing process. (For further discussion, see *Column and margin,* pp. 51–52.)

Typographic grids exist in a nearly infinite number of configurations, accommodating a wide range of design needs. Figure **70** presents a small sampling of grids that range from one to sixteen modules.

67.
Horizontal lines running along the x-axis, and vertical lines running along the y-axis are the elements composing a basic grid.

68.

text columns

column intervals

flow line

spatial zone

grid modules

margins

68.
The typographic grid is a structure with features specifically suited to the physical properties of typographic elements.

69.
Margins function within grids to set the typographic stage; they may be dynamically asymmetrical or quietly symmetrical.

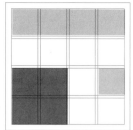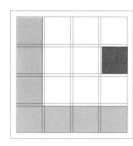

71.
Spatial interaction and
compositional balance are
achieved when modules de-
fine void spaces that are
integral to the geometry of
the page.

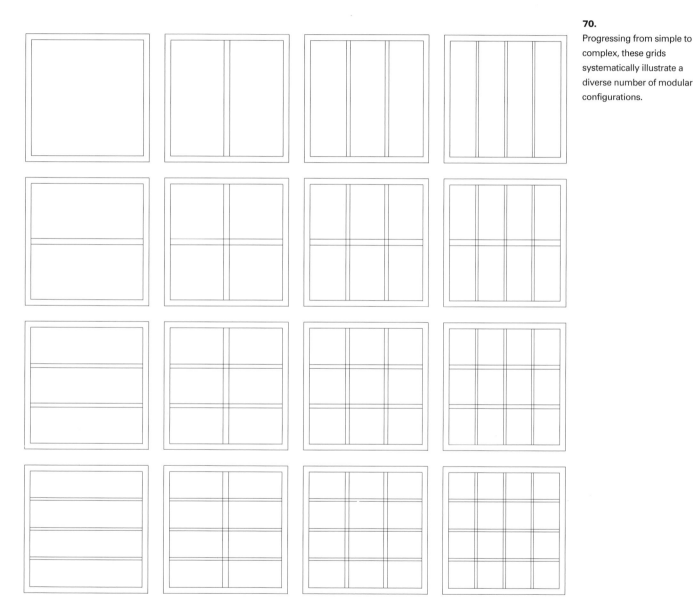

70.
Progressing from simple to
complex, these grids
systematically illustrate a
diverse number of modular
configurations.

These modules, which are constructed with horizontal and vertical lines, represent the type and
image areas of the grid. Variations in both the size
and shape of modules and the intervals of space
separating them are shown. Modules may be combined into a variety of sizes and configurations. It is
the designer's task to transform the rigid structure
of the grid into a lively pattern of positive and negative modular combinations (Fig. **71**). Generally, as
the number of modules within a grid increases, so
too does the designer's flexibility in organizing the
elements and achieving dynamic scale contrasts.
However, a point of diminishing returns is reached
when a grid is inappropriately complex for the content. Careful study of the content will reveal the
most appropriate grid for the occasion.

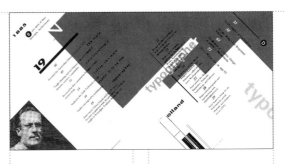

74.
Dynamic spatial forces are generated by diagonal grid divisions. (Designer: Eric Cruz)

Modular relationships can be established without the use of the traditional typographic grid. A grid ratio, which is a mathematical relationship between two or more grid measurements, governs the size and placement of typographic elements. The ratio X:2X (one unit to two units) indicates the relative size of grid dimensions (Fig. **72**). This stepped progression of X:2X establishes an underlying modular system among the parts.

The type area within a grid is comprised of vertical columns. The width of text columns and the intervals between them should promote optimum legibility when required. The size of type should be measured on the column width to achieve the ideal number of characters per line. Once these factors are considered, column widths may comprise any number of modules within the grid (Fig. **73**).

Grids may consist of primary and secondary divisions of space. For example, the grid used in this book consists of two columns as the dominant structure, with an optional structure of five columns (note the visible grid lines on this page). Concurrent grids not only provide added flexibility, they also enable the designer to layer typographic elements, achieving an illusion of three-dimensionality.

Departing from the conventions of the traditional grid, which is characterized by horizontal and vertical relationships, it may be desirable to employ dynamic structural divisions based upon the diagonal and the circle, or hybrid combinations of spatial divisions (Fig. **74**). Again, the designer should be keenly aware of the appropriateness of such approaches in light of the context of the problem.

Grids allow for the distribution of typographic elements into a clearly intelligible order. Within the internal structure created, headlines, text, captions, images, and other parts of the message are integrated. The areas occupied, which correspond to specific modules or groups of modules, are referred to as spatial zones. After identifying all the parts of a message, the designer assigns them to specific zones. The result is a logical hierarchy of parts and information that is more accessible to the reader.

The book *American Graphic Design Timelines* features a highly flexible grid that makes it possible for readers to compare and contrast timelines of several design and related themes, including major events in world and U.S. history, cultural events, American graphic designers, companies, organizations, and publications (Figs. **75–77**). In addition to the timelines, each section contains a number of other informational components that are accommodated by the grid. The American graphic designers section, for example, includes a headline (the designer's name), quotation, reproductions of characteristic work, captions describing the work, a narrative reviewing significant contributions to the field, and a biographical timeline. Timelines in all

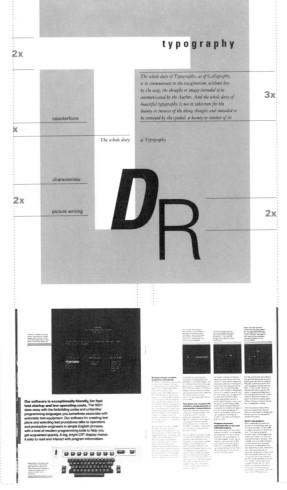

72.
This exploratory composition exhibits modular relationships among elements. (Designer: Debra Thompson)

73.
This layout, characterized by a rhythmic tension of typographic and photographic elements, demonstrates legible text settings on columns of single and triple module width. (Designer: John Kane)

77.
As the pages of the book turn, timelines can be compared one with another due to the interactive grid system.

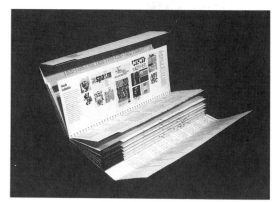

sections are organized in a nine-column grid, with each column corresponding to a decade in the twentieth century. As readers turn the pages, this time-oriented structure remains constant from section to section, making it possible for information to be studied in context. Events on the timeline related to topics elsewhere in the book are keyed by a page number printed on a color-coded square. Depending upon need, several pathways through the book may be taken by readers. It may be read traditionally as a linear narrative from section to section, or it may be used as a reference book where readers make specific connections by comparing the information found on the timelines.

Flow lines are boundaries that divide pages or spreads into major zones. When applied consistently throughout a publication, these boundaries unify pages and promote visual flow. In *American Graphic Design Timelines,* flow lines establish essential boundaries for the major zones of the book. As a result, the information flows naturally through the publication, and readers confidently move from one section to another without getting lost.

In the tradition of modern design, the spatial zones within a typographic grid are not violated. The designer works within the grid framework to objectively present information, while utilizing the principles of ABA form to establish relationships between the parts and to embue the composition with rhythmic and textural variety. But rules can be broken and risks are possible; skilled designers are capable of violating the grid to optimize clarity and maximize visual effect.

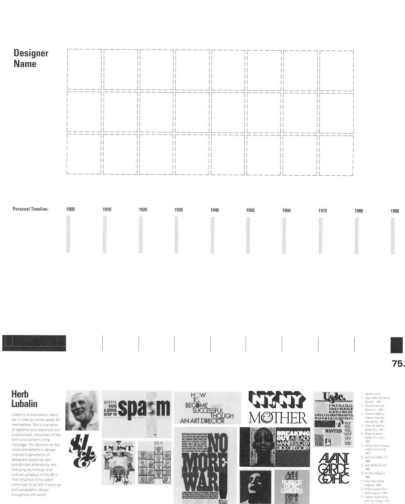

75.
All parts of the information are assigned a "home" in the publication. While these zones are separated from one another spatially, the grid unifies them through visual alignments. (Designer: Keith Jones)

76.
This spread demonstrates how the typographic and photographic information is applied to the grid. Events in the timeline related to subjects elsewhere in the book are keyed by page numbers located in an index at the bottom of the page.

DE STIJL

81.

ping pong
　　ping pong ping
　　pong ping pong
　　　　ping pong

78.

The typographic message is verbal, visual, and vocal. While typography is read and interpreted verbally, it may also be viewed and interpreted visually, heard and interpreted audibly. It is a dynamic communication medium. In this sense, early twentieth-century typography became a revolutionary form of communication, bringing new expressive power to the written word. Consider the concrete poem "ping pong" (Fig. **78**). The geometric structure of this poem is composed of a repetition of the words *ping* and *pong*. As these words are repeated, they signify the sound of a bouncing ping-pong ball, and the circular letters *p, o,* and *g* reflect the shape of the ball. The full impact of this poem is achieved when it is read aloud. By hearing the sounds and viewing the typographic forms, the typographic message is strengthened.

Significant departures from the use of conventional typographic forms occurred in Europe at the beginning of the twentieth century. During this activist period, experimentation in all the visual and performing arts was affected by potent social and philosophical changes, industrial and technological developments, and new attitudes about aesthetics and modern civilization. Typographic design was pulled into this artistic revolution as poets and visual artists realized that both meaning and form could be intensified in typographic communications.

The Futurist manifesto, written by the Italian poet Filippo Marinetti in 1909, profoundly influenced thinking in Europe and Russia. Futurism praised technology, violence, danger, movement, and speed. Futurist typography, known as "free typography," demonstrated these ideas in a highly expressive manner (Fig. **79** and see Chapter 1, Fig. **125**). The chill of a scream was expressed in bold type, and quick impressions were intensified through italics. Letters and words raced across the page in dynamic motion.

Among the movements affected by Futurism were Dadaism in France, Switzerland, and Germany; de Stijl in Holland; and Constructivism in Russia. Each of these historical movements has had a penetrating effect upon typography. Artists and

designers associated with these movements saw typography as a powerful means of conveying information relating to the realities of industrialized society (Figs. **80–82**; also see Chapter 1, Figs. **129–35**). They disdained what typography had become: a decorative art form far removed from the realities of the time. The architect Otto Wagner further emphasized that "all modern forms must be in harmony with the new requirements of our time. Nothing that is not practical can be beautiful." Written in 1920, the second de Stijl manifesto clearly demonstrated the concern for a new, expressive typography (Fig. **83**). With dramatic changes taking place in the form and content of typography, the typographic message became a multifaceted and expressive form of communication. Typography needs to be read, seen, heard, felt, and experienced.

78.
"ping pong" (Poet: Eugen Gomringer)

81.
Title lettering for *De Stijl.* (Designer: Theo van Doesburg)

80.
Cover of the first issue of *Der Dada.* (Editor: Raoul Hausmann)

79.
Les mots en liberté futuristes. (Designer: Filippo Marinetti)

82.
Constructivist cover design for *Veshch, Gegenstand, Objet.* (Designer: El Lissitzky)

BERLIN 1922

OBJET

ВЕЩЬ

№ 3

GEGENSTAND

REVUE●INTERNATIONALE●DE L'ART●MODERNE
МЕЖДУНАРОДНОЕ●ОБОЗРЕНИЕ●СОВРЕМЕННОГО●ИСКУССТВА
INTERNATIONALE●RUNDSCHAU●DER KUNST●DER GEGENWART

84.
Solidarity logotype.
(Designer: Jerzy Janiszewski)

THE WORD IS DEAD...
THE WORD IS IMPOTENT
asthmatic and sentimental poetry
the "me" and "it"
   which is still in common use
    everywhere...
is influenced by an individualism fearful of space
    the dregs of an exhausted era...

psychological analysis
and clumsy rhetoric
have KILLED THE MEANING OF THE WORD...

the word must be reconstructed
    to follow the SOUND as well as
    the IDEA
if in the old poetry
    by the dominance of relative and
    subjective feelings
the intrinsic meaning of the word is destroyed
we want by all possible means
    syntax
    prosody
    typography
    arithmetic
    orthography
to give new meaning to the word and new force
to expression

the duality between prose and poetry can no longer
be maintained
the duality between form and content can no longer
be maintained
Thus for the modern writer form will have a directly
spiritual meaning
it will not describe events
it will not *describe* at all
but ENSCRIBE
it will recreate in the word the common meaning of
events
a constructive unity of form and content...

Leiden, Holland, April 1920.

   Theo van Doesburg
   Piet Mondrian
   Anthony Kok

As a dynamic representation of verbal language, typography must communicate. This functional role is fulfilled when the receiver of a typographic message clearly and accurately understands what is in the mind of the transmitter. This objective, however, is not always accomplished. With a proliferation of typographic messages littering the environment, most are missed or ignored. The messages that are noted, possessing effective qualities relating to form and content, are appropriate to the needs of both message transmitter and message receiver.

The impact of an effective typographic message cannot be easily measured. Some may assume that since printed and broadcast messages are ephemeral, they have little impact upon their audience. This assumption is false. Because typographic ephemera are rhetorical, they often have a long-range effect upon a message receiver, influencing change within the context of social, political, and economic events. The symbol of solidarity expressed by Polish workers (Fig. **84**), the social statements made with graffiti in urban environments, and the typography on billboards aimed at passing motorists all operate as purposeful messages directed toward a predetermined audience within a specific context.

Effective typographic messages result from the combination of logic and intuitive judgment. Only the neophyte approaches this process in a strictly intuitive manner; a purely logical or mechanical procedure undermines human expression. Keeping these two extremes in balance requires the use of a functional verbal-visual vocabulary capable of addressing a broad spectrum of typographic communication.

83.
De Stijl manifesto of 1917.

87.

| to scrape | to crease | to peel | to melt | to splinter |

Verbal/visual equations

Language, in any of its many forms, is a self-contained system of interactive signs that communicate ideas. Just as elocution and diction enhance and clarify the meaning of our spoken words, typographic signs can be manipulated by a designer to achieve more lucid and expressive typographic communication.

Signs operate in two dimensions: syntactic and semantic. When the mind is concerned with the form of a sign, it is involved with typographic syntax. When it associates a particular meaning with a sign, it is operating in the semantic dimension.

All objects in the environment can potentially function as signs, representing any number of concepts. A smog-filled city signifying pollution, a beached whale representing extinction, and confetti implying celebration, each functions as a sign relating a specific concept.

Signs may exist at various levels of abstraction. A simple example will illustrate this point. Let us consider something as elemental as a red dot. It is a sign only if it carries a particular meaning. It can represent any number of things: balloon, ball, or Japanese flag. The red dot becomes a cherry, for example, as the mind is cued by forms more familiar to its experience (Fig. **85**).

The particular syntactic qualities associated with typographic signs determine a specific meaning. A series of repeated letters, for example, may signify motion or speed, while a small letter in a large void may signify isolation. These qualities, derived from the operating principles of visual hierarchy and ABA form, function as cues, permitting the mind to form concepts. Simple syntactic manipulations, such as the repetition of letters, or the weight change of certain letters, enable words visually to mimic verbal meaning (Fig. **86**). In another example, the letter *E* has been visually altered, relating it to the meaning of specific descriptive words (Fig. **87**).

85.
Signs exist at various levels of abstraction. A form is a sign, however, only when it carries a message. As the mind is cued by forms familiar to experience, information is conveyed.

86.
Simple syntactic manipulations are controlled by such factors as repetition, size change, position change, or weight change. These enable words to mimic verbal meaning visually.

87.
These elaborations of the letter *E* express a variety of concepts. (Designers: Carol Anthony, Linda Dronenburg, and Rebecca Sponga.)

leav e

in ter val

di e t

ststutter

dro p

86.

85.

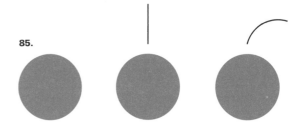

88.
Typographic signs combine
to form a more complex sign,
suggesting a decorated
Christmas tree. (Designer:
Donna Funk)

In language, signs are joined together to create messages. Words as verbal signs, grouped together in a linear fashion, attain their value vis-a-vis other words through opposition and contrast. Words can also evoke meaning through mental association. These associative relations are semantically derived. Since typography is both visual and verbal, it operates in a linear fashion, with words following each other in a specific sequence, or in a nonlinear manner, with elements existing in many syntactic combinations. For example, in the visual poem "O Christmas Tree," the choice of the typeface, Futura Light, is very important. The capital letter *O* is a perfect circle, signifying ornaments; the linear strokes of other letterforms suggest the texture of evergreen needles (Fig. **88**). This typographic message is derived from the mental associations formed by contrasting typographic signs.

Two terms important to the understanding of signs are denotation and connotation. When considering the meaning of typographic signs, denotation refers to objective meaning, the factual world of collective awareness and experience. For example, a denotative interpretation of a yellow *O* would be: "This is a yellow letter *O*" or "This is a yellow circle." Connotative interpretations of the yellow *O* might be: "This is the sun, a slice of lemon, or a golden ring." Connotative observations are often conditioned, for they relate to overtones and are drawn from prior personal experience.

Typographic signs are both verbal and visual. The associations formed between the verbal and visual attributes are verbal/visual equivalencies, which are found in a variety of configurations. These reveal the associative nature of signs composing the typographic message and help us further understand its multifaceted attributes. Figures **89–101** illustrate the nature of some of these verbal/visual equations.

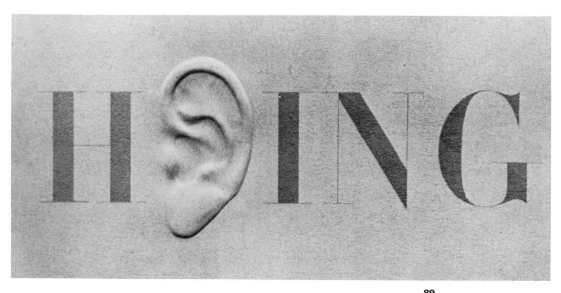

89.
Visual substitution: The visual
sign of an ear is substituted
for the letters *E, A,* and *R.*
(Designer: Lou Dorfsman)

91.
Simultaneity: The numeral *8* functions as the letter *g* in this logotype used for a group exhibition of paintings by the early twentieth-century American art group, The Eight.

92.
Visual transformation: A mother, father, and child are suggested through the visual transformation of the letters *l* and *i*. (Designer: Herb Lubalin)

Families

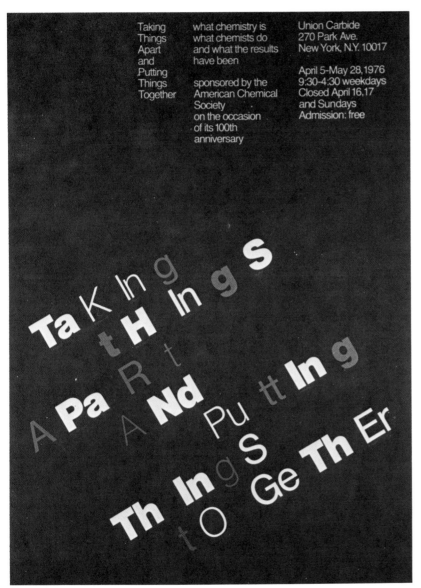

Taking
Things
Apart
and
Putting
Things
Together

what chemistry is
what chemists do
and what the results
have been

sponsored by the
American Chemical
Society
on the occasion
of its 100th
anniversary

Union Carbide
270 Park Ave.
New York, N.Y. 10017

April 5-May 28, 1976
9:30-4:30 weekdays
Closed April 16,17
and Sundays
Admission: free

90.
Visual substitution: The visual sign of a compass is substituted for the letter *A* and an inverted cone is substituted for the letter *V*. (Designer: Harold Burch)

93.
Visual exaggeration: The irregular syntactic treatment of typographic signs exaggerates the process of taking things apart and putting things together. (Designer: Steff Geissbuhler)

the American premiere at the Depot in Urbana
of the play by Marcel Achard

translated by Sue Huseman Moretto
directed by Jose Moretto

October 31, November 1, 2, 3 1974
November 7, 8, 9, 10
at 8:00 pm, Friday and Saturday also at 10:30 pm

tickets at Record Service
704 South Sixth Champaign
and at the Depot 223 North Broadway
on nights of performance

Fools' Play

95.
Form combination: Visual and verbal signs are combined into a single typographic statement, creating trademarks which suggest the nature of various industries: an electrical contractor, a maker of plastic fibers for carpets and draperies, and a lithographic printer. (Designer: Don Weller)

95.

96.
Form combination: Verbal signs are combined with visual signs (cables). The resulting forms suggest the qualities of cable transmission. (Designers: Jerry L. Kuyper and Sheila de Bretteville)

96.

97.
Parallel form: The Olivetti logotype and electronic calculator have similar visual characteristics which parallel each other. (Logotype design: Walter Ballmer)

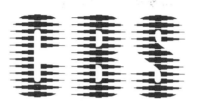

97.

98.
Verbal / visual correspondence: The syntactic qualities of this typographic sign correspond to the graffiti found in an urban environment. (Designer: Jeff Barnes)

99.
Verbal / visual correspondence: The visual characteristics of this typographic sign correspond to the form of a zipper. This is achieved by a repetition of letters and a horizontal shift within the word. (Designer: Richard Rumble)

98.

94.
Visual exaggeration: The repetition and playful treatment of typographic forms effectively reinforces the content of the drama *Fool's Play,* for which this poster was designed. (Designer: David Colley)

ZIIIIIIIIIIIIPPPER

99.

american library association

Gandhi, **Garbo** *and* Poe

to

go

100.

Unity 1974

Anspach
Grossman
Portugal
Inc

101.

100.
Verbal/visual correspon-
dence: The visual qualities of
the typefaces chosen for the
signs *Gandhi, Garbo,* and *Poe*
make direct reference to time
and culture. The message is
further strengthened by the
sounds associated with the
words. (Designer: David
Colley)

101.
Verbal/visual correspon-
dence: The visual repetition
of this word—unified by the
shared letters *u* and *n*—express the concept of unity.
(Designer: Steff Geissbuhler)

Function and expression

Functionalism is a design term that has commonly been used to describe the utilitarian and pragmatic qualities inherent in designed objects. During the twentieth century, functionalism has generally been equated with purposeful, unornamented simplicity; however, functionalism is a subjective term that varies according to the needs of a user.

For example, if comfort in the design of a chair is defined as a soothing softness, an upholstered, automatic recliner, complete with footrest and vibrator, would exemplify a comfortable, functional chair.

In contrast to the automatic recliner is the red/blue chair, designed by Gerrit Rietveld in 1918, which is a central artifact of the de Stijl movement. This movement sought a restrained expression of universal harmony, and the creation of a new philosophy for living (Fig. **102**). At first glance, the red/blue chair's hard, flat surfaces would seem to be very uncomfortable. This common reaction, however, is uninformed. Rietveld intended for his chair to promote alert mental activity through firm support. The seat and backrest planes are attached at only one edge; therefore, the naturally pliable wood adjusts to the user's weight. In this regard, the chair functions according to Rietveld's intentions. In an interior environment, Rietveld's red/blue chair has the presence and visual harmony of a piece of sculpture. The needs for a functional object (seating) *and* for aesthetic experience are fulfilled by this one piece.

In typography, function is the purposeful communication of information to a specific audience. Although the range of possible typographic design solutions is infinite, the appropriateness of a solution always depends upon the purpose for which it was intended. Varying degrees of formal reduction or elaboration can be effective when solving specific typographic-design problems.

102.

102.
Red/blue chair, 1918.
(Designer: Gerrit Rietveld)

105.

An announcement for a retrospective exhibition of record album design has been influenced by Russian Constructivism. A playful integration of horizontal and vertical typographic elements contrasts with circular forms suggesting records. (Designer: Paula Scher)

104.

A vocabulary of functional typography is used in an expressive and experimental manner to communicate the content of the typographic journal, *Typografische Monatsblatter*. (Designer: Willi Kunz)

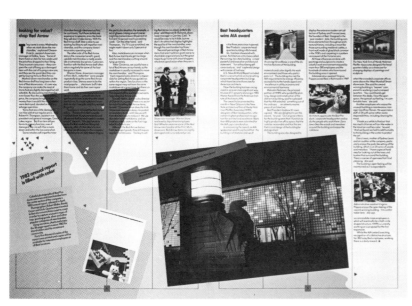

106.

Best Times, a Best Products employee publication, communicates about corporate activities. Visual richness and reader interest are achieved through the use of abstract forms and color, photography, and typographic variety. (Designer: Rob Carter)

103.

The *Minneapolis Tribune* is an example of a functional newspaper design having legibility and clarity. All typographic elements conform to a well-defined grid, and a specific visual hierarchy determines the importance of each story. (Design director: Michael Carroll)

Formal reduction can be used to create optimum clarity and legibility, presenting complex information, such as news or scientific data, in a clear and straightforward manner. Orderly presentation guides the eye from one part to another, without a loss of interest in content (Figs. **103** and **104**).

Another approach, expressionism, accomplishes its purpose through formal elaboration and ornamentation, creating visual impact. When appropriate, attention can be given to experimental, expressive, and ornamental forms, in addition to the verbal considerations. Ornament serves a variety of practical needs. Because it is semiotic, iconographic, and historical, it identifies the object with which it is associated. Ornament can place an object in time, reveal its purpose, and clarify its structure (Figs. **105–107**). The formal elaboration of objects in architecture, industrial design, and the fine arts can significantly influence typographic development. Figures **71** and **119** (Chapter 1) and **108–110** possess strong ornamental qualities. Innovative typography can emerge when a designer fully understands communication needs and is able to assimilate a diversity of visual ideas.

On this subject, Ladislav Sutnar commented that "an eccentric visual scandal or visual shock of the outrageous and of the unexpected can catch the attention of the astonished eye . . . it may also delight the eye to see a fresh design concept or a message so orderly presented as to make comprehension fast and easy." A designer can avoid conventional solutions to typographic problems when innovation is appropriate. A single approach to typographical design, induced by stylistic convention and predetermined formulas, is a routine activity lacking the vitality of meaningful typographic invention. Sound principles and a trained vision should supersede dependency upon preconceived formulas. For typography to be truly functional, satisfying the needs of an audience, a designer must understand both the verbal and the visual attributes of a typographic message.

TM
SGM
RSI

Typografische Monatsblätter
Schweizer Grafische Mitteilungen
Revue Suisse de l'Imprimerie

109.

The Best Products corporate headquarters makes a strong decorative statement while providing a functional work environment. (Architect: Hardy Holzman Pfeiffer Associates)

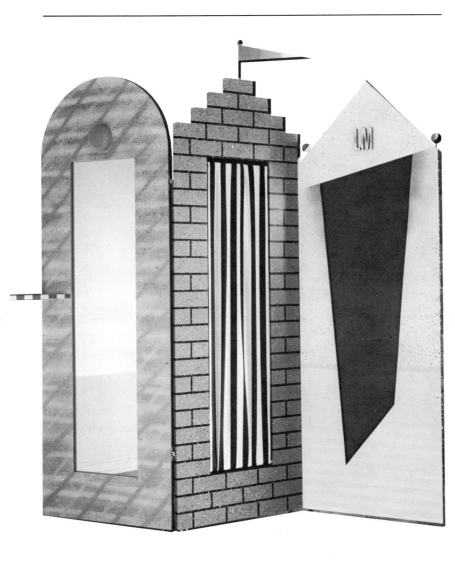

107.

A diversity of shape, tone, and texture in this exhibition poster parallels the range of visual art on display. (Designer: Wolfgang Weingart)

110.

The ornament of this late nineteenth-century French maquetry cabinet expresses the spirit of its time. (Designer: Eugene Gaillard)

110.

108.

Lively geometric form and pattern characterize this folding screen. (Designer: Daniel Friedman)

Typographic legibility is widely misunderstood and often neglected by designers. Yet it is a subject that requires careful study and constant evaluation. Legibility represents those qualities and attributes inherent in typography that make type readable. These attributes make it possible for a reader to comprehend typographic forms with the least amount of difficulty.

Typographers and designers have a responsibility to communicate as clearly and appropriately as possible. This responsibility is suggested by Henry David Thoreau in *Walden:* "A written word is the choicest of relics. It is something at once more intimate with us and more universal than any other work of art."

aadddd

1.
As the top stroke of the letter *a* rises to become the ascender of the *d,* the intermediate forms are not easily deciphered by the reader.

As signs representing sounds in spoken language, letters are basic to legible typography. The primary purpose of a letterform is to convey a recognizable meaning to the mind. Therefore, letterforms must be designed with clarity, each being distinct within the alphabet. The contrast among individual characters makes it possible for the reader to decipher written information without confusion.

The most legible typefaces are those timeless examples characterized by three qualities upon which legibility is dependent: contrast, simplicity, and proportion. These typefaces exemplify beautiful and functional letterforms. A close look at typefaces such as Garamond, Baskerville, and Bodoni will reveal why their forms are as vital now as when they were first designed. (See the type specimens in chapter eight.) The use of well-designed typefaces, however, is no guarantee that typography will be legible. Effective typography depends upon such factors as the communications context and the subtle adjustment of letterforms and their spatial relationships, each of which may have an effect upon how easily typography is read. Making type legible is a masterful achievement, requiring a process of intelligent decision making.

In the strictest sense, legible typography is a means of communicating information objectively. However, typographic designers sometimes bend the traditional criteria of legibility for expressive purposes. Designers, with their instinctive curiosity, have experimented with typography, playing with forms, imposing new meaning, and changing the standards of typographic communication. Innovative typography always poses fresh questions, challenges edicts of the past, and redefines the concepts of legibility and functionality.

This chapter approaches legibility as an art of spatial synthesis. As an art, it is not absolute. Therefore, information derived from legibility research should be considered only a guideline. The knowledge designers have of legibility is based upon a legacy of typographic history and a keen awareness of the visible world. This knowledge will continually evolve, creating new standards for readability and functional typography.

Distinguishing characteristics of letters

The alphabet consists of twenty-six letters, each of which has evolved over the centuries to a unique place within this system of signs. This evolution has occurred gradually. It is no accident that the individual shapes of letterforms have developed out of a need to improve the communication process. As the alphabet has evolved, it has become a flexible system of signs in which all letters are distinct, yet all work together harmoniously as visible language.

In spite of the innumerable variations of size, proportion, weight, and elaboration in letterform design, the basic structure of each letterform must remain the same. For example, the capital *A* always consists of two oblique strokes joined at the top and connected by a horizontal stroke at their midsection. Sufficient contrast must exist between the letters in a font so that they can be easily distinguished (Fig. **1**).

2.
Four groupings show the structural relationships of all letters in the alphabet. The divisions are based upon the dominant strokes of each letter.

il
acegos
bdfhjmnpqrtu
kvwxyz

EFHILT
COQS
BDGJPRU
AKMNVWXYZ

3.
The upper halves of words
are read with ease, while the
lower halves are less legible.

Letters can be clustered into four groups, according to their contrasting properties. These are letterforms with strokes that are vertical, curved, a combination of vertical and curved, or oblique (Fig. **2**). From these groupings, one notices that letters are not only similar in many ways but that there are also some important differences. Obviously, letters with similar characteristics are more likely to be confused, while letters with distinct qualities provide contrast within a word. Letters within a word are most legible when they are taken, in equal number, from each group.

A closer look at the alphabet reveals additional characteristics distinguishing letters. The upper halves of letters provide more visual cues for letter recognition than the lower halves (Fig. **3**). Likewise, the right halves of letters are more recognizable than the left halves (Fig. **4**). Dominant letters within the alphabet that aid in word recognition are those that have either ascenders or descenders. Through tests, researchers have contributed valuable information about the comparative legibility of each letter in the alphabet. Findings vary only slightly. Lowercase letters can be rank ordered according to their distinctiveness as follows: *d k m g h b p w u l j t v z r o f n a x y e i q c s*. This varies, however, with different typefaces.

The most frequently used letters, such as the vowels *a e i o u,* are among the most illegible, and *c g s x* are easily missed in reading. Other letters that often cause confusion and are mistaken for one another are *f i j l t.* For example, the words *fail, tail,* and *jail* each begin with letters of similar shape and could easily be misread. The eye could possibly perceive *f* as *t,* or *t* as *j* (Fig. **5**). The designer should carefully study the words in display typography to identify such potential problems in legibility.

4.
More letters remain
recognizable when only their
right halves are exposed;
however, there are exceptions (*b, p*).

fail
tail
jail

5.
Words have a tendency to be
misread and confused with
each other when composed
of letters of similar shape.

7.

As with the changing position of the dancer, subtle changes in the drawing of the forms and counterforms significantly affect perception.

6.

7.

DANCER

DANCER

DANCER

G
DANCER
DANGER
G

shape

SHAPE

8.

Word recognition is based on word structure, a combination of word shape (defined by the contours of the letters) and internal word pattern. The word set in lowercase letters is more distinct than the word set in all capitals, because its irregular word shape makes it more recognizable.

The perception of a letter is based upon the form/counterform relationship. Counterforms are as significant to legibility as the shapes of the letters themselves. This principle relates to all aspects of visual phenomena. A dancer manipulates space with the body, "making shape," defining, and redefining space (Fig. **6**). If the shape of a letter is changed, so is the way in which that letter is perceived. Letter shapes are cues that distinguish one letter in the alphabet from another (Fig. **7**).

Much controversy has surrounded the issue of the comparative legibility of serif and sans-serif typefaces. One argument claims that serif text type is more readable because the serifs reinforce the horizontal flow of each line. Serif typefaces also offer more character definition: for example, the serif on the bottom horizontal stroke of a capital *E* accentuates the difference between it and a capital *F*. However, the relative legibility between serif and sans-serif typefaces is negligible. Reader familiarity and the control of other legibility factors (to be discussed later) are far more significant than the selection of a serif or sans-serif typeface. (See the text-type specimens in Chapter Eight to compare the legibility of serif and sans-serif type.)

The nature of words

While individual letters as discrete units, affecting all other spatial and aesthetic considerations, are the basis for a discussion of legibility, one reads and perceives words and groups of words and not just letters. In discussing typographic legibility, Frederic Goudy observed that "a letter may not be considered apart from its kinsmen; it is a mere abstract and arbitrary form far remote from the original picture or symbol out of which it grew, and has no particular significance until it is employed to form part of a word."

There are two important factors involved in the reading process: word shape and internal pattern. Words are identified by their distinctive word shapes, strings of letters which are instantaneously perceived, permitting the reader to grasp content easily (Fig. **8**). Counterforms create internal word patterns that provide cues for word recognition.

O R D W
R D W O
D W O R
R O W D
W O R D
O W R D
9.

When these internal spaces are altered sufficiently, the perceptual clarity of a word may also be altered. The weight of letters is vital to word recognition and influences an adequate internal pattern. The combination of word shape and internal pattern creates a word structure, an all-inclusive term describing the unique composition of each word (Fig. **9**).

Capital and lowercase letters

If a text is set entirely in capital letters, it suffers a loss of legibility and the reader is placed at a significant disadvantage. Type set in this manner severely retards reading—more so than any other legibility factor. Figure **8** demonstrates that a word set in all capital letters is characterized by a straight horizontal alignment, creating an even word outline with letters of similar shape and size. A reader is not provided with the necessary visual cues that make words recognizable.

TEXT SET IN ALL CAPITAL LETTERS ALSO USES A SIGNIFICANTLY GREATER AMOUNT OF SPACE THAN TEXT SET IN LOWERCASE LETTERS OF THE SAME SIZE. AS MUCH AS 35 PERCENT MORE SPACE CAN BE CONSUMED WHEN USING ALL CAPITAL LETTERS.

On the other hand, text set in lowercase letters forms words that are distinct, based upon their irregular word shape and internal pattern. A variety of letter shapes, ascenders, and descenders provides rich contrasts that assure satisfactory perception. Once a specific word shape is perceived, it is stored in the reader's memory until the eye confronts it again while reading. A reader can become confused if a word takes on an appearance that differs from the originally learned word shape.

Interletter and interword spacing

The spacing of letterforms has a significant impact on legibility. Most readers are unaware of the typographic designer's attention to this detail. Minute spatial relationships are controlled to create not only readable but beautiful and harmonious typographic communication. It takes great skill to specify spaces between letters and words,

determining proper spatial relationships. Letters must flow rhythmically and gracefully into words, and words into lines.

Typographic texture and tone are affected by the spacing of letters, words, and lines. When the texture and the spatial intervals between typographic elements are consistent, the result is an easily readable text. Texture is also affected by qualities unique to the design of specific typefaces. Sometimes designers arrange type for specific spatial effects, sensitively balancing norms of legibility with graphic impact. (See the text-type specimens in Chapter Eight.)

Too much or too little space between letters and words destroys the normal texture intended by the typeface designer. As you read this sentence, notice that the narrow letter and word spacing causes words to merge together visually. L i k e w i s e ,   t h e   v e r y   w i d e   l e t t e r s p a c i n g   o f   t h i s   s e n t e n c e   a l s o   d i s r u p t s   t h e   r e a d i n g   p r o c e s s .

There is often a danger of misfit letter combinations, which, in earlier typesetting systems, such as linotype, could not be easily corrected. (If the type size is small and evenly textured, this is a minor problem.) With phototypesetting and digital typesetting, these details can be corrected easily. The kerning of specific letter combinations can be programmed into the typesetting system. As type is set, appropriate letterspacing appears automatically (Fig. **10**).

9.
Letters can be grouped in a myriad of combinations. Those which are perceived as having meaning are words with which we have become familiar over time. They form a distinct and familiar shape.

Reading is disrupted by inappropriate wordspacing.

10.
Misfit letter combinations and irregular spacing can be a problem, particularly for display type. Optical adjustments should be made to achieve spatial consistency between elements.

SPACING

SPACING

EdwardoJohnston,oaocalligrapher, advocatedoaowordospaceoequaloto aolowercaseoo.

11.

AaronrBurns,rarcontemporary typographer,rsuggestsrwordrspacing equalrtorarlowercaserr.

Space between letters and words should be proportional to the width of letters. This proportion is often open to personal judgment (Fig. **11**). With experience and practice comes an understanding of the spacing that is suitable to a particular design project.

Type size, line length, and interline spacing
Critical to spatial harmony and legibility is an understanding of the triadic relationship of type size, line length, and interline spacing. When properly employed, these variables can improve the legibility of even poorly designed letterforms or enhance the legibility of those forms considered highly legible.

It is difficult to generalize about which sizes of type should be used, how long lines should be, or how much space should be inserted between lines. These decisions are based upon comparative judgments. The guidelines discussed in this section can never replace the type designer's sensitively trained eye for typographic detail. The normal reading distance for most printed matter is from twelve to fourteen inches, a fact to be kept in mind when making decisions about type size, since it affects the way in which a specific type size is perceived.

Text type that is too small or too large makes reading difficult. Small type reduces visibility by destroying counterforms, which affect word recognition, while large type can force a reader to perceive type in sections rather than as a whole. According to legibility research, the most legible sizes of text type at normal reading distances range from 9 to 12 point. This range results from the wide variation of x-height in different typefaces, that is,

when typefaces of the same point size are placed side by side, they may appear to be different sizes, because their x-heights vary radically. This is important to keep in mind when selecting typefaces and sizes.

An interesting comparison is the relationship between Univers 55 and Baskerville. Univers 55 has a very large x-height, with short ascenders and descenders. It appears much larger than Baskerville set in the same size, which has a smaller x-height and large ascenders and descenders. (See text column specimens in Chapter Eight.)

Type sizes larger than 12 point may require more fixation pauses, making reading uncomfortable and inefficient. A fixation pause occurs when the eye stops on a line of type during reading, actually perceiving the meaning of groups of words. When there are fewer fixation pauses, there is greater reading efficiency and comprehension. When text type is smaller than 9 point, internal patterns can break down, destroying legibility. The reading audience is also a major consideration. For example, children learning to read need large type sizes in simple formats, as do adults with poor eyesight.

An appropriate line length is essential for achieving a pleasant reading rhythm, allowing a reader to relax and concentrate on the content of the words. Overly short or long lines will tire a reader. Excess energy is expended when reading long lines, and it is difficult to find the next line. A short column measure requires the eye to change lines too often, and there is an inadequate supply of horizontal perceptual cues. Compare the legibility of this paragraph with the legibility of Figures **12** and **13**.

An appropriate line length is essential for achieving a pleasant reading rhythm, allowing a reader to relax and concentrate on the content of the words. Overly short or long lines will tire a reader. Excess energy is expended when reading long lines, and it is difficult to find the next line. A short column measure requires the eye to change lines too often, and there is an inadequate supply of horizontal perceptual cues.

13.

An appropriate line length is essential for achieving a pleasant reading rhythm, allowing a reader to relax and concentrate on the content of the words. Overly short or long lines will tire a reader. Excess energy is expended when reading long lines, and it is difficult to find the next line. A short column measure requires the eye to change lines too often, and there is an inadequate supply of horizontal perceptual cues.

12.

Interline spacing intervals

Interline spacing intervals

14.

Certainly, every typographic problem has its own legibility requirements. The following data can serve as a point of departure in determining how to create legible typography. Line length is dependent upon both the size of type and the amount of space between lines. When working with the optimum sizes of 9-, 10-, 11-, and 12-point text type, a maximum of ten to twelve words (or sixty to seventy characters) per line would be acceptable. This would equal a line length of approximately 18 to 24 picas. An optimum line length for the average 10-point type is 19 picas.

The amount of interline spacing is dependent upon several factors. Generally, lines with no added space between them are read more slowly than lines with added space. Proper interline spacing carries the eye naturally from one line to the next. When there is inadequate space between lines, the eye takes in other lines as well. If lines are too widely spaced, a reader may have trouble locating the next line. As column measure increases, the interline spacing should also increase to maintain a proper ratio of column length to interline spacing.

Typefaces with larger x-heights need more interline spacing than those with smaller x-heights. Also, when working with display types, the frequency with which ascenders and descenders occur makes a difference. They can optically lessen the amount of white space between lines. Optical adjustments in display types should be made when spaces between lines appear inconsistent because of ascenders and descenders (Fig. **14**). Generally, the maximum line length for text type with a small x-height—used without interline spacing—is about sixty-five characters. When text type with a large x-height is used without interline spacing, legibility is diminished when line length exceeds about fifty-two characters.

Research has shown that for the optimum sizes of text type (9, 10, 11, and 12 point), one to four points of interline spacing can be effectively added between lines to increase legibility. Remember, this is not to say that type set outside these optimum specifications will be illegible, for critical judgment can ensure legible typography without inhibiting fresh approaches.

Weight

When considering the legibility of a typeface, the thickness (weight) of the strokes should be examined. A typeface that is too light or too heavy has diminished legibility. Light typefaces cannot be easily distinguished from their background, while a typeface that is too heavy has a tendency to lose its internal pattern of counterforms.

Weight can be used advantageously to provide contrast and clarity between typographic page elements such as titles, headlines, and subheads. A heavier or lighter weight can emphasize one piece of information over another, thereby making information more comprehensible.

Extreme thick and thin strokes within letters of a particular typeface make reading more difficult, preventing smooth transitions from one word or group of words to the next. Thin strokes are less visible, creating confusion with letters of similar shape. When a typeface with extreme contrasts between thick and thin strokes is used in a text setting, a dazzle or sparkle effect is created. The reader begins to have difficulty distinguishing the words, and legibility decreases significantly.

Character width

The shape and size of the page or column can influence the selection of character width. For example, a condensed typeface might be selected for a narrow page or column, achieving proportional harmony and an adequate number of characters and words to the line.

The width of letters is also an important legibility factor. Generally, condensed type is more difficult to read. A narrower letter changes the form/counterform relationship, causing letters to have an extreme vertical posture that can alter eye movement and reading patterns, diminishing legibility.

Italics

Similar to other situations where typeforms deviate from a reader's expectations, italics impede reading. An extreme italic slant can slow the reading process and is disliked by many readers. However, italic type can be very effective when used as a means of providing emphasis.

Typefaces of median weight are most legible.

In text type, weight change significantly affects legibility.

In text type, legibility is affected when condensed or expanded typefaces are used.

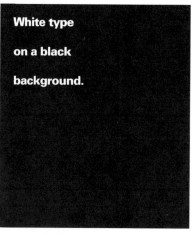

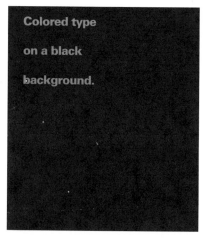

Color combinations

When reading large amounts of text, people prefer black type on white backgrounds, and they are used to seeing this relationship. Large amounts of text are most legible as black on white, rather than the reverse. However, extreme black and white contrast can contribute to dazzle or sparkle. For example, reading a large amount of text on glossy bright-white paper is more difficult than reading the same text printed on uncoated paper. Type and its background can take various forms—from ink on paper to light on a cathode-ray tube. In all cases, the relationship between type and background is important to legibility.

If an appropriate type size and weight are chosen, the selection of a color combination for type and its ground is possible without a disturbing loss of legibility. Combinations of black, white, and color are often used for both type and ground (Fig. **15**).

Legibility and the grid

In discussing the grid, Josef Muller-Brockmann stated, "Information presented with clear and logically set out titles, subtitles, texts, illustrations, and captions will not only be read more quickly and easily, but the information will also be better understood and retained in memory." As a valuable framework for structuring typographic and pictorial elements, the grid produces a cohesiveness that can improve legibility and the communication of ideas.

In a rapidly changing information environment, designers must constantly reassess the nature of typographic legibility. As technology changes, so do communication techniques and methods. Today, legibility research must proceed beyond the realm of printed communications into the world of electronics, for words that once appeared primarily on paper are now found on the cathode-ray tube. Legibility concerns extend into all media, including videographics, television broadcasting, computer graphics, film, and laser graphics. Although the information found in this chapter relates mainly to printed communications, many of the principles and factors concerning typographic legibility apply to other media.

15.

Compare the legibility of
the justified and unjustified
columns.

Justified and unjustified typography

Traditionally, it was common practice to set type in a justified alignment. This was done for reasons of efficiency; in addition, it was more familiar and was considered to be more refined. In the 1920s, designers began to question this typographic convention and experiment with alternative text-setting styles. Unjustified and asymmetrical typography began to find widespread acceptance. Among experimental typographic designers was Herbert Bayer, who said, "I have long believed that our conventional way of writing and setting type could be improved for easier reading. In my first typographic works in the early twenties, I started to abandon the flush-left-and-right system for short lines of text and have introduced the flush-left system, leaving a ragged-right outline."

There are appropriate reasons for setting either justified or unjustified typography, but type set flush left and ragged right promotes greater legibility. If properly used, flush-left, ragged-right typography provides visual points of reference that guide the eye smoothly down the page from line to line. Because each line is either shorter or longer than the next, the eye is cued from one to another. In a justified setting, all lines are of equal length. Lacking are visual cues that promote easy reading.

With the use of unjustified typography, wordspacing is even, creating a smooth rhythm and a consistent texture. The indiscriminate placement of additional space between words in order to justify lines causes awkward gaps or "rivers" in paragraphs, which are disruptive to reading. Hyphenations at the end of lines should be used whenever possible to keep wordspacing consistent.

When setting ragged-right text, care should be taken not to rag the type too much. Uncontrolled line breaks of erratic rhythm can create awkward spaces that inhibit reading. In ragged-right type, care should be given to the selection of interline spacing, for it influences legibility and appearance. Spatial consistency and rhythmic line breaks influence typographical decisions.

The breaking of lines can be determined by the author's meaning rather than by appearance. This method, sometimes referred to as "thought-unit" typography, arranges lines into discrete parts related to the meaning of the text. Ragged-right lines may be of any length, with line breaks that are logical and focus on the intended message of the writer (Fig. **16**).

Paragraphs and indentions

An important goal for a designer is to distinguish typographically one thought from another, clarify content, and increase reader comprehension. Clear separation of paragraphs in a body of text is one way to accomplish this goal.

It is common practice in the design of books, magazines, and newspapers to indent each paragraph, usually with moderate indention of one to three ems. It is also typographic practice *not* to indent the first paragraph in an article, chapter, or advertisement so that the square corner of the first column can be maintained.

Paragraphs can also be separated by inserting additional space between them. This space should be proportional to the amount of interline spacing, which corresponds to the vertical measurement of the typographic grid. Paragraphs are often separated by one line space. This method should be avoided if the original copy is full of short, choppy paragraphs. Spaces between such paragraphs could be very disturbing, consuming too much space. Indentions and additional linespace are also used to establish order within complex tabular matter, such as financial charts and scientific data.

16.

Thought-unit typography
from the Washburn College
Bible. (Designer: Bradbury
Thompson)

1:1 In the beginning
God created the heaven and the earth.

2 And the earth was without form, and void;
and darkness was upon the face of the deep.
And the Spirit of God
moved upon the face of the waters.

3 And God said,
Let there be light:
and there was light.

4 And God saw the light, that it was good:
and God divided the light from the darkness.

5 And God called the light Day,
and the darkness he called Night.
And the evening and the morning
were the first day.

6 And God said,
Let there be a firmament
in the midst of the waters,
and let it divide the waters from the waters.

7 And God made the firmament,
and divided the waters
which were under the firmament
from the waters
which were above the firmament:
and it was so.

8 And God called the firmament Heaven.
And the evening and the morning
were the second day.

9 And God said,
Let the waters under the heaven
be gathered together unto one place,
and let the dry land appear:
and it was so.

10 And God called the dry land Earth;
and the gathering together of the waters
called he Seas:
and God saw that it was good.

11 And God said,
Let the earth bring forth grass,
the herb yielding seed,
and the fruit tree yielding fruit after his kind,
whose seed is in itself, upon the earth:
and it was so.

12 And the earth brought forth grass,
and herb yielding seed after his kind,
and the tree yielding fruit,
whose seed was in itself, after his kind:
and God saw that it was good.

This is Garamond
This is Garamond
This is Garamond
17.

a b c d e f g
h i j k l m n
o p q r s t u
v w x y z

18.

17.
Three typefaces have the same name, but significantly different properties. The size, weight, width, and shape of characters differ from one to the other.

18.
The lowercase *i*, *j*, and *l* appear out of place due to the presence of serifs in an otherwise sans-serif typeface. Also, the *m* and *w* appear darker in tone than their neighbors.

Legibility and electronic page design

Electronic page design offers designers more possibilities for type manipulation than ever before, resulting in an obligation to know more about the cultural and formal evolution of typography than in times past. Without adequate knowledge of typographic legibility, it is easy for designers to blindly follow fads, succumb to common visual cliches provided by software, or worse yet to thoughtlessly yield to the built-in defaults of a computer application. Legibility is a concern that should be continually addressed as technology changes. Because designers now work at a keyboard, they are directly responsible for composing legible type—a task once accomplished by sending specifications to a compositor at a typesetting firm.

As a result of desktop technology and type-design software, new typefaces and revivals of old typefaces are being released at an unprecedented rate. Some of these are well designed, others are not. Many typefaces share the same name from foundry to foundry, yet in design some of these faces are far removed from the the original (Fig. **17**). It is not enough to make typeface selections on the basis of a name; designers should make visual comparisons before deciding upon which typefaces are most suitable.

Well-drawn typefaces possess the following optical characteristics: crisp edges without stair-stepping, no out-of-control pixels, curves with smooth and flowing thick-to-thin transitions, bowls of curved characters that slightly extend beyond the baseline and meanline, form and counterform relationships that provide consistent texture and color, characters that do not "dance" up and down on the baseline, and the absence of "black sheep" characters that visually stray from the rest of the letters due to an anomalous shape (Fig. **18**).

AS WITH DECORATIVE AND NOVELTY FACES, MANY TYPEFACES EMPHASIZE VISUAL EMBELLISHMENT AT THE EXPENSE OF LEGIBILITY. THE PRACTICE OF INTENTIONALLY USING BLOCKY BIT-MAPPED LETTERS FOR LARGE AMOUNTS OF TEXT, FOR EXAMPLE, SHOULD BE AVOIDED. WHILE THE LETTER "Y" IN FIGURE **19** IS ELEGANT AS A GEOMETRIC FORM, IT LACKS THE PROPORTIONAL QUALITIES INHERENT IN LEGIBLE LETTERS. AS DISPLAY TYPE, THESE TYPEFACES SHOULD BE USED SPARINGLY AND ONLY WHEN THEIR VISUAL TEXTURES ENHANCE OR SUPPORT THE CONTENT.

The tools of desktop software enable type to be outlined, stretched, rotated, skewed, mirrored, placed on a curved baseline, and manipulated in innumerable other ways. Upon determining the objectives, requirements, and limitations of the typographic problem at hand, designers can creatively employ these tools while also addressing legibility needs. In that it is a property of typography to *express* ideas visually, these tools should be used for this purpose. However, when using such tools, it is desirable to make typography as legible as possible by adhering to the legibility factors discussed earlier in this chapter, and to maintain the proportional integrity of letterforms. Even though type set on a curved baseline, for example, is not as legible as type set on a horizontal baseline, it can be made more legible by carefully spacing the letters and choosing a well-designed typeface. Figures **20–23** present a variety of electronic type manipulations with accompanying alterations for improved legibility.

A major factor influencing the legibility of type is resolution. Where fewer pixels are available to describe letters, resolution decreases. To compen-

Form/counterform irregularities creating an uneven texture, jagged curves disrupting harmonious thick-to-thin transitions, and a font comprising only capitals make this type less legible.

19.
The same typeface as shown above, but much enlarged. Note the extreme distortion of the letter *Y*.

24.

The letter *G* enlarged to show how a hinted type outline activates pixels to more closely resemble the actual letter. Shown from left to right are pixels activated by an unhinted type outline, a type outline reshaped by hinting, and pixels activated by a hinted type outline.

sate for this problem, type designers reshape the outlines of characters—a process called "hinting"— to create the best possible image for the output device. Hints alter the actual outlines of letters so that selective pixels are activated, thus improving the legibility of letters on the screen and in low-resolution output devices (Fig. **24**).

High-resolution imagesetters produce type far exceeding the quality generated by lower-resolution laser printers. Particularly in smaller sizes of type, low-resolution output combined with the way in which devices physically produce hardcopy, encourage counterforms to fill in, letters within words to touch one another and the strokes of letters to be rounded at the terminals. The result is spotty and difficult to read text type, problems that are accentuated in the use of bold and condensed letters. This would not be such a problem were it not for the fact that low-resolution laser printers are used as a practical means of setting type for materials ranging from in-house publications to business letters. Whether low-resolution printers are used for proofing or for final output, adjustments should be made to ensure improved legibility. In time, the resolution problem will become less of an issue as first-generation laser printers are replaced with those of higher resolution.

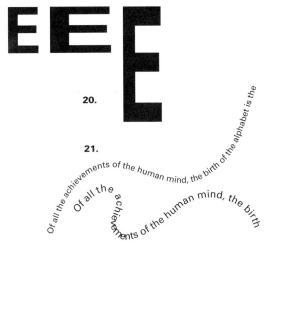

20.

21.

22.

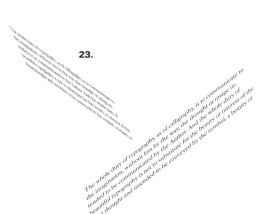

23.

20.

When letters are stretched horizontally or vertically on a computer to create condensed and expanded letters, their proportions change. When stretched horizontally, vertical strokes thicken; when stretched vertically, horizontal strokes thicken.

21.

Type improperly scaled on a tightly curved baseline causes characters to awkwardly bump into each other (bottom). Smaller type on a similar curve flows smoothly and consistently (top).

22.

Type skewed to the degree that it is no longer readable (top). Type similarly skewed, but word pictures are preserved enough to ensure legibility (bottom).

23.

Several skewed lines of type suggest a textural plane floating in space. Due to the degree of skew and the proximity of the lines one to another, the type is totally unreadable (left). By increasing the interline spacing, changing the weight of the type, and regulating the degree of skew, lines can still be read (right).

5   Typographic Technology

The invention of typography has been called the beginning of the Industrial Revolution. It is the earliest mechanization of a handicraft: the hand-lettering of books. Typographic design has been closely bound to the evolution of technology, for the capabilities and limitations of typesetting systems have posed constraints upon the design process. At the same time, typesetting has offered creative challenges as designers have sought to explore the limitations of the available systems and to define their aesthetic and communicative potential.

From hand composition to today's electronically generated typography, it is important for designers to comprehend the nature and capabilities of typographic technologies, for this understanding provides a basis for a thoughtful blending of design and production.

Hand composition

The traditional method of setting foundry type by hand is similar to the method used by Gutenberg when he invented movable type in 1450. For centuries, hand composition was accomplished by assembling individual pieces of type into lines. A typographer would hold a composing stick (Fig. **1**) in one hand while the other hand placed type selected from a type case (Fig. **2**) into the stick. Type was set letter by letter, line by line, until the desired setting was achieved. When it was necessary to justify a line, additional spaces were created in the line by inserting metal spacing material between words. Letterspacing was achieved by inserting very thin pieces of copper or brass between letters until words appeared to be evenly spaced. When

additional space between lines was desired, strips of lead were inserted between the lines until the type column was the proper depth. By adding lead, the exact proportion and size of the column could be formed, assuring readability through consistent spacing.

Once type was set, it was "locked up" in a heavy rectangular steel frame called a chase (Fig. **3**). This was done on a table called a stone. The type was surrounded by wood or metal spacing material, called furniture, and the contents of the chase were made secure by tightening steel, wedgelike devices called quoins. After the type was secured in the chase, it was ready to be transferred to a press for

2.
Type case.

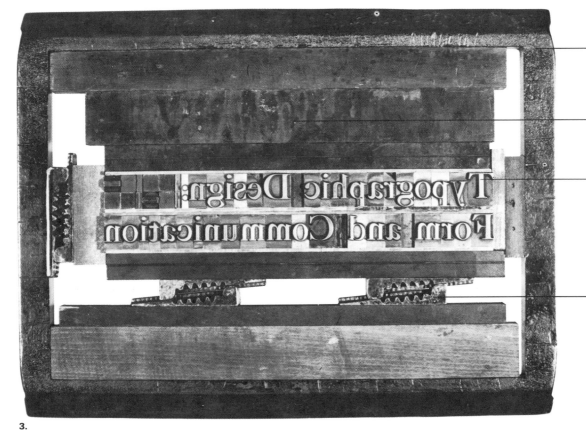

Chase

Wood furniture

Type

Quoins

3.
A chase containing type "locked up" and ready for printing.

printing, and after printing, the individual pieces of type were distributed back into the type case by hand.

Hand composition was tedious and time consuming. When typesetting became automated as a result of the invention of Linotype and Monotype machines, hand composition was used only for setting small amounts of type or for display type. Currently, hand composition is obsolete as a practical means of setting type, but as an art form there has been a revival. Private presses produce limited-edition books and a variety of experimental materials by hand. Many of our typographic conventions and traditions have their origins in the rich heritage of handset metal type.

Linotype

One of the most profound developments in typesetting technology was the invention of the Linotype machine (Fig. **4**) by Ottmar Mergenthaler in 1886. This machine represented the first great step toward typographic automation. Its name was coined because it produced a single line of type to a predetermined length specified by the keyboard operator.

The operation of the Linotype was based on the principle of a circulating matrix. Each time a key was pressed, a single brass matrix (Fig. **5**) was released from an overhead magazine, divided into ninety vertical channels, each containing matrices for one character. The magazine was the character storage case for the machine. Once an entire line had been typed, the matrices moved into an automatic casting mechanism where the line of type was cast from molten lead. As each line was being cast, the operator typed the next line. After the casting process was complete, cast lines of type called slugs (Fig. **6**) were ejected from the mold, and the matrices were automatically returned to their appropriate slot in the magazine for reuse.

The advantages of machine composition as compared to hand composition were obvious. It was faster and more accurate; the problem of type distribution (returning characters to the type case) was eliminated, for the cast lines of type were

99

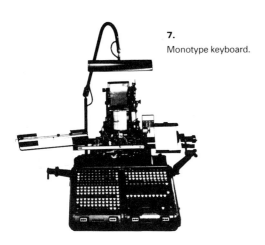

7.
Monotype keyboard.

simply melted, and the lead was reused. Justification of type was automatic, eliminating the tedious process of inserting spaces between letters and words. A standard Linotype could cast lines up to thirty picas in length.

An important development for linecasting type was the Teletypesetter. This perforated tape-driven machine—an attachment to Linotype and Intertype—was introduced in 1928. Tape, which was punched by a machine similar to a standard typewriter, could be generated from a distant office and transmitted to the linecaster by wire, which made the machine invaluable to news services.

Monotype

Another significant achievement leading to fully automated typesetting was the Monotype machine, invented by Tolbert Lanston in 1887. This machine cast one character at a time rather than an entire line. It was composed of two parts: a keyboard and a typecaster (Figs. **7**). When an operator typed at a keyboard, a perforated paper tape was generated. This coded tape was used to drive the second part of the system—the typecaster. Compressed air, blown through the punched holes of this revolving spool of coded paper, determined which characters would be cast by the typecaster. Actual casting of type occurred when hot metal was forced into matrices from the matrix case (Fig. **8**). Once the cast characters had cooled, they were placed into a metal tray called a galley, where the lines were assembled. Monotype lines could reach a maximum length of about sixty picas.

Monotype became an efficient way to set type for several reasons. Corrections could be made by changing individual letters instead of complete lines. Therefore, complex typesetting, such as scientific data and tabular information, was easier. The Monotype matrix case held many more characters than a Linotype magazine, and the casting machine was relatively fast, casting one hundred fifty characters per minute. Since the system consisted of two separate machines, an operator could generate type away from the clatter of the casting machine. In fact, several operators could keyboard information for later setting.

8.
Monotype matrix case.

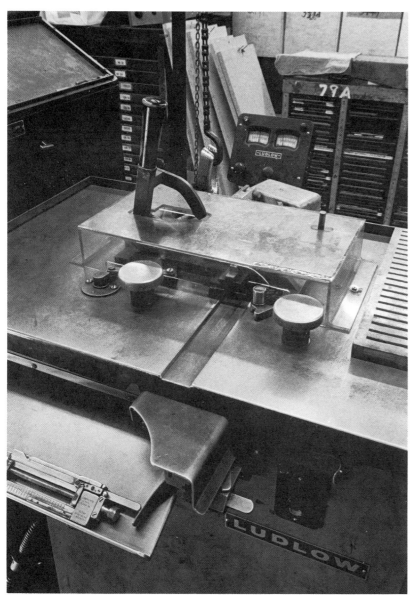

Ludlow

Ludlow, a semiautomatic linecaster, is another machine that found a place in the development of automated typesetting (Fig. **9**). Unlike the Linotype and Monotype, the Ludlow did not have a keyboard but combined both hand and machine production. An operator took matrices from a matrix case similar to a handset type case and placed them into a special composing stick, one by one. The stick would automatically justify or center lines by inserting blank matrices where necessary. Once a line of matrices was assembled, it was placed into a casting device where it was auto-matically cast into slugs. If a correction was necessary, matrices were inserted into the stick, cast, locked up, and printed. Although partially automated, this process was time consuming. Distributing the matrices back into the type case by hand added to the production time.

Type produced by the Ludlow machine ranged from 6 to 144 point. Its major use was to produce display type for headlines and other purposes requiring larger typefaces. As was true in the case of handset composition, the Ludlow was neither practical nor efficient for setting large volumes of type.

9.
Ludlow linecaster.

Phototypesetting

Light
source

Negative
film matrix

Lens system
for enlarging
or reducing

Photographic
paper or film

11.
Photo-optical system.

Optical
negative

Image transfer

Digitized image

Cathode-ray-
tube scan

Lens system

Photographic
paper or film

12.
Photo-scanning system.

Although some research in the area of phototypesetting had been done as early as the 1880s, the practicality of this new form of typesetting was not fully recognized until the close of World War II. Printing technology advanced from letterpress to the photographic process of offset lithography; typesetting underwent a similar technological change.

Phototypesetting and digital typesetting are currently the primary methods of setting type in the graphic arts. Since the development of Intertype's Fotosetter and Mergenthaler's Linofilm, the first generation of keyboard phototypesetters, introduced in 1950, numerous other systems have been developed (Fig. **10**). Typesetting speed, character definition, and ergonomics (the relationship between man and machine) have continued to improve. Despite varying degrees of electronic sophistication among systems, phototypesetting can be divided into two basic classes: photo-optical systems and photo-scanning systems.

Photo-optical systems

Photo-optical systems store characters in the form of a master font on film, discs, grids, strips, or drums (Fig. **11**). These negative images are the "matrices" of phototypesetting systems. They are optically projected onto photographic film or paper. A variety of sizes of type can be obtained from a single master font in most systems. An operator enters text and specifications at an editing terminal. Advanced computer technology is used to control this typesetting process.

Photo-scanning systems

Photo-scanning systems store characters in the form of a master font, not unlike those of photo-optical systems (Fig. **12**). However, characters are not photographically projected onto film or paper; rather, they are scanned electronically and broken down into either dots or lines. These digitized characters are then projected onto a cathode-ray tube from which they are optically projected onto photographic paper or film. Once the characters have been digitally generated, their appearance can easily be altered. Weight, width, and slant can be changed automatically. Photo-scanning systems operate at much higher speeds than photo-optical systems.

10.
Linofilm machine.

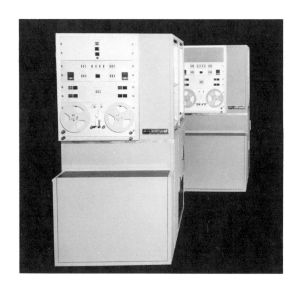

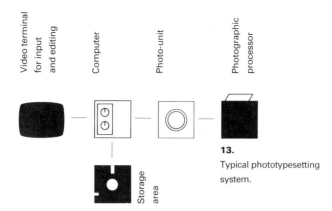

Video terminal for input and editing

Computer

Photo-unit

Photographic processor

Storage area

13.
Typical phototypesetting system.

System components

Typically, a phototypesetting system is composed of five parts, which perform input, output, editing, and storage functions (Fig. **13**).

Keyboard and visual display terminal (VDT). Copy is typed at the keyboard and viewed on the VDT. Although keyboards vary from one system to another, their basic function is to enter and edit text. While a phototypesetter keyboard is similar to a typewriter's keyboard, additional keys are provided to perform special functions. The editing capabilities of a terminal save considerable time and effort. Words, lines, and paragraphs can be added, deleted, and moved from one area of the screen to another with ease. Changes can be made at the keyboard before type is processed.

Storage area. Storage is a very important part of the editing system of a phototypesetter and may or may not be a part of the VDT. Input is stored temporarily in the computer's memory or permanently on a magnetic disk or on tape. If at a later date the type needs to be altered, the contents of the disk or tape are simply loaded into the computer and changes are made at the keyboard.

Computer. This component, which is connected to the VDT, relays signals between the keyboard, the screen, memory, photo-unit, and processor.

Photo-unit. The photo-unit is the part of the system that actually generates type. A photo-optic system, for example, would optically expose an entire character from a photographic negative onto paper or film.

Processor. After type has been set, the exposed film or paper is developed in a photographic processor. This may be a part of the typesetter, or it may be a separate unit.

A machine that combines all the above components into one unit is called a direct-entry phototypesetter. These machines are very popular for a number of reasons. They are small, affordable, easy to operate, and capable of handling difficult typesetting demands. Since input and output are shared by a single unit, a direct-entry machine can be used as a word processor and editing terminal that produces high-quality type. Some units can connect with other word processing terminals, enabling input from more than one operator. Other units have full-page display capabilities. Called area composition terminals, these units enable complete page makeup and presentation on a visual display terminal.

Phototypesetting systems, especially those of newspapers and other large publishers, can be part of complex and extensive networks, with links to word processors and mainframe computers. Text generated at one location can be transferred to another via telephone modem or satellite.

The advantages of phototypesetting over hot-metal composition are obvious. Phototypesetters are highly flexible and very fast. The typical phototypesetter can set as many as five hundred characters per second, while hot-metal machines may set only five characters per second. Hot-metal machines are operated mechanically; phototypesetters are controlled and operated electronically. Type generated from a phototypesetting system takes up very little physical space because its final form is a film or paper proof. In contrast, the space required to store lead slugs is enormous. Another major advantage of phototypesetting is that text input uses computerized editing capabilities. This speeds up the process of entering the text considerably, as corrections are made electronically at the keyboard.

Typography created by phototypesetting is free of the physical restrictions inherent in lead type. There is flexibility in the spacing of typographic elements through kerning, letterspacing, overlapping, interline spacing, and special effects such as runarounds (type that runs around another element such as a photograph or illustration). A designer should understand the capabilities and limitations of typesetting technology so that it can be controlled and used to a greater advantage.

Display photographic typesetting

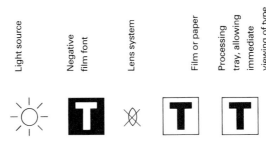

15.
Typical display photographic typesetter.

A rapid increase in the use of display photographic typesetting during the 1960s brought new design capabilities for the designer in display typography (Fig. **14**). As with keyboard phototypesetters, a light source projects the image of a letterform from the film font through a lens system onto photographic paper or film. There is no keyboard; each character from the film font is brought into position by the operator using hand controls. Because the operator is able to see the recently set characters as they develop photographically, letterspacing can be precisely controlled (Fig. **15**).

The numerous design advantages of display photographic systems led to their becoming the dominant method for headline typesetting within a few years. Instead of being bound by the sizes of handset composition, the designer could now specify any enlargement or reduction of the master font—which has capitals about one inch high—from twice up to four times down with perfect sharpness. Unlike metal display fonts, which have a limited number of characters, display phototype offers an unlimited supply. Spacing flexibility was a major innovation, for display type could now overlap, touch, and be set at any interletter-spacing interval specified by the designer. The constraints of blocks of metal yielded to the elasticity of photo-graphic processes, and innovative designers rapidly explored new possibilities. The lens system enables letterform distortion. Characters can be expanded, condensed, italicized, and even backslanted (Fig. **16**). The tremendous expense of introducing new metal typefaces, requiring punches, matrices, and cast letters in each size, was replaced by one economical film font. As a result, the introduction of new typefaces and revivals of earlier styles greatly increased.

14.
Display photographic typesetter.

16.

Normal		aaaaaaaaa
Expanded	8°	aaaaaaaa
	16%	aaaaaaaa
	24%	aaaaaa
Condensed	8%	aaaaaaaaaa
	16%	aaaaaaaaaaa
	24%	aaaaaaaaaaa
Backslant	10%	aaaaaaaaa
	16%	aaaaaaaaa
	24%	aaaaaaaa
Italic	10%	aaaaaaaaa
	16%	aaaaaaaa
	24%	aaaaaaaa

Digital typesetting

The digital computer in combination with the high-resolution cathode-ray tube (CRT) and laser, revolutionized the communications industry. Because digital computers have no mechanical parts and are entirely composed of electronic components, they set and process type at speeds never thought possible. In addition, the text type from digital typesetters has now been developed to rival the quality of phototype.

Knowledge of digital-computer functions is critical to an understanding of digital typesetting. A digital computer is an electronic device that uses electricity to process information. It can perform repetitive logical and arithmetic operations and store the results of those operations in memory. A computer system is composed of hardware, software, and firmware. Hardware consists of the physical components of a computer; software is the program data which controls the operation of the hardware; firmware is software in hardware form.

The computer component that controls all other parts, performs logical operations, and stores information is the central processing unit (CPU). All components that do not belong to the CPU are called peripherals. A typical digital-typesetting system is composed of a CPU and various peripherals that perform functions necessary to the setting of type—for example, editing and storing text, displaying text on a screen, and printing typeset copy.

A CPU consists of three interdependent components: arithmetic-logic unit (ALU), main memory, and control unit. These three components work together to control the operations of the computer. The ALU performs both arithmetic and logical functions such as adding two numbers together and determining which of two numbers is the greatest. In the main memory, called the random-access memory (RAM), data is stored and retrieved by the control unit. This unit also governs the functions of ALU and RAM. Consisting of these three parts, the CPU is the brain of a computer. It controls all functions, including the generation and setting of type in a digital-typesetting system.

A digital-computer system is based on the biconditional state of electronic circuitry. An electronic line can exist in only one of two states: it is either on or off. Each on/off state represents one binary digit or bit, enabling a computer to operate within the laws of the binary-number system. The binary system is a base-2 numbering system using only two numbers, 0 and 1. These numbers coincide with the biconditionals: off and on, respectively. The binary system is the exclusive language of any digital computer.

A computer communicates and processes information through the use of data structures. These are bits that have been grouped together into various configurations large enough to store significant information. The smallest bit structure is a byte, which consists of a group of bits linked together, such as the ASCII code (American Standard Code for Information Interchange, an information code in which the numbers zero to one hundred twenty-seven represent alphanumeric characters on the keyboard). These data structures are binary codes representing characters or numbers. Translating our alphanumeric characters into the binary system enables computers and people to communicate.

In digital typesetting, when the operator punches a key to enter a letter or issue a command (such as line length or paragraph indent), the computer receives it as a binary code. Once information has been entered, it can be stored, edited, and sent to a peripheral device for typesetting.

A digital-typesetting system encodes typographic characters digitally on a grid, defining the shape of each letter as a certain number of distinct points. Every detail of a letter is defined, including horizontal strokes, vertical strokes, and curves. The coded characters are stored electronically as digital instructions designating the x and y coordinates of the character on the grid. These instructions are then sent to a CRT, where the character is generated onto the screen.

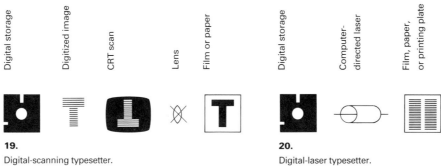

19.
Digital-scanning typesetter.

20.
Digital-laser typesetter.

A CRT is much like a television set. It has a vacuum tube with a cathode at one end and a plate of phosphorous and aluminum at the other. When the CRT receives the digital instructions from the computer, defining the shape of the characters, the cathode emits a beam, which scans the tube in a series of parallel back-and-forth sweeps. The cathode beam is programmed to be either on or off, depending upon the design of the letterforms that have been digitally encoded into the computer. When the beam is on, it excites the phosphorous and aluminum plate. The light emitted by the plate defines each character being typeset. The type is then digitally exposed to photographic paper.

The level of resolution in digital letterforms is an important consideration. Basically, the more dots or lines used to describe a letterform, the higher the resolution becomes. Because letters are constructed on a grid, the curved lines consist of a series of stair-stepped contours (Fig. **17**). When more dots are used to represent a curve, the curve appears smoother to the eye. Large characters require more dots than do small characters to achieve a refined appearance. The quality of a letterform is determined not only by its original design, but also by its digital resolution (Fig. **18**). The designer of digital type must consider digital technology and its effect upon the resolution of letterforms.

One major difference between digital type and phototype is the manner in which type is stored. Rather than storing master fonts on photographic disks, drums, grids, or strips, digital master fonts can be stored electronically as bit patterns on a magnetic disk. Some machines are capable of storing hundreds of fonts, with each size stored independently.

Scanning and laser systems
There are two classes of digital typesetters: digital-scanning systems and digital-laser systems. In digital-scanning systems (Fig. **19**), photographic characters are digitally scanned and recorded electronically on a magnetic disk or tape. The characters are translated into a grid of extremely high resolution and are transmitted as a set of instruc-

tions to a CRT. Next, the characters are generated onto the CRT by a series of scan lines. The letterform images are then projected from the CRT onto paper, film, or an electrostatic drum. Because the output type is digital, it can be modified automatically to reflect a number of typographic variations. For example, it can be made heavier, lighter, slanted, condensed, or expanded at the command of the operator.

Digital-laser systems (Fig. **20**) also store characters digitally, but do not employ a CRT to generate characters. A laser beam scans photographic paper as it reads digital information stored in the typesetter. As the paper is scanned, a series of dots forming the characters are exposed to the paper. The information controlling the laser includes the typographic font and spacing, such as hyphenation, justification, kerning, and letterspacing.

Because digital typesetting is so fast, it is particularly suited to industries requiring the processing of enormous amounts of information, such as news services and publishing companies. However, smaller offices and type houses are also using digital type because of its efficiency.

Direct-entry digital typesetters (Fig. **21**) are similar to direct-entry phototypesetters, for they are both self-contained. However, direct-entry digital typesetters are much faster and more versatile. Because they generate modified characters and a wider range of sizes and spatial intervals, direct-entry digital typesetters bring greater flexibility to the typesetting process (Fig. **22**).

18.
Examples of digital letterforms, demonstrating decreasing resolution, from top to bottom, as the number of elements is reduced.

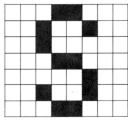

17.

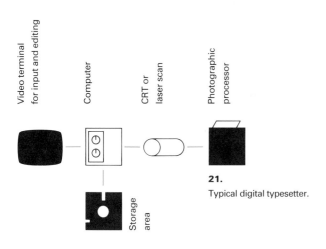

Video terminal
for input and editing

Computer

CRT or
laser scan

Photographic
processor

21.
Typical digital typesetter.

Storage
area

22.
An infinite variety of letterform alteration is possible
with digital typesetters.

ABabABabABabABabA

ABabABabABabABabABabAB

ABCabcABCabcABCabcABCab

ABCabcABCabcABCabcABCabcABCab

ABCabcABCabcABCabcABCabcABCabcABCabcAB

ABCDabcdABCDabcdABCDabcdABCDabcdABCDabcd

ABCDEabcdeABCDEabcdeABCDEabcdeABCDEabcdeABCDEabc

ABCDEFabcdefABCDEFabcdefABCDEFabcdefABCDEFabcdefABCDEFabcdef

ABCDEFGabcdefgABCDEFGabcdefgABCDEFGabcdefgABCDEFGabcdefgABC

ABCDEFGHabcdefghABCDEFGHbcdefghABCDEFGHabcdefghABCDEFGHabcdefghABCDE

ABCDEFGHIJabcdefghijABCDEFGHIJabcdefghijABCDEFGHIJabcdefghijABCDEFGHIJabcdefghijABCDEFGHIJa

ABCDEFGHIJKLabcdefghijklABCDEFGHIJKLabcdefghijklABCDEFGHIJKLabcdefghijklABCDEFGHIJKLabcdefghijklABCDEFGHIJKLabcdefghijkl

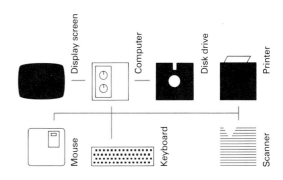

24.
Electronic page design workstation

23.
This Next computer monitor displays type in true WYSIWYG, for the dots-per-inch resolution is the same as its laser printer.

Digital typesetting moved onto the designer's desktop with the development of more powerful personal computers and software applications during the last decade. This major leap forward in typographic technology makes it possible to design entire pages on a computer screen, then electronically output them onto paper, film, or even printing plates. Electronic page design, also called desktop publishing, eliminates the need for pasteup, which is the hand-assembly of elements in position for reproduction as a page. Type size, style, spacing, and position can be changed, then viewed on the screen immediately, bringing unprecedented control and freedom to typographic design. Advances in technology are bringing typography closer to WYSIWYG, an expression meaning "what you see is what you get;" that is, the image on the computer monitor (Fig. **23**) is identical to the image that will be printed as final output.

Hardware components

Hardware, the physical component of the system, consists of the computer and the peripheral devices (Figs. **24** and **25**) that connect to it. Available peripherals include input devices, which are used to feed information into the computer, and output devices, which produce the final product.

Central processing unit. This electronic microprocessor chip does the actual work of the computer by receiving, processing, and storing information. It functions in a manner similar to the CPU of a digital typesetter, discussed earlier.

Input devices. These generate information for processing by the CPU and display on a screen, which uses a cathode-ray tube to produce a visual display of data. The keyboard contains alphabetical and numeric keys to input data. In addition, it contains special keys to perform specified functions, such as arrow keys to direct a pointer around the screen, and a command key that is held down while other keys are pressed, enabling them to send commands to the computer. The mouse is a hand-held device that is moved about the desktop;

it controls the movement of a pointer on the screen. A button on the mouse is clicked on elements to select them. When the mouse button is held down, elements on the screen can be moved by moving the mouse. Graphics tablets operate in a manner similar to a mouse, but use a stylus or pointer touched to a flat surface to input information. Scanners are devices which convert images or text into digital form so that they can be stored and manipulated by the computer.

Information storage devices. A disk is a round platter with a magnetic coating similar to recording tape, on which information from the computer is stored in the form of magnetic impulses. A disk drive reads information from, and writes information onto, disks. Floppy disks are portable and housed in a 3.5-inch hard plastic case; they are inserted into a disk drive, which reads the information on the disk. Hard-disk drives have large rigid disks permanently mounted within the computer or in a separate case. Hard disks have large storage capacity and fast operating speed. Removable hard-disk cartridges combine the portability of floppy disks with the large storage capacity of hard-disk drives. The development of new information storage devices using compact disks and optical, rather than magnetic, systems promises even greater speed and the storage of massive amounts of data.

Output devices. After a design is completed, output devices are used to convert the screen image to printed output. A dot matrix printer composes characters and image into a pattern of dots. The measure of quality for typographic output is the number of dots per inch (dpi); this determines the resolution of the image. A pin-strike printer uses a series of small pins that strike against an inked ribbon, transferring dots of ink onto paper to form the image. Many pin-strike printers have 72 dpi resolution, identical to the dpi of low-resolution screens.

25.
This designer's workstation combines a Macintosh IIci computer with a keyboard, mouse, and internal floppy and hard-disk drives. The image is displayed on a high-resolution SuperMac color monitor. An external HD Index removable cartridge drive permits the storing and transporting of large documents. A Sharp scanner is used to scan images and text and store them as digital data.

A laser printer creates images by drawing them on a metal drum with a laser. Dry ink particles are attracted to this image, which is then transferred to paper in a process similar to a photocopying machine. The first-generation laser printers' 300 dpi resolution was called "near typeset quality." The ability of laser printers to output pages combining text and images was made possible by the development of interpretive programming languages that provide a software interface between page-design programs, discussed below, and output devices. The first page-description programming language, PostScript™ by Adobe Systems, Inc., was specifically designed to handle text and graphics and their position on the page; QuickDraw™ by Apple Computer is another programming language that enables the rapid display of typographic elements on a screen.

Imagesetters are high-resolution output devices (Fig. **26**) that consist of two components, a raster image processor (RIP) and a recorder or exposure unit. The RIP is a computer that uses a page-description language (see below) to convert the data files from the designer's workstation into an electronic pixel pattern of the page. Every single point on the page, whether part of a letterform or a pictorial image, is positioned in this pattern, which is sent to the exposure unit as a bit-map of raster lines. A bit-map is a computerized image "made up of dots." Exposure units from various manufacturers use different technologies, such as cathode-ray tube (CRT), gas laser, laser diode, or light-emitting diode (LED), to record the RIP-composed page on photographic paper or film, plain paper, or even a printing plate.

Imagesetters produce very high resolution 1270 or 2540 dpi output. Imagesetters output type and halftone images in their final reproduction position, and some can output color separation negatives as well. The speed of digital typesetters is rated in characters per second, but imagesetters are rated in inches per minute since they output an entire bit-mapped page. Early imagesetters were not capable of the typographic refinement of digital typesetters; however, steady improvement in hardware and software has closed the gap in quality. Imagesetter output of electronically designed pages has rapidly replaced traditional composition and pasteup.

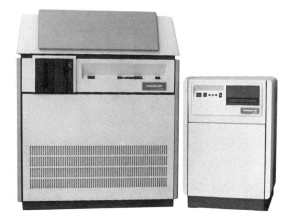

26.
The Linotron 300 imagesetter, shown with its raster image processor, outputs complete pages at 1270 or 2540 dpi resolution.

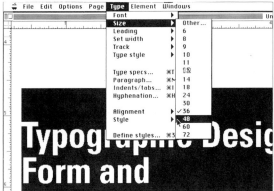

27.

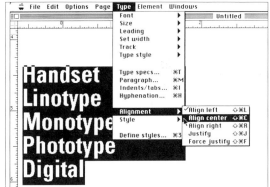

28.

Many typesetting firms have service bureaus to offer imagesetter output for their clients, and large advertising agencies and graphic-design offices have installed imagesetters within their firms. Typefaces are stored electronically in either bit-mapped or outline data form. Bit-mapped fonts are made up of dots and usually require a separate data set for each size of the typeface. Outline fonts are stored as instructions for drawing the outline of each character, using bezier curves to drawn non-uniform curves (as opposed to uniform curves, which are called arcs). Bezier curves are defined by four points, and their use enables computers to generate smooth images of complex letterforms.

Software
The instructions that tell the computer what to do are called software. An application program is software used to create and modify documents. The principle types of applications used in typographic design are word processors, drawing and painting programs, and page-layout software.

Word-processing programs are used to type in text, then edit, change, move, or remove it. Word-processing software can check grammar and spelling and suggest synonyms. Most text is written with a word-processing program, then transferred to a page-layout program for design.

Drawing and painting programs are used to create images. Early paint programs created images as a series of bit-mapped dots, while drawing programs generated objects that are treated as mathematically defined line and arc segments rather than a series of dots. A rectangle created in a paint program can have its corner erased, but in order to move it, all the dots composing it must be selected; by contrast, an object-oriented rectangle can be selected by clicking anywhere on it, then moving it about the space. However, you can not erase or change details. Most drawing and painting programs can generate and manipulate type, and

advanced versions often combine the features of object-oriented draw programs along with bit-mapped paint programs.

Page-design programs are used to design pages of typography and combine images with them. The type font, size, and leading can be selected, and text type can be flowed into columns running from page to page. Elements can be moved about the page, and templates of grid lines and standard repeating elements such as page numbers can be established. The screen image provides immediate feedback about the page design since all the elements are visible in their final sizes and spatial positions, and their attributes are capable of infinite change. The paper or film output is in final form, ready for reproduction.

The differences between word-processing programs and page-design programs are decreasing as each incorporates features from the other in updated versions. In general, word-processing programs have greater control over the editing process, while page-design programs have greater control over page composition. For example, in page-design programs an element can be selected with the mouse and moved anywhere on the page, but word-processing programs do not have this capability.

Page-design programs were made possible by the development of interpretive programming languages that provide a software interface between page-design programs and output devices.

The new computer-graphics technology has rapidly expanded the range of typeface design as well, for typeface design programs permit more rapid development of a new font than was possible with earlier technologies, while font editors allow the customization of individual letters or entire fonts to meet the needs of a user.

27.
The type menu lists parameters that can be changed on type that has been selected. Here the user has chosen *Size* and clicked the mouse button on *48* to change the selected type from *36* to *48* point.

28.
The type menu is being used to change the alignment of the selected type from *Align left* to *Align Center*.

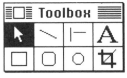

29.
When toolbox icons are selected, the mouse-controlled pointer becomes the selected tool. Top row: pointer tool, diagonal line drawing tool, perpendicular line drawing tool, and text tool. Bottom row: Rectangle drawing tool, round-cornered rectangle drawing tool, oval drawing tool, and cropping tool.

The history of writing is, in a way, the history of the human race, since in it are bound up, severally and together, the development of thought, of expression, of art, of intercommunication, and of mechanical invention.

The history of writing is, in a way, the history of the human race, since in it are bound up, severally and together, the development of thought, of expression, of art, of intercommunication, and of mechanical invention.
30.

30.
The top specimen has an undesirable widow. By changing the tracking of the second line in the bottom example by -1.5 (-1.5 / 200 em), the spatial interval between characters is deleted slightly, setting the type tighter and pulling the widow up to the last full line.

31.
Using a drawing program, the designer has joined the baseline of the type with an oval and a curved line.

The user interface

A typographic designer's computer workstation has an intuitive user interface; this means the tools are easy to use, permitting the user to focus upon the task at hand. A desktop pasteup metaphor is employed. The user sees the page surrounded by a desktop where elements can be created, held to one side, and then placed into position on the page. This metaphor to traditional pasteup has made it easier for the designers accustomed to traditional methods to design and assemble pages.

In page-design programs, a menu bar across the top of the screen lists major titles. The user moves the mouse to place the pointer on an item on the screen to be changed, then selects it by clicking the mouse button. Then, the pointer is placed on a menu title, and the mouse button is clicked, causing a list of commands to pop down. Under the type menu in one page-design program, for example, a list of commands for making changes to type that has been selected pops down. The user can change the type style, size (Fig. **27**), color, or alignment (Fig. **28**). Page layout programs also have a palette of tools that are represented by icons (Fig. **29**). After a tool icon is selected, the mouse is used to perform that operation.

Advanced page-design programs permit unprecedented flexibility in typographic design. Minute adjustments of typographic spacing are possible.

Type can be set in sizes from 2 points to 720 points and leaded from -1080 to +1080 points. Letterspacing can be controlled by manually kerning in increments of 1/20 or 1/200 em. The user can create kerning tables that automatically kern letter pairs. Tracking can be edited by selecting a range of characters (Fig. **30**), then changing the tracking in increments of 1/20 or 1/200 em as well.

Many programs provide the designer with unique capabilities for the manipulation and distortion of typographic forms. Lines of type can be joined to circular, oval, or irregular baselines (Fig. **31**); letterforms can be stretched and distorted in numerous ways (Fig. **32**). Page-design programs compose elements on a page in layers, so elements can be overlapped and layered in space (Fig. **33**). These electronic page-design capabilities are a mixed blessing, for while they can expand the creative range of typography, they can also produce awkward spatial arrangements and typographic forms that are hard to read.

DISTORT TYPE
DISTORT TYPE
DISTORT TYPE
DISTORT TYPE

32.
The bottom letterforms have been stretched excessively, causing the optical relationships to become distorted. The cross bar of the *T* has become too thick, while the *S* and *O* extend too far above and below the baseline.

33.
In contrast to the two-dimensional plane of traditional typographic technology, computer software permits the layering of information in space. (Designer: Erika Maxwell)

33.

Each major typographic process has its own place in the evolution of technology. Increased efficiency, control, flexibility, and the design of letterforms have been affected by continuous research and innovation. The nature of the typographic image has been changed as well (Fig. **34**). The microphotographs by Mike Cody demonstrate the differences. Letterpress printing of metal type impressed the letterform into the fibers of the paper. Phototype, usually printed by offset lithography, provides a precise image with a comparatively smooth contour. As the microphotographic enlargement shows, digital type evidences the stepped contour caused by the digitization of the image into discrete elements. In the most advanced digital-typesetting systems, the discrete elements are so small that they become indiscernable to the naked eye.

Technology develops rapidly, and designers must work to keep abreast of innovations that influence the design process and the typographic image. Designers should view typographers as partners in the design process, for their specialized knowledge of the typesetting system and its capabilities, along with an understanding of typographic refinements, can help the designer achieve the desired quality of typographic communication.

34.
Microphotographic
enlargement of letterforms.

Metal type on newsprint.

Metal type on coated paper.

Phototype.

Digital type.

The rapid advance of technology and the expanding role of visual and audiovisual communication in contemporary society have created new challenges for typographic education. Faced with the complex communications environment and the changes that are occurring and are anticipated, how can a designer nurture sensitivity to typographic form and communication? An appreciation of our typographic heritage, an ability to meet the standards of contemporary design practice, and an innovative spirit in facing the challenges of tomorrow are required.

The following assignments, ranging from basic theoretical exercises to complex applied projects, provide an overview of contemporary typographic design education. Responsible design education is composed of perceptual and conceptual development, technical training, and an ability to solve complex design problems. These projects were selected with emphasis upon building the perceptual and conceptual abilities that provide a foundation for effective and innovative typographic design practice.

Generation of a typographical sign from a gestural mark

P. Lyn Middleton

North Carolina
State University

Students were asked to make gestural question marks (Figs. **1–3**), giving consideration to the visual-design qualities of their sketches. Proportion, stroke weight, negative space, and details such as the relationship of the dot to the curved gesture were evaluated. One of the student's question marks was selected and became the basis for designing a freehand typographic sign.

Students generated a variety of graphic signs, exploring a range of forms that can function as a question mark. Executing the typographic version develops visual and manual acuity, and an understanding of the differences between written and typographic signs.

1.
Designer: Alexandre Lock.
2.
Designer: Maxine Mills
3.
Designer: Angela Stewart

1.

2.

3.

Letter/digit configurations

Urban letterform studies

Rob Carter

Virginia Commonwealth
University

Thomas Detrie

Guest Lecturer
Winter Session in Basel
Rhode Island
School of Design

Visual configurations were invented by combining a letter from the English alphabet with a single-digit number (Figs. **4–7**). Scale, proportion, weight, and shape relationships between two different signs were explored.

Objectives of this exercise include introducing letterform drawing and drafting skills, using typographic joinery to unify the two distinct forms into a visual gestalt, and understanding the variety of spatial relationships that can exist among characters.

4.
Designer: Penny Knudsen
5.
Designer: Penny Knudsen
6.
Designer: Colene Kirwin
7.
Designer: Linda Evans

8.

Letterforms in an old section of a European town were studied and documented through drawing, rubbings, and found material. A black-and-white letter composition was developed, depicting graphic qualities found in the assigned area (Fig. **8**).

On a formal level, compositional issues such as dynamic asymmetrical composition and form-counterform relations are explored. On an interpretive level, the ambiance of a historical area is translated into a typographic configuration.

4.

5.

6.

7.

8.
Designer: J. P. Williams

Inventing sign systems

Greg Prygrocki

North Carolina
State University

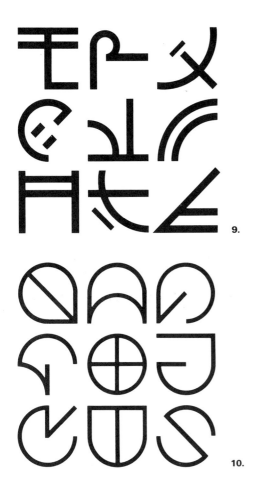

9.

10.

A set of nine signs were invented (Figs. **9–10**). Each was required to be a distinctive mark, with unique optical characteristics, yet harmonious with all the other signs and clearly recognizable as part of the set.

The focus of this project is to make students aware of the properties that bring unity to any typographic system. These include stroke weight and direction, stress, form repetition, and intersection.

9.

Designer: Joe Easter

10.

Designer: Paul Dean

Letterform analysis

Ben Day

Boston University

A modular grid of horizontal, vertical, and diagonal units was established and used to draw variations of a letterform (Fig. **11**). The sans serif *E* has been transformed into expanded and condensed variations. A grid sequence from four to twelve vertical units and from five to ten horizontal units was used. In Figure **12**, the form has been elaborated upon by opening the space between the vertical stroke and the three horizontal strokes.

The purpose of this project is to understand the allowable tolerence for the alteration of letterform proportions without losing sign legibility. In addition, the internal structure of a letter is analyzed and manipulated. This project introduces students to the formal variety that is possible and to the process of logo design.

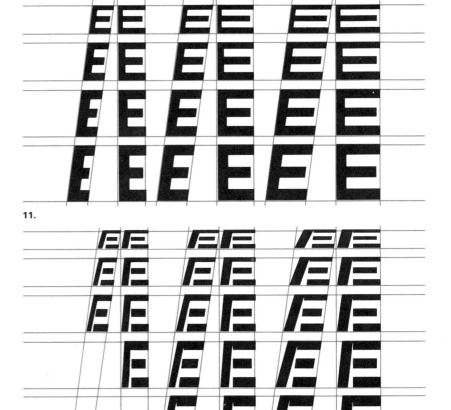

11.

12.

Designer: Tim Barker

Visual organization and grid structures

Greg Prygrocki

North Carolina State University

Students developed linear grid structures, then created a series of plates, organizing found typographic materials into spatial compositions based upon this underlying structure (Figs. **13** and **14**).

This project introduces the grid structure as a formal design element. The grid module is the basic compositional unit, bringing order to the arrangement. Students consider contrast, structure, positive and negative space, balance, texture and tone, and rhythm as design properties.

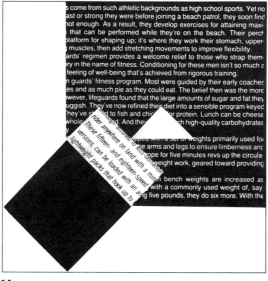

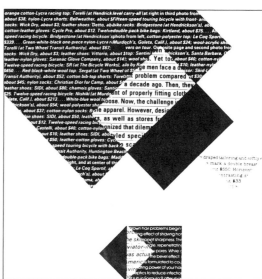

13.
Designer: Craig McLawhorn
14.
Designer: Matt Monk

14.

Repetition and pattern making

Typography and image transformations

Greg Prygrocki

North Carolina
State University

Gordon Salchow

University of Cincinnati

17.

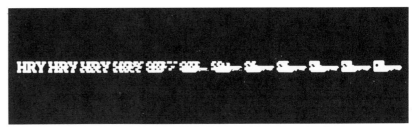

18.

An understanding of the structural nature of letterforms was investigated by using form repetition to create a clearly definable pattern (Figs. **15** and **16**). Through the rotation and repetition of letterforms, the student can acquire increased sensitivity to letterform structure and skill in alignment.

A letter has been altered in a series of steps until it is transformed into a simple object, an abstract shape, or another letterform (Figs. **17-19**). An understanding of typographic sequencing, permutation, and kinetic properties is developed. Students can gain an awareness of form and counterform relationships and the unity that can be created in complex configurations.

15.
Designer: Elizabeth McPherson

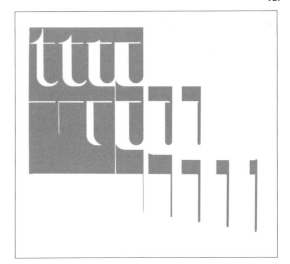

19.

16.
Designer: Kim Marlatt

17.
Designer: University of Cincinnati Sophomore
18.
Designer: University of Cincinnati Sophomore
19.
Designer: University of Cincinnati Sophomore

Experimental compositions with found typography

Katherine McCoy

Cranbrook Academy of Art

Using all of the typography found on a product label, a grid-based composition was produced exploring size relationships, spatial interval, and weight (Fig. **20**). A second composition was generated with more dynamic movement and scale change (Fig. **21**). Visual notations were made of each, analyzing eye movement, massing, and structure (Figs. **22** and **23**). Tone, texture, and shape are substituted for the typographic elements.

This project is designed to encourage an understanding of the abstract properties inherent in existing typographic forms. An exploratory attitude toward space and visual organization is developed.

20.

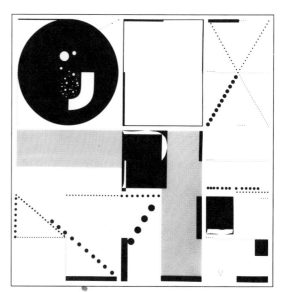

21.

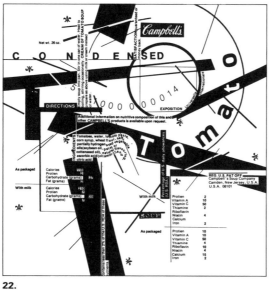

22.

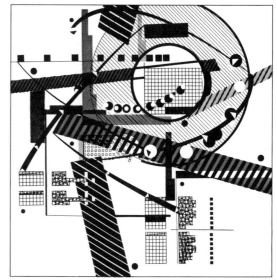

23.

20-23.
Designer: Ryoji Ohashi

**Unity of form
and communication**

Christopher Ozubko

University of Washington
at Seattle

After selecting a historical
event as subject, students
were asked to develop a
typographic message using
the visual properties of type
and space to amplify content
(Figs. **24–27**). This project
develops an understanding of
the inventive potential of
typographic form. As a
message carrier, typography
can intensify and expand
content and meaning.

24.
Designer: Steve Cox
25.
Designer: Kyle Wiley
26.
Designer: Bill Jolley
27.
Designer: Susan Dewey

24.

25.

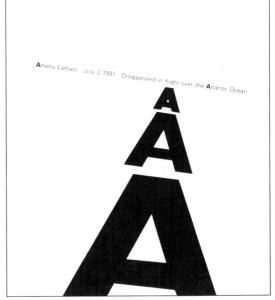

26.

27.

**Expressive typography:
form amplifies message**

Douglas Higgins

University of Cincinnati

Design students were introduced to computer typography in a project that explored the potential of computer techniques to intensify typographic messages. Content derived from scientific newsletters was used to create typographic identifiers that clearly summarize factual information contained in the article. By employing a source of subject matter that is usually designed routinely, the temptation to appropriate a solution was minimized.

Special attention was given to the role of visual hierarchy and typographic contrast while developing computer drafting skills useful in professional practice. The ease with which the computer generated variations facilitated visual refinements.

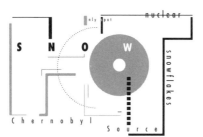

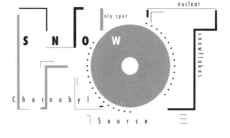

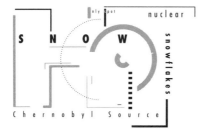

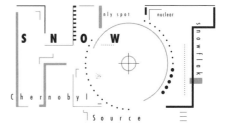

28.

29.

30.

28.
Designer: University of
Cincinnati Junior
29.
Designer: University of
Cincinnati Junior
30.
Designer: University of
Cincinnati Junior

Computer improvisation and manipulation

Douglas Higgins

Ringling School
of Art and Design

Two letterforms in structural opposition were combined to create a "seed" configuration (Figs. **31** and **32**). Successive improvisations depart from the original while preserving the basic structural form, as basic computer operations are learned (Fig. **33**). Parallels are established between typographic concepts and computer techniques needed to explore them. Electronic pages layout software was used to document the entire design process in book form.

Using a computer to deconstruct and manipulate digital type images allows students to hasten their understanding of letterform analysis and elemental structures governing each letter's legibility. Assignment goals include an understanding of letterform complexities and using forms inherent in a letter's design as points of departure for applied problem-solving.

31.
Designer: Michelle Carrier
32.
Designer: Teresa Leard
33.
Designer: Teresa Leard

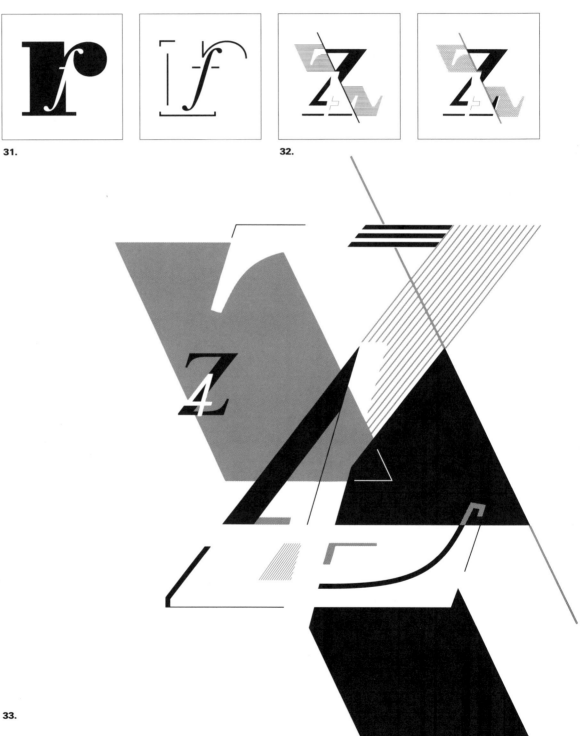

31.

32.

33.

**Typographic variations
through changing parameters**

Rob Carter

Virginia Commonwealth
University

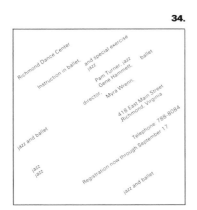

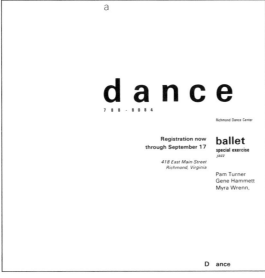

Using descriptive copy from a small newspaper advertisement, students designed a series of typographic messages. These variations were generated through changing problem parameters in a progressive series. Parameters for the examples shown here are as follows: same type size and weight (Fig. **34**); same type size, different weight (Fig. **35**); different type size and weight (Fig. **36**); different size and weight, varied letterspacing for emphasis (Fig. **37**); and interpretive manipulation of type to reinforce the message (Fig. **38**).

The objective is to make students aware that a visual hierarchy can be created by changing typographic parameters. Students learn that an infinite number of possible solutions to each problem is available. A typographic designer can generate and evaluate these possible solutions for their communicative effectiveness.

34.
Designer: Michelle Teten
35.
Designer: Michelle Teten
36.
Designer: James Creps
37.
Designer: Michelle Teten
38.
Designer: Colene Kirwin

Legibility, readability, and expression

Philip B. Meggs

Virginia Commonwealth University

Dozens of typographic permutations were made on the computer to explore legibility, readability, expression, and their interaction. Legibility is the clarity with which signs can be deciphered; readability is making material attractive and inviting to readers; and expression is using artistic means to reveal attitudes or feelings. Students were challenged to make the most legible possible typography by manipulating and critically evaluating typeface selection, spacing parameters, and line length. Each student chose the most legible solution (Fig. **39**), then used display type, spatial interval, rules, and so on, to make readership more inviting (Fig. **40**).

Scale, spatial manipulation, and textural contrasts were manipulated to intensify expression (Figs. **41** and **42**), ranging from subtle variations to bold experiments. This problem encourages students to consider legibility, readability, and expression as interactive characteristics that can be controlled and increased through a design decision-making process.

39.
Designer: John Bielik
40.
Designer: Keith Jones
41.
Designer: Nancy Seigler
42.
Designer: Joe Scuderi

39.

40.

41.

42.

Poem and news combinations

Jan Boterman

Gerrit Rietveld Academy
Amsterdam

Using a standard-size sheet of paper, folded at one-third its size, students were challenged to lay out two contrasting communications—a poem and a news item—on the same subject. Time and sequence were introduced through the use of the folded sheet. In Figure **43**, a line of poetry, "He that knows that enough is enough, always has enough," is combined with a newspaper headline: *Meer Geld* ("More money"). Figure **44** shows a sound poem of repeating sounds that translate, "That small round part is dealt out." The second item describes the type of poem structure that is present in the sound poem.

The keystone of this project is an editorial and syntactical problem: combine two messages into a single typographic expression while maintaining their uniqueness. Production was by letterpress. Selection of paper stock and ink color appropriate to the message were important considera-tions.

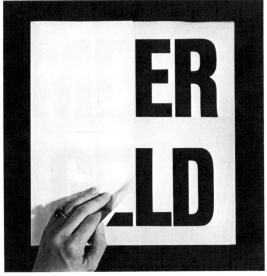

43.

44.

43.
Designer: Allan Tan
44.
Designer: Rijk Boerma

Typographic cubes

R. Roger Remington

Rochester Institute
of Technology

A visual presentation combining typography, images, and symbols was created as an extension of a self-assessment study by advanced design students (Figs. **45–47**). The students made a formal analysis of their past experiences and future goals. This part of the project stressed research and information gathering. The collected materials were evaluated for their communicative effectiveness in a complex design.

Transforming diverse information into a three-dimensional cube poses a complex design problem. Each side of the cube functions as part of a totality; the four contiguous sides are graphically and communicatively integrated.

45.

46.

47.

45.
Designer: Beth April Smolev
46.
Designer: Katherine St. James
47.
Designer: Bruce Morgan

Calendar typography

Josef Godlewski

Indiana University

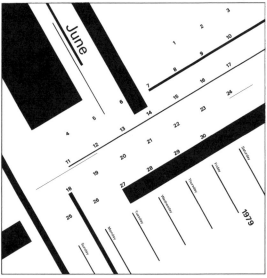

Calendar pages were designed using typographic elements to organize the space and direct eye movement on the page (Fig. **48**). Emphasis was placed upon experimentation, creating unity and movement on each page, and developing a visual elaboration over twelve pages. A grid structure was established and used to achieve diversity and order within a sequence of twelve designs. Graphic elements were limited to typography and rules.

This assignment enables students to explore interrelationships between graphic elements and the surrounding space.

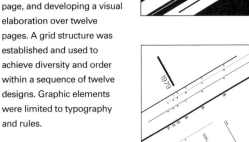

48.

48.
Designer: Jean Brueggenjohann

Interpretive typography:
form and content

John DeMao

University of Illinois
at Chicago

Using only typography, students arrived at appropriate interpretations of the essential character of a renowned work of literature (Figs. **49–51**). They were asked to respond to the story by manipulating letterforms in a figurative and expressive way.

Distortion and alteration of letterforms achieve visual dynamics and intensify the meaning of the title. An awareness of the potential correspondence between typographic form and verbal content is developed.

49.
Designer: Mark Signorio
50.
Designer: Cindy Kim
51.
Designer: Karl Knauz

49.

50.

51.

Typeface history posters

Type specimen book page

Jan Baker

Rhode Island
School of Design

Jean Brueggenjohann

Boston University

Each student in the class was assigned a typeface to study and use in a poster design, communicating its essential characteristics (Figs. **52** and **53**). Letterforms that reveal the unique properties of the typeface were emphasized. The typeface name and entire alphabet were required components of the design.

This project enables students to establish a visual hierarchy in a poster format, while introducing them to the visual characteristics of typefaces.
52.
Designer: Holly Hurwitz
53.
Designer: Luci Goodman

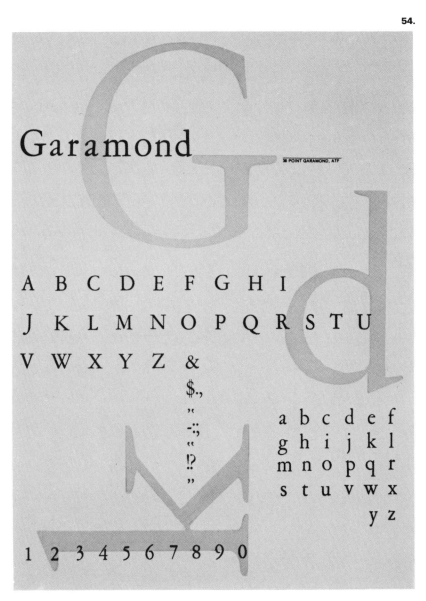

54.

52.

53.

A specimen book page was developed using the typeface name, complete upper- and lowercase alphabets, numbers, punctuation, and display letterforms selected to convey the visual properties of the font (Fig. **54**).

Objectives of this project include: the establishment and use of a simple grid, the clustering of elements to create typographic densities, and expressing the nature of the typeface through an overall patterning. A one-

color reproduction restriction enables the students to explore the potential of screen tints.
54.
Designer: Joyce Hempstead

Jan Baker

Rhode Island
School of Design

David Colley

University of Illinois
at Champaign-Urbana

An abecedarian primer was designed and printed by letterpress (Fig. **55**). Each student researched a topic, then developed a sequence of twenty-six pages presenting information about the subject. The example shown presents the historical evolution of each letterform in the alphabet; other student research included music, animals, the Amazon, and teaching the alphabet to pre-school children.

Combining display and text type into cohesive page layouts, integrating the left- and right-hand pages, and creating a visual flow in a serial progression are project objectives. Students learn how to translate their subject research into a typographic format.

55.

Designer: Susan Limoncelli

A series of posters was designed to encourage local high school students to attend symphony concerts (Fig. **56**). Emphasis was placed on writing interpretive copy and selecting typefaces appropriate to that message. Diversity of expression to parallel the concert season was an important consideration. (These posters were printed by offset and donated to the symphony.)

This project introduces the student to the importance of the message in typographic communication. Language devices including metaphor, sound repetition, and rhyme were used to make the content memorable. The relationship of form and meaning was addressed; the nature of each composer's music was considered in the selection of typeface, size, placement, and color. In the examples shown, typographic dissonance in the Stockhausen poster parallels the composer's musical dissonance; word substitution occurs in the Brahms poster; and an auditory double meaning is found in the Bach poster.

56.

Designer: University of Illinois undergraduate students

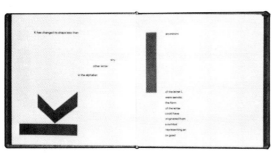

55.

56.

Type chronology booklet

R. Roger Remington

Rochester Institute
of Technology

A comparative study of ten typefaces was made by each student. The information was organized chronologically in a booklet with four pages devoted to each typeface. In Figure **57**, the opening spread juxtaposes descriptive text and a complete font opposite a large letterform. The following spread contains a historical application of the type opposite a contemporary application created by the student.

This problem develops research skills, an understanding of typographic history, and an ability to work with different typefaces. Large amounts of complex data are organized; a consistent format is developed; diversity is created within this format.

57.

57.
Designer: Heinz Klinkon

Thematic exhibition posters

Alston Purvis
and Jean Brueggenjohann

Boston University.

An extensive research project investigated the traditions of design in early New England. The results were presented in a series of exhibition posters (Fig. **58**). Emphasis was placed upon the integration of images and type into cohesive compositions.

In this advanced self-initiated project, the student made use of principles of grid organization to bring unity to each poster. Since the artifacts shown varied widely in design and format, major compositional axes (composed of a horizontal flow line one-third from the top and a central vertical division) were used as a structural theme unifying the series.

58.
Designer: Suzanne Perry

Ben Day

Virginia Commonwealth
University

Student teams researched an
epoch of European cultural
history, then formulated an
itinerary for a journey
through Europe to major
sites. A visual and verbal
timeline was designed, outlining the journey for a
potential traveler. Each timeline begins with a map of
Europe and ends with a
poster composition of the
final destination. Figure **59**
shows a segment of a tour of
early cultures; in Figure **60**
the final destination on a tour
of early twentieth-century
architecture is seen.

Background and pictorial research, image selection, and
organization of complex data
on a grid are addressed in
this project. Functional communicative considerations
and expressive graphic interpretation are emphasized.

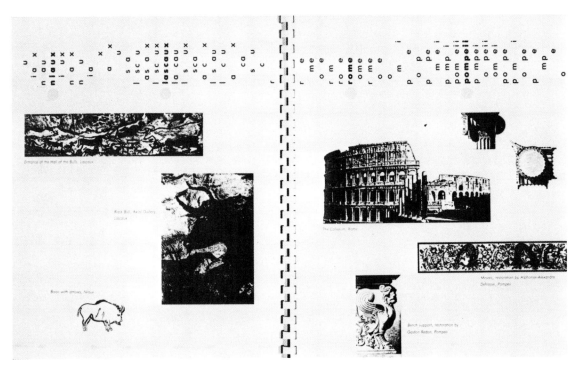

59.

60.

59.
Designer: Lark Pfleegor
60.
Designer: Michael Fanizza

7 Case Studies in Typographic Design

Many of the educational projects in the preceding chapter represent theoretical and exploratory investigations. They are structured to teach typographic history, theory, spatial concepts, form, and meaning. The goal of typographic education is to prepare young designers for the complexity of applied problem solving. The case studies presented in this chapter describe specific typographic design problems encountered in professional practice. The nature of each problem is analyzed, and the rationale for the solution is discussed.

These six studies cover a wide range of typographic design: a visual identification system, an exhibition catalogue, a book design, permutations of a title page, typographic motion picture titles, and a large-scale publication program. Each of the examples presents a different aspect of the broad scope of typography in our contemporary communications environment, and each fulfills a human commmunicative need with functional clarity and sensitivity.

A new logotype and graphic standards for the National Aeronautics and Space Administration were created by the design firm Danne and Blackburn Inc., of New York City. A graphic-standards manual was developed to instruct individuals throughout the NASA organization on the proper application of the unified visual communications system. The continued evolution and implementation of this design system has been the responsibility of NASA graphics coordinator Robert Schulman. By designating an individual at each NASA location (usually the section head of the graphics department) with responsibility for implementation and maintenance of the graphics system, Schulman was able to develop a network of professionals who are closely involved in NASA visual communications on a daily basis.

The first element in a visual-identity system is the visual identifier: a sign, symbol, or uniquely designed word called a *logotype.* It is used in a consistent, repetitive manner to establish and maintain a unified image and immediate identification. The NASA logotype is the dominant element in the visual-communications system (Fig. **1**). In it the agency initials are reduced to their most elemental forms. The resulting simplicity enables the logotype to be reduced to small sizes and to be readily identified from afar on signs, aircraft, and vehicles. The angled junctions of strokes in the capital *N* and the apexes of the *A*s are replaced by curved forms. This reduces the contrast between the letterforms, making the *N* and *A*s more harmonious with the *S.* The strokes are all of one width, evoking qualities of unity and technical precision. The crossbars from the two *A* forms are deleted, giving them a vertical thrust which sug-

gests rocketry and space flight. The sum of these design devices is visual cohesiveness and expressiveness. Although the stylization is very pronounced, readability and legibility are maintained.

A key to the effectiveness of the NASA system is the consistent use of the agency name and the identification of NASA centers. Subtle visual relationships are important. The name is set in Helvetica Light, which has letterforms compatible to the logotype but has definite weight contrast

4.

1.

2.

NASA
National Aeronautics and
Space Administration

3.

NASA
National Aeronautics and
Space Administration

John F. Kennedy Space Center

(Fig. **2**). The stroke weight of the logotype, the x-height of the lowercase letters, and the spatial interval between the bottom of the logotype and the topmost lowercase letters are virtually identical in measure. This repetition of spatial interval links the logotype and identifying name together. When the name of a NASA center is added to the logotype, contrast is achieved through the use of Helvetica Medium (Fig. **3**). Note that the interval between the agency name and the center name is a one-line space. However, this is measured to the x-height of the lowercase letters of the center name (*not* the top of the capitals) to achieve optical, rather than mathematical, evenness of the spatial intervals.

Two colors are designated for use in NASA graphics: a warm, lively red and a medium shade of warm gray. The consistent use of color is another unifying element in the visual-communications system. Careful guidelines govern the use of color and ban incorrect graphic treatments, such as outlining the logo, superimposing a pattern or texture over the logo, running it uphill, adding perspective shadows, or placing it in a circle, square, or plaque. Formulation of these regulations is critical to the success of the visual-identification program. Without clear and concise guidelines detailing all typographic treatments for visual identification, personnel throughout NASA's worldwide system might deviate, resulting in a dilution of the system's effectiveness.

Publications are the largest visual communications area. The *NASA Graphic Standards Manual* specifies criteria for routine printed material. For example, stationery has a logotype of 5/6-inch capital height with 10/12 Helvetica Light and Medium upper- and lowercase typography (Fig. **4**). Secondary typography is always set in 7/8 Helvetica Light upper- and lowercase typography. The left margin of the typography establishes the typing margin. Line spaces are used instead of paragraph indents. This combines typography and typewriting into a unified presentation.

The NASA logotype is often used as a "stem word" in conjunction with Helvetica type to form publication titles (Fig. **5**). This technique is limited

NASA Tech Briefs

National
Aeronautics and
Space
Administration

5.

Before   After

6.

7.

to ongoing periodicals and requires approval of the NASA graphics coordinator to ensure appropriate treatment. In some organizations, the graphic-standards manuals rigidly specify grid structures and text-type sizes for all publications. At NASA, the manual provides general guidance to allow a measure of flexibility in the design of publications. The logotype and accompanying typographic elements must be used consistently to create a strong, integrated family of publications. The level of graphic improvement and consistent identi-fication achieved by the NASA program is evi-denced by the redesign of a mission operation report (Fig. **6**) and in the application of the system to routine printing materials. While Helvetica is designated as the primary typeface, the manual recommends Futura, Garamond, and Times Roman as possible alternatives in special cases where the character of one of these faces might be more appropriate. The *NASA Graphic Standards Manual* presents grid systems for use in publica-tions design.

Environmental applications include signage, ve-hicle identification, and aircraft. The NASA system involves simple, functional signs employing flush-left, ragged-right Helvetica (Fig. **7**). In accordance with governmental regulations, vehicle identifica-tion consists of four elements: government-use identification, logotype, agency identification, and installation identification (Fig. **8**). Careful design specifications are also detailed for NASA aircraft (Fig. **9**). A white fuselage top, a blue stripe around the aircraft perimeter, a gray fuselage underside, and a red NASA logo on the tail are consistent design elements. This basic scheme adapts well to a wide range of aircraft. However, the proportions of the stripes vary widely when applied to aircraft sizes and shapes from small single-engine aircraft to the Boeing 747 photographed carrying the space shuttle *Enterprise* (Fig. **10**). Spacecraft marking, of necessity, is different on each vehicle. Flight en-gineers and scientists designated only a few areas on each spacecraft for graphics.

9.

10.

As shown on the *Enterprise,* the NASA logo, American flag, "United States," and vehicle name are carefully placed to conform with technical requirements and to be harmonious with the overall form and shape of the spacecraft. The NASA logo is in gray to avoid visual conflict with the red stripes of the flag. The logotype and Helvetica Medium typeface ensure continuity with all other NASA graphics.

The NASA visual-identification system has proven strong and resilient. It is both consistent and easily identifiable, yet the system has allowed for a wide variety of applications over the years.

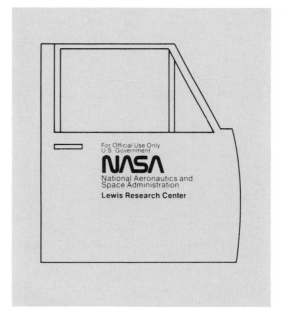

8.

For a major exhibition presenting work from two decades by the Fluxus group of artists, designers Katherine McCoy, Lori Barnett, Lyn Silarski, and Ken Windsor were commissioned to design a four-hundred-page exhibition catalogue. The Fluxus experimental art group was founded in 1962 by George Maciunas. International in scope and nurtured by the early twentieth-century art movements, Fluxus issued several manifestos, published inexpensive editions of artist's works, musical scores, and documentation of events. It provided a focus for expermentation that challenged accepted notions about art and the art experience.

The catalogue provides a record of hundreds of works from the exhibition. In addition, it serves as a permanent documentation of the Fluxus movement. The challenge facing the design team was to organize a large quantity of diverse information into a legible and coherent format, while capturing the vitality and spirit of the Fluxus movement. The catalogue is divided into five sections: a history of Fluxus, including philosophy, attitudes, influences, and purposes; a portfolio of over five hundred Fluxus Editions and related works; a presentation of Fluxus periodicals and documents; an illustrated record of Fluxus performance events; and a chronology of Fluxus performances.

Clearly, a format design was needed that could unify the breadth of information and imagery, while allowing design flexibility. A format was developed for nine-by-ten inch pages, using primary and secondary divisions of space. Each page has four vertical columns, with a secondary division of eight columns. Horizontal structure is achieved with a "floating" modular spatial division, which accommodates a diversity of content, form, and scale. Fluxus was greatly involved with process; therefore, the design process of this catalogue has been revealed by printing the grid structure for the pages in a subtle, screened tint. Thus, the construction lines for the pages are visible and become design elements. Unity is achieved through the repetition of a vertical black band down the left-hand side of each page. Key information appears on this band. A ruled line

11.

12.    **13.**

transverses the top of each page, with the page number placed in the top left-hand corner. Consistent use of condensed sans serif type lends further unity.

The front and back covers signify the content and mood of the publication. The front cover reproduces a 1963 photograph by George Maciunas, depicting a front door with a figure peering through the mail slot (Fig. **11**). The image communicates on several levels. It invites the reader to enter the world of Fluxus. The weathered, knobless door with a latch hanging below the mailslot without apparent purpose evokes a Dada-like visual irony, and the person peering from within is an ambiguous image, defying a specific interpretation. The stepped red box (containing the title) and the black band on the right establish the typographic format and graphic theme within. The back cover expresses a parallel but contrasting visual theme (Fig. **12**).

The complete history of Fluxus is presented through contributions by artists and poets from around the world. Manifestos (Fig. **13**) and philosophic observations (Fig. **14**) by members of the group are reproduced as full-page statements. The poetic energy and visual texture of the originals are preserved.

The section-divider pages are solid black, in contrast to the lighter tone and texture of the book (Figs. **15** and **16**). Stepped contour shapes provide spaces for each section's title typography.

The section entitled "Fluxus Editions and Related Works" presents an illustrated checklist of five hundred thirty items (Fig. **17**). Unity within complexity is achieved by the repetition of similar graphic elements. The designers placed the catalogue numbers in small white rectangles along the left-hand black bands. In the first grid column, typography identifies the artist, title, date, and dimensions of the work. Media and descriptive copy are placed in the second column. Rules are

15.

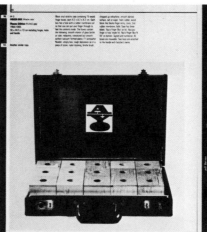

16.

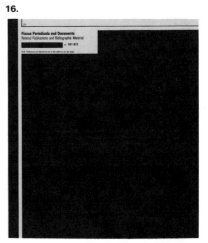

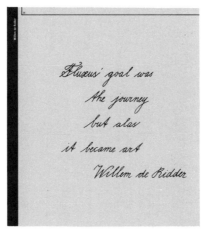

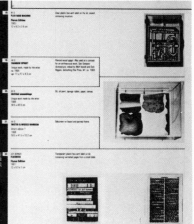

17.

14.

used to divide each page clearly into zones separating the works. The reader quickly understands the system and can connect the typography and images without difficulty.

This format continues into the sections presenting periodicals, documents, and performances, where illustrations include posters, invitations, and other artifacts relating to the events (Fig. **18**). A playful typographic vitality, expressive of the nature of the performances, characterizes these materials.

The final section is a typographic presentation of a "working document," a chronology of the Fluxus movement (Fig. **19**). The reader must turn the book to read the information. The primary division of space splits each page into two long columns upon which the programs are listed, separated by heavy rules. Three columns divide each program into areas for artists, work, and performers. As in the catalogue material, use of a bolder typeface gives appropriate emphasis to titles.

In determining the typographic schema and format of this book, the designers have been sensitive to the nature of the exhibition and the attitudes and philosophies of the Fluxus art movement. The exploratory innovations of the Fluxus group made appropriate the design team's decision to create a book that displays its grid organization. In addition, the flexibility of the modular spatial divisions clearly separates each work from others on the page. It allows page arrangements and grid manipulations to reflect the diversified content.

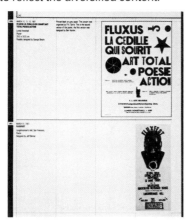

18.

1962

This chronology of Fluxus performance must be viewed as a working document. It is in no way complete, nor should the information in it be considered as accurate. Some of the events listed did not occur. Frequently programs were changed at the last minute, performers were unable to attend or other problems came up. What we have done is to gather as much information as possible that was available to us, and organize it into a form that can be added to, corrected, deleted and debated.

Jon Hendricks
New York, June 5, 1981

JUNE 9, 1962
KLEINER SOMMERFEST
Galerie Parnass, Wuppertal-E.
Revised Program:
'Apres John Cage'

Artist	Work	Performers
George Maciunas	Einführung: Neo-dada in New York	
Benjamin Patterson	Duo	
Benjamin Patterson	Variation für Kontrabass	
George Maciunas	Hommage à Adriano Olivetti	
Terry Riley	Ear Music	
Dick Higgins	Constellation No. 2	
Jed Curtis	Tribut	

JUNE 16, 1962
NEO-DADA IN DER MUSIK
Kammerspiele, Düsseldorf
Program:

Artist	Work	Performers
1. Nam June Paik	One for Violin Solo	N.J. Paik
2. George Brecht	Word Event	
3. Nam June Paik	Sonata Quasi Una Fantasia	N.J. Paik
4. Nam June Paik	read music 'Do it yourself — Antworten an La Monte Young — gelesen von C. Caspari	
5. Composition Anonyme: Simultaneous performances		
Sylvano Bussotti	Pak piece 62	C. Caspari
Jed Curtis	Saint Anthony's Blues	Jed Curtis
Dick Higgins	Danger Music Structure	J. Flemm
Toshi Ichiyanagi	Violin Piece	J.G. Fritsch
Jackson MacLow	poem	W. Kirchgässner
George Maciunas	piano piece No. 8 / No. 12	George Maciunas / H.v. Alemann
Nam June Paik	aus 'Bagatelles americaines'	N.J. Paik / Fr. Reddemann / Tomas Schmit / Batzing / Bonk
Benjamin Patterson	Paper Musik	Alvermann / Schneider / Weselina / Schilder u.a. etc.
Benjamin Patterson	Disturbance from 'Lemons'	A. Falkenstörfer / Benjamin Patterson
Dieter Schnebel	Visible Composition for Conductor	H. Reddemann
Wolf Vostell	'KLEENEX' décollage	W. Vostell
La Monte Young	For Flynt 566 chant of death	N.J. Paik u.a. etc. / J.G. Fritsch
6. Nam June Paik	smile gently—or etude platonique NO. 5	

JULY 3, 1962
SNEAK PREVIEW: FLUXUS
Performed in various locations around Paris
Organisé par la Galerie Legitime (Robert Filliou)
In conjunction with the opening of Ben Patterson's exhibition at the Galerie Girardon, Paris

Artist	Work	Performers
George Brecht	Comb Music	
George Brecht	Drip Music	
Joseph Byrd	Piece for Richard Maxfield	
John Cage	Music for Marrying Maiden	
Walter de Maria	Boxes	
Walter de Maria	Signs	
Robert Filliou	Le Voyage de la Galerie Legitime	
Robert Filliou	An Auction	
Dick Higgins	Requiem for March 17, 1848	
Dick Higgins	Symphony No. 3	
Dick Higgins	Constellation No. 4	
Toshi Ichiyanagi	Music for Piano No. 7	
Toshi Ichiyanagi	Stanzas	
Allan Kaprow	Stockroom	
Takehisa Kosugi	Micro 1	
Charles Mac Dermed	Dance not for Dancers	
George Maciunas	Solo for Lips and Microphone	
Jackson MacLow	Letters for Iris Numbers for Silence	
Richard Maxfield	Pastoral Symphony	
Richard Maxfield	Night Music	
Simone Morris	Dance Constructions	
Benjamin Patterson	Paper Piece	
Benjamin Patterson	Variations for Contrabass	
Yasunao Tone	Costumes	
La Monte Young	Composition 1960, #4	
Toru Takemitsu	Water Music 1960	

SEPTEMBER 1 – SEPTEMBER 23, 1962
FLUXUS INTERNATIONALE FESTSPIELE NEUESTER MUSIK
Hörsaal des Städtischen Museums, Wiesbaden

Performers for the 14 concerts, as listed in *Happening & Fluxus*, included:
Dick Higgins, Alison Knowles, Nam June Paik, Emmett Williams, Arthur Koepcke, Wolf Vostell, Robert Filliou, George Maciunas.

SEPTEMBER 1, 1962 7:30 PM
FLUXUS INTERNATIONALE FESTSPIELE NEUESTER MUSIK
Hörsaal des Städtischen Museums, Wiesbaden
Announced program:
Konzert nr. 1, Klavier Kompositionen - U.S.A

Artist	Work	Performers**
John Cage	31' 57.9864"	
Philip Corner	Klavier Tangkeren	
Philip Corner	Flux	
Philip Corner	Form nr. 7	
Philip Corner	Form nr. 14	
Terry Riley	Konzert für 2 Pianisten un Tonband	
T. Jennings	Klavier Stücke	
Jed Curtis	Klavier Stücke	
Griffith Rose	2. Ennead	
Dick Higgins	Constellation nr. 1	
La Monte Young	566 für Henry Flynt	
La Monte Young	Klavier Stücke für David Tudor nr. 2	
George Brecht	Fünf Klavier Stücke 1961	
George Brecht	Drei Klavier Stücke 1962	

Performers:
K.E. Welin
F. Rzewski
plus the Fluxus group

SEPTEMBER 1, 1962 8:00 PM
FLUXUS INTERNATIONALE FESTSPIELE NEUESTER MUSIK
Hörsaal des Städtischen Museums, Wiesbaden
Announced program:
Konzert nr. 2, Klavier Kompositionen - Japan

Artist	Work	Performers**
Toshi Ichiyanagi	Musik für Klavier nr. 1 bis nr. 7	
Yoriaki Matsudaira	Instruktionen für Klavier	
Shinichi Matsushita	Mosaiken	
Yoko Ono	Ein Stücke um den Himmel zu Sehen	
Keijro Sato	Calligraphy	
Yuji Takahashi	Ekstasis	
Toru Takemitsu	Klavier Entfernung und Übergang	
Yasunao Tone	Klavier Ton-Mit Tonband	
George Yuasa	Projection Esemplastic I, II und III	

Performers:
K.E. Welin
plus the Fluxus group

SEPTEMBER 2, 1962 2:30 PM
FLUXUS INTERNATIONALE FESTSPIELE NEUESTER MUSIK
Hörsaal des Städtischen Museums, Wiesbaden
Announced program:
Konzert nr. 3, Klavier Kompositionen - Europa

Artist	Work	Performers**
K.H. Stockhausen	Klavierstück IV	
G. Ligeti	Trois Bagatelles	
G.M. Koenig	2 Klavier Stücke	
Konrad Boehmer	Klangstück	
Konrad Boehmer	Potensal	
Jan Morthenson	Couranta	
Lars J. Werle	Grüße für Pianist	
Michael von Biel	Ein Buch für Drei	
Dieter Schnebel	Reactions (für einen instrumentalisten & publikum)	
Dieter Schnebel	Visible Musik für 1 Dirigenten und 1 Instrumentalisten	

Performers:
K.E. Welin
plus the Fluxus group

The U.S. National Park Service
Unigrid System

21.
Ten basic publication
formats are derived from
the Unigrid structure.

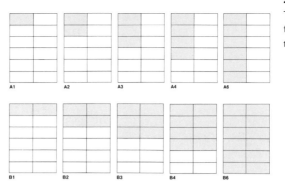

A1 A2 A3 A4 A6

B1 B2 B3 B4 B6

21.
Ten basic publication
formats are derived from
the Unigrid structure.

The United States National Park Service (NPS) developed the Unigrid System as a design system to unify the design of hundreds of site folders, while bringing harmony and economy to its publications program. Unigrid (Fig. **20**) is based on a sheet 965 by 1270 millimeters (about 16.5 by 23.5 inches), which folds into 12 panels that are 99 by 210 millimeters (about 4 by 8.25 inches). Ten basic formats (Fig. **21**) can be derived from the Unigrid ranging from one-panel leaflets to 12-panel fold-out broadsides. Each side of a folder is treated as a unified graphic surface that is completely unfolded by the user, just as one fully opens a map. The fold lines and the panels they create become background rather than a dominant structure, because the typical folder user quickly unfolds it to its full size; users rarely open a folder panel by panel. These standard formats permit great production economy because paper can be purchased in volume in two flat sizes or in web rolls. Most folders are printed in five of the available formats, further simplifying planning.

Grid modules for the folder formats measure 7 picas wide and 80 points high. Vertical spaces between modules are 1 pica wide; horizontal spaces between modules are 10 points high. Horizontal measurements are always made in picas, while vertical measurements are always made in 10-point units or modules. These spatial intervals provide a structure for organizing type, illustrations, photographs, and maps into an orderly whole.

Helvetica was selected as the type family for the Unigrid System because of "its crisp, clean details and typographic texture that make it esthetically pleasing and easy to read." It was also determined that Helvetica would strengthen and unify the NPS map series that accompanies the folder program. Other considerations are Helvetica's clearly defined hierarchy of sizes and weights with predictable results, large x-height with good line strength and consistent color, and outstanding printing characteristics. Text type is usually set in 8/10 or 9/10 Hevetica or Helvetica Medium in columns two or three modules wide (15 or 23 picas wide, measuring two or three modules plus spatial intervals

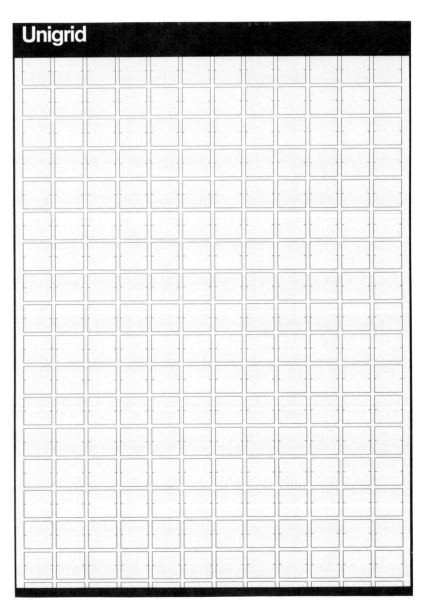

Unigrid

20.
The Unigrid was created by
Massimo Vignelli (consult-
ing designer), Vincent
Gleason (art director), and
Dennis McLaughlin (graphic
designer).

22 and 23.

Copy the Unigrid on the preceding page onto transparent material and place it over these folders to study the underlying structure of the designs.

24.

The black bars and consistent typography on folder covers become a visual identification.

between them). Text type is often justified, and columns are aligned top and bottom to create horizontal movement. Sometimes the last column will run short. One line space, rather than indentations, are used to separate paragraphs.

Captions are set one or two modules wide (7 or 15 picas wide) in 7/7, 7/8, or 8/9 Helvetica Regular or Medium, and may be either roman or italic. This variety of weight, posture, and leading provides flexibility to create a value and texture that complements and contrasts with other typographic and pictorial elements. Captions are set rag right, and this helps create a strong separation between text and captions, as do contrasts between text and caption textures, weights, and line lengths.

Major display type can be set in 12-, 18-, or 24-point Helvetica Medium and is often positioned 10 points above the related text on a horizontal band of white space, frequently 40 points high, running above the text. The variety of display sizes gives the designer the flexibility needed to create appropriate scale relationships between display type, the size of the folder, image sizes, and density of text type. The margin below the text type is always a spatial interval at least 20 points high.

The cover panels of all folders have a 100-point black band that bleeds at the top and on both sides. Titles reverse from this bar and are set in standard sizes of Helvetica Medium for park names with fewer than twelve letters. When site designation and location appear reversed from the black bar, these are set in 12/14 or 8/9 Helvetica Medium and align on the seventh grid module. Service designations are the same size and align on the tenth grid module. Cover panel type is always positioned 10 points down from the top edge of the band. This horizontal black band with its standardized title type becomes a consistent visual identification device for the National Park Service. Horizontal movement is accentuated through the placement of the type, the horizontal margins, and internal

24.

bars that divide the space into zones of information. These bars correspond to the title bar and may be complementary colors, contrasting colors, or black. These bars are 25 points wide, and one is always placed across the bottom of the folder. Display type is sometimes reversed from the bars.

The Unigrid System emphasizes clarity by clearly separating the elements. Type seldom overlaps images, and maps are not obscured by picture inserts or overlaps. Neutral grays and beiges, used to create backgrounds behind text areas or unify groups of images, are part of a standard palette of twenty-four colors, created from four-color process inks and a limited selection of secondary colors. This color palette creates continuity between various park publications.

Planning layouts are created using computer-generated typography, images, map windows, and the master grid sheets. A typesetter with a contract to set National Park Service typography uses electronic page makeup to format and position type, rules, and bars, providing repro-quality output for mechanicals.

Standardized formats and typographic specifications enable National Park Service designers to focus on content and design, rather than developing formats and specifications for each project. The Unigrid System is flexible, permitting unique solutions appropriate to specific messages, while leading to consistent graphic excellence and a unified visual identification.

Massimo Vignelli was the inventor and remains consulting designer for the Unigrid System. The program gained its vitality because the original design team remained intact over the first dozen years, and included Vincent Gleason (chief), Melissa Cronyn, Nicholas Kirilloff, Linda Meyers, Dennis McLaughlin, Phillip Musselwhite, and Mitchell Zetlin.

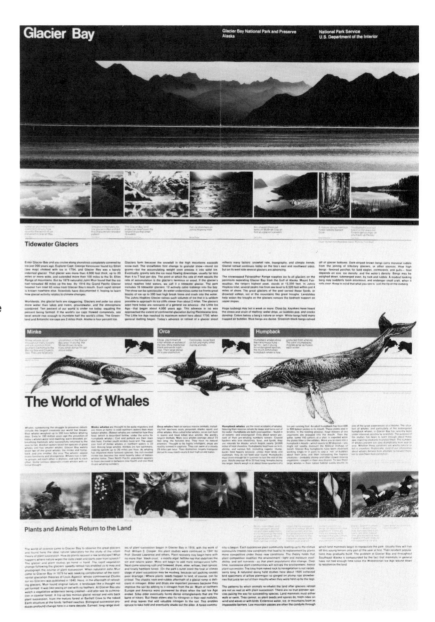

23.

143

The range of potential solutions to a typographic problem is seemingly infinite. Variations, permutations, and transformations can be developed, exploring changes in both fundamental aspects and subtle details. In this case study, designer Thomas Detrie has developed a sequence of solutions for a title-page design. Detrie's approach to the design process is based on his beliefs that "solutions come from within the problem" and "ideas come from working with the material and are not supplied or preconceived."

The problem-solving sequence is a three-stage design process: preliminary exploration, message investigation, and visualization of solutions. In his preliminary exploration, Detrie considered the nature and content of the problem and made sketches to explore possible directions. Typographic information (title, subtitle, authors, and publisher) was assigned priority. Detrie raised the question, "For the book *Basic Typography,* what is basic to typography that can be signified in a visual solution?" His answer established parameters appropriate to the given problem: a right-angled system, black on white, printed and unprinted areas, and a clear message. These considerations became the criteria for the investigation.

To investigate the range of typographic possibilities for the clear presentation of the manuscript, actual type was set and used in the initial visualizations for accuracy. A sans-serif face was chosen, and the message was printed in three sizes and two weights for use as raw material in these typographic studies. While maintaining the message priorities determined in the first stage, a variety of visual solutions were executed. Decisions were made through subtle comparisons of type sizes and weights to select those that provided the best visual balance and message conveyance. Detrie did not place the type upon a predetermined grid; rather, he allowed the organizational structure to evolve from the process of working with the type proofs. Selecting the basic typographic arrangement was an intermediate step in the design process (Fig. **25**).

Next, Detrie developed a series of variations of this arrangement by investigating the application of horizontal and vertical lines, positive and negative shapes with positive type, and positive and negative shapes with positive and reversed type. Figure **25** shows nine permutations with the application of vertical lines to the basic typographic schema. Permutations range from type alone to the addition of linear and rectilinear elements to a solid black page with reversed type (Fig. **26**). A graded arrangement of twenty-four of the many solutions is shown in Figure **27**. Observe the horizontal and vertical sequencing.

Unlimited solutions are possible in typographic design, and selection becomes an integral part of the design process. Not every possible solution is appropriate; the designer must continually evaluate each one against the problem criteria. The significance of Detrie's investigations lay in the workings of the design process.

This project commenced in the postgraduate program in graphic design at the Basel School of Design, Switzerland. The encouragement and criticism of Wolfgang Weingart are gratefully acknowledged.

25.

26.

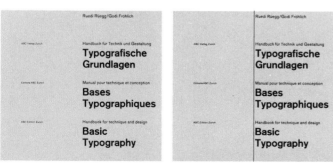

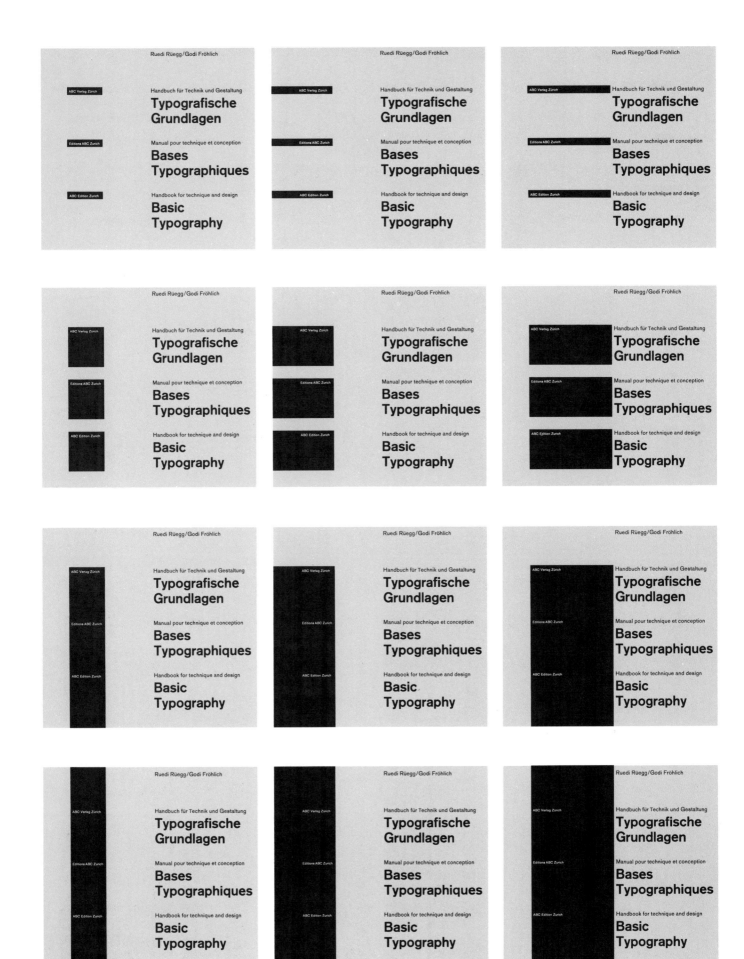

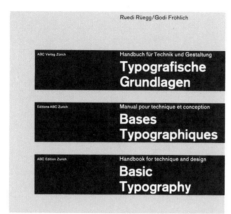

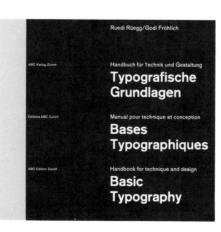
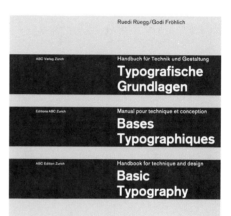

Referring to a movie advertisement that used letterforms "painted by light," typographic historian Beatrice Warde wrote that "after forty centuries of the necessarily static Alphabet, I saw what its members could do in the forth dimension of Time, 'flux,' movement. You may well say that I was electrified." Through advanced animation and computer-graphics techniques, graphic designers are transforming typographic communication into kinetic sequences that might almost be called "visual music."

Richard Greenberg, Director/Designer of R/Greenberg Associates in New York City, has emerged as a leading innovator on the frontier of cinematic graphic design for film titles, movie previews, special effects, and television commercials. Greenberg considers film titles to be a "visual metaphor" for the movie that follows, setting "the *tone* of the movie. You have to take the people who have just arrived at the theater and separate them from their ordinary reality—walking on the street, waiting in line; you bring them *into* the movie. You want to tell them how to react: that it's all right to laugh, that they are going to be scared, or that something serious is going on."

In the titles for the Warner Bros. film *Superman— the Movie,* bright blue names and the Superman emblem streak through space like comets, stop for

a moment, then evaporate into deep space (Fig. **28**). The speed and power of this film's fantasy superhero are evoked. This effect is accomplished by tracking rear-illuminated typography in front of an open camera lens. Each frame captures a streak of light that starts and stops slightly before the light streak recorded on the next frame. When shown at twenty-four frames per second, this series of still images is transformed into a dynamic expression of zooming energy.

A very different mood is expressed by Greenberg in his title designs for the PolyGram Pictures production, *Making Love* (Fig. **29**). Four red dots appear on the black screen and begin to move, forming abstract lines. As the sequence continues, the word *LOVE* emerges and fills the screen in elegant sans serif letterforms having slightly tapered terminals. Then widely letterspaced capitals spell out the first word of the title.

For the Warner Bros. movie, *Altered States,* the title sequence opens with a wide-angle image of a researcher in an isolation tank (Fig. **30**). Super-imposed over this image, the two words of the title—transparent, as if they are windows cut from a black background—overlap each other as they slowly move across the screen. The film credits are superimposed in white typography in front of this lively pattern of typographic forms and counter-

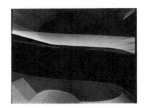

28.

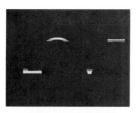 

29.

30.

forms. Behind the title the background slowly darkens while the camera pulls away from it, causing the letterforms to become smaller and smaller. Finally, the complete title, *Altered States,* appears in its entirety before the totally black screen. In the title, set in Avant Garde Demi, the right stroke of each capital *A* is deleted. The repetition of this unusual configuration unifies the two words and serves to make the title a unique and memorable signification.

An ominous and mysterious mood is created in the title sequence for the Twentieth Century-Fox production *Alien* (Fig. **31**). As the camera tracks across a barren landscape, the title emerges before the void of deep space. One by one, small white rectangles appear and undergo a metamorphosis, forming a five-letter title letterspaced across the screen. In a dynamic change of scale and orientation for the audience, the landscape transforms into the egg of an alien. The sequence closes as an internal blast of light rips through the shell of the egg. The dramatic intensity of this final scene is strengthened by its contrast with the quietude of the initial sequence.

In contrast to the otherworldly aura created by the *Alien* film titles, Greenberg's film trailer and television promotion for the Universal Studios production *Jaws 3-D* combines straightforward ocean

footage and typographic animation with documentary conviction (Fig. **32**). The trailer begins with a black screen. The first stroke of the Roman numeral III fades in, revealing a calm sky and placid ocean as the voiceover speaks of the terror of the original *Jaws* motion picture. Next, another stroke fades in as the voiceover recalls the excitement of *Jaws II.* Then the center stroke fades in, revealing a distant figure moving through the ocean toward the viewer. As the viewer becomes aware that the figure is a shark's fin, the middle stroke of the roman numeral bursts outward, filling the frame with the menacing form. As the shark's fin turns, it becomes the curve of the letter *J* in the *Jaws 3-D* logo. The perspective configuration of the logo becomes a powerful signification of dimensionality, an appropriate expression of the intense spatial illusionism of the 3-D cinematography used in this film.

The time-space orientation of kinetic media enables the typographic designer to add motion, scale change, sequence, and metamorphosis to alphabet communication. As demonstrated by the work of Richard Greenberg, this opens new vistas of expressive communication.

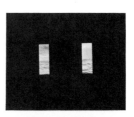

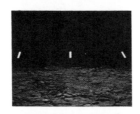

32.

31.

Book design for
Listen Up: The Lives of Quincy Jones

33.
Type was expanded and condensed by computer to form a column, but the designers were very careful to minimize awkward optical distortions.

34.
Quincy Jones's friends call him "Q"; this inspired the large red *Q* on the cover, which is repeated on the title page.

The release of a major motion picture about musician and composer Quincy Jones was accompanied by an oversized book. Design director Kent Hunter and designers Thomas Bricker, Riki Sethiadi, and Johan Vipper of the Frankfurt Gips Balkind design office responded to the structure and content of the movie, which had a syncopated rhythm of rapid cuts, musical performances, and interviews. This inspired a lively design approach using typography for expression and interpretation. The background material for this 192-page montage included hundreds of photographs, long and short quotations gleaned from the film soundtrack and 800 pages of transcripts, and a lengthy essay by jazz journalist George Nelson.

Jazz albums from the 1950s and 1960s influenced the use of the sans serif Franklin Gothic type family, especially its condensed versions, for display type. This was combined with Sabon old style for the running text. A lively dissonance resulted from the contrast between Franklin Gothic's bold verticality and Sabon's lighter, more organic forms. On the book jacket (Fig. **33**), a vertical column of type was printed in red over a photograph of Jones. This typographic configuration was also used on the sound-track packaging and movie publicity to unify graphics for the book, film, and recording.

Upon opening the book (Fig. **34**), the reader experiences dynamic typographic scale, including: informational copy on the brown-and-black jacket flap; the blue-and-black shapes of the words "Quincy Jones" printed on the inside of the jacket; and a large red *Q* that wraps around the front and back book cover.

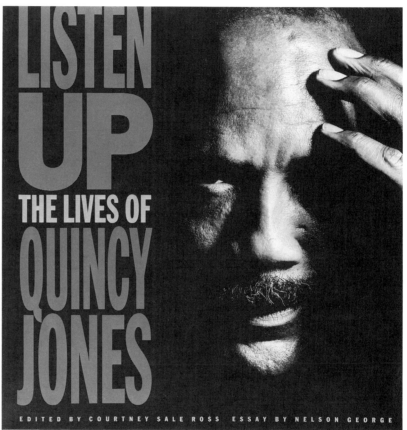

33.

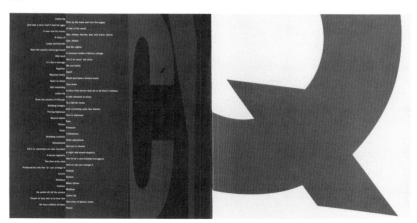

34.

35.

Large outline letters were freely arranged on the computer screen to create an electronic collage using a drawing program. The areas were then filled with colors.

36.

The light texture of widely leaded gray Sabon is punctuated by red Franklin Gothic Condensed; two bleed photographs give the layout a lateral expansiveness.

37.

A dozen full-page bleed photographs of musicians each have a large color initial letter, the musician's name, and a narrow column of Franklin Gothic Condensed text superimposed over the image.

35.

The book is divided into seven chapters representing periods of Quincy Jones's life and work, entitled Early years, Player, Film scorer, and so on. Each section opens with a large typographic design (Fig. **35**) of overlapping letters in black, gray and a bright color, such as red in the first title page shown here, opposite a full-page photograph. Quiet pages (Fig. **36**) are introduced periodically as calm areas after more complex, energetic pages to bring variety to the visual flow; that is, sequential movement, repetition, and rhythm from spread to spread. Unity within tremendous diversity is achieved through the repetition of several themes throughout the book. These include a series of full-page bleed photographs of musicians accompanied by Quincy Jones's remembrances (Fig. **37**), and pages combining one or more small photographs with quotations from the movie as well as other sources (Fig. **38**).

The essay takes about one fourth of the book's pages. This running text was placed on gray rectangles (Fig. **39**). These rectangles containing text type help the reader find the essay after it skips several pages. The essay becomes a thread running throughout the book, contributing to the visual flow. The content suggested typographic themes to the designers. A double-page spread (Fig. **40**) uses type to express the cadence and dissonance of rap music.

The back cover (Fig. **41**) is a typographic montage of words expressing music and life. This typographic montage reappeared in animated form for the film titles, further tying the two works together. Typographic experimentation to express content and a thorough understanding of electronic page design enabled the design team to make *Listen Up: The Lives of Quincy Jones* an outstanding example of innovative typography.

If Ray had followed the strict commercial line, he may have had more hits, but he would have had less meaning. People buy an armful of Ray Charles cassettes or discs, and what they're buying is an armful of **integrity.** –Jesse Jackson

"Every music has its soul. And if you really are sincere and surrender to it and explore it, it's all soulful." –Ray Charles

When he became the vice president in charge of **A***rtists &* **R***epertoire of Mercury Records, the first black person to reach that level, I absolutely was so proud, it was just unbelievable. And then he says, "I'm going out to Hollywood!!"–Lloyd Jones*

I just dropped everything and just took that chance. I said, "Maybe I won't make it out there, but **I'm going!"** –Quincy

36.

37.

38.

Quotations from the movie expressing contradictory opinions about Jones's trumpet-playing skills are asymmetrically composed around a centrally placed photograph. Scale, weight, and color are used to emphasize key words in the comments.

39.

Negative leading was specified on the computer, squeezing interline space from between the lines to create a rhythmical cadence.

40.

Typography becomes a visual metaphor for the auditory intensity of rap music. The text type's alignment and structure are influenced by the large letters and words.

38.

"Quincy was a **tremendous** jazz trumpet player." – Lionel Hampton

"He **wasn't that good** a trumpet player." – Bobby Tucker

"Turned out to be a **marvelous** trumpet player." – Clark Terry

"He was a **horrible** trumpet player." – Billy Eckstine

39.

YOU GOTTA WRITE YOUR OWN TICKET IN THIS LIFE BECAUSE IF YOU DON'T THEN SOME-BODY IS DEFINITE-LY GONNA WRITE A TICKET FOR YOU, AND YOU AIN'T GONNA RIDE FIRST CLASS. YOU'LL JUST FALL VICTIM TO WHATEVER THE STREET DICTATES TO YOU INSTEAD OF TRYING TO DIC-TATE SOMETHING TO THE STREET. – MELLE MEL

Weather Report founder Josef Zawinul, the rap rhymes intercut with brief solos by each of the legends named. The voice of Pee Wee Marquette, Birdland's immortal doorman, is heard as well. All this rapping leads to "Birdland" itself. Zawinul, who comes from the same jazz world as Quincy, wrote the song a decade ago, and it has since become a standard in the post-acoustic jazz repertoire. Quincy gives it new life by having Gillespie, Moody, George Benson, Vaughan, and Fitzgerald all take solos. The conjunction of these elements creates a fantastic, pungent effect, a time warp of tunes and tones. For fans of rap and aficionados of jazz, such a collaboration is totally unexpected. But throughout Quincy's life, he's never stopped with what is. He's always tried to find out what might be. Labels don't matter. For Quincy, good music is good music, and that's all he's ever made.

FAST FORWARD

It's winter in Southern California. Quincy Jones sits in front of a picture window overlooking the city of Los Angeles. The view is exhilarating. It's just finished raining, and for a few hours this smoggy metropolis has clean, clear air. You can see all the way downtown, but Quincy, curled up in a backless chair, his glasses perched on the tip of his nose, could not care less. Instead, he scans *Variety, Hollywood Reporter, Radio & Records,* and *Billboard.* Finally the phone rings. He scribbles down some numbers, his eyes narrow — and then he smiles.

The latest chart position of his latest release is coming in through *Billboard's* computer network. He studies the stats with the anxious eye of a rookie producer, then he begins working the phones. When he talks to friends and colleagues in the industry, Quincy isn't cocky or overconfident. He speculates on how competing projects may affect the record's sales. He gives and receives suggestions on the next single to release. He gossips, analyzes, schemes, and ▶ PG 170

40.

41.
Layering, overlapping, and extreme scale changes were qualities generated using the capabilities of electronic page design.

41.

The typographic specimens in this chapter were selected from outstanding type families to provide examples of major classifications: Old Style, Transitional, Modern, Egyptian, and Sans Serif. Old Style is represented by ITC Garamond, a recent redesign with a large x-height and a weight range popular in recent decades. By contrast, the specimens of Baskerville, the Transitional face displayed here, have the letter proportions of traditional typography. The strong geometric stress and thick-and-thin strokes of the Modern category are demonstrated by Bodoni. Egyptian is represented by specimens of a recent type family, ITC Lubalin Graph, which has slab serifs and the geometric construction found in much twentieth-century design. The Univers family, known for the design cohesion among its members, represents the Sans Serif category.

More extensive specimens of ITC Garamond and Univers than of the other families are shown. They are typical of the two most widely used categories. Enlarged fonts are included for study and tracing purposes. Text specimens are shown with 1-, 2-, and 3-point interline spacing. Eight full columns of text type are included for comparison and for layout purposes. Additional display fonts are shown in approximately 30-point type. These materials have been carefully selected to provide a compendium of the essential qualities of typographic form.

ORONTII FINEI

DELPHINATIS, REGII MATHEMA=
TICARVM PROFESSORIS, DE
ARITHMETICA PRACTICA
LIBRI QVATVOR.

LIBER PRIMVS, DE INTEGRIS: HOC EST,
eiusdem speciei, siue denominationis tractat numeris.

❦De fructu, atǫ dignitate ipsius Arithmeticæ: Proœmium.

NTER LIBERALES MA=
thematicas, quæ solæ disciplinæ vocâtur,
Arithmeticam primum locum sibi vendi=
casse: nemo sanæ mentis ignorat. Est enim
Arithmetica omnium aliarum disciplina=
rum mater, & nutrix antiquissima: nume=
rorū qualitates, vim, & naturam, ac id ge=
nus alia demonstrans, quæ absolutum vi=
dentur respicere numerum . Cuius prin=
cipia tanta excellunt simplicitate , vt nul=
lius àrtis videatur indigere suffragio: sed cunctis opituletur artibus. Ad
cuius puritatem illud etiam plurimum facit: quoniam nulla diuinitati
adeò cónexa est disciplina, quantùm Arithmetica. Nam vnitas omniū
numerorū radix & origo, in se, à se, ac circum seipsam vnica vel impar=
tibilis permanet: ex cuius tamen coaceruatione, omnis cósurgit & ge=
neratur, omnísque tandem in eam resoluitur numerus. Quemadmo=
dum cuncta quæ seu discreta, siue composita inspectentur Vniuerso, à
summo rerum conditore in definitum digesta, redactáve sunt, & demū
resoluenda numerum. ❦Quot autem vtilitates cognita, quótve laby=
rinthos ignota præbeat Arithmetica: conspicere facile est. Numerorū
etenim ratione sublata, tollitur & musicarum modulationū intelligen=
tia: geometricorum, cælestiúmve arcanorum subtilis aufertur ingres=
sio: tollitur & vniuersa Philosophia , siue quæ diuina, seu quæ contem=
platur humana: imperfecta relinquitur legū administratio, vtpote, quæ

Dignitas
arithmeticę.

Fructus
arithmeticę.

A.iij.

Old Style

ITC Garamond

Page three, *Arithmetica* by
Oronce Fine, printed by
Simon de Colines in Paris,
1535.

Although Old Style typefaces trace their development to the printers of the Italian Renaissance, their heritage extends to an earlier time, for Roman inscriptional letterforms inspired their capital-letter design. The Caroline Minuscules from medieval manuscripts inspired writing styles during the fifteenth century, and these became the model for Old Style lowercase letters.

Many Old Style typefaces bear the name of Claude Garamond, a leading typeface designer and punch-cutter working in Paris when the book *Arithmetica* was printed (Fig. **1**). In the heading material, the designer has used bold capitals for the author's name, two sizes of capitals for the title, and italics

for a subhead. The spatial intervals between these units have been established with great care. Fleurons (printer's flowers), paragraph marks, a woodcut headpiece, and a large initial bring vibrancy to this elegant example of French Renaissance book design.

ITC Garamond, presented here, was designed by Tony Stan for the International Typeface Corporation. The first four fonts in the family were issued in 1975. ITC Garamond has a large x-height and shortened ascenders and descenders. The complete type family has sixteen fonts, light, book, bold, and ultra, each with an italic, and a companion series of eight condensed versions.

abcdefgh
ijklmnop
qrstuvw
xyz$1234
567890;:!?

ABCDEF
GHIJKL
MNOPQ
RSTUV
WXYZ&

abcdefghijklmn
opqrstuvwxyz
ABCDEFGHIJK
LMNOPQRSTU
VWXYZ$12344
567890(.,""''-;:!)?&

72 Point

abcdefghijklmn
opqrstuvwxyz
ABCDEFGHIJK
LMNOPQRSTU
VWXYZ$12344
567890(,'"",;.:!)?&

abcdefghijklmnopq
rstuvwxyzABCD
EFGHIJKLMNOPQ
RSTUVWXYZ$123
44567890(.,""";:!)?&

abcdefghijklmnopqrstu
vwxyzABCDEFGHIJK
LMNOPQRSTUVWXYZ
$12344567890(.,""";:!)?&

abcdefghijklmnopq
rstuvwxyzABCDE
FGHIJKLMNOPQR
STUVWXYZ$1234
567890(,'""-;:!)?&&

abcdefghijklmnopqrstu
vwxyzABCDEFGHIJK
LMNOPQRSTUVWXYZ
$12344567890(,'""-;:!)?&&

36 Point

abcdefghijklmnopqrstuvwxyz
ABCDEFGHIJKLMNOPQRSTUV
WXYZ$12344567890 (.,""-;:!)?&

30 Point

abcdefghijklmnopqrstuvwxyz
ABCDEFGHIJKLMNOPQRSTUVW
XYZ$12344567890 (.,""-;:!)?&

24 Point

abcdefghijklmnopqrstuvwxyz
ABCDEFGHIJKLMNOPQRSTUVWXYZ
$12344567890 (.,""-;:!)?&

18 Point

abcdefghijklmnopqrstuvwxyz
ABCDEFGHIJKLMNOPQRSTUVWXYZ
$12344567890 (.,""-;:!)?&

abcdefghijklmnopqrstuvwxyz
ABCDEFGHIJKLMNOPQRSTU
VWXYZ$1234567890(.,'""-;:!)?&

abcdefghijklmnopqrstuvwxyz
ABCDEFGHIJKLMNOPQRSTUVW
XYZ$12344567890(.,'""-;:!)?&

abcdefghijklmnopqrstuvwxyz
ABCDEFGHIJKLMNOPQRSTUVWXYZ
$12344567890(.,'""-;:!)?&

abcdefghijklmnopqrstuvwxyz
ABCDEFGHIJKLMNOPQRSTUVWXYZ
$12344567890(.,'""-;:!)?&

72 Point

abcdefghijklmno
pqrstuvwxyz
ABCDEFGHIJKL
MNOPQRSTUV
WXYZ$123456
7890(,'""-;:!)?&

72 Point

abcdefghijklm
nopqrstuvwx
yzABCDEFGH
IJKLMNOPQ
RSTUVWXYZ
$1234567890

48 Point

abcdefghijklmnopqrstuv
wxyzABCDEFGHIJKL
MNOPQRSTUVWXYZ
$12344567890(.,""''-;:!)?&

30 Point

abcdefghijklmnopqrstuvwxyz
ABCDEFGHIJKLMNOPQRSTUVWXYZ
$12344567890(.,""''-;:!)?&

18 Point

abcdefghijklmnopqrstuvwxyz
ABCDEFGHIJKLMNOPQRSTUVWXYZ
$12344567890(.,""''-;:!)?&

---

48 Point

abcdefghijklmnopqrs
tuvwxyzABCDEFGH
IJKLMNOPQRSTUVW
XYZ$12344567890

---

30 Point

abcdefghijklmnopqrstuvwxyz
ABCDEFGHIJKLMNOPQRSTUVW
XYZ$12344567890(.,""''-;:!)?&

---

18 Point

abcdefghijklmnopqrstuvwxyz
ABCDEFGHIJKLMNOPQRSTUVWXYZ
$12344567890(.,""''-;:!)?&

72 Point

abcdefghijkl
mnopqrstuv
wxyzABCDEF
GHIJKLMNO
PQRSTUVW
XYZ$123456

abcdefghijklmnop
qrstuvwxyzABCDEF
GHIJKLMNOPQRST
UVWXYZ$123456
7890(.,""''-;:!)?&

abcdefghijklmnopqrstuvwxyz
ABCDEFGHIJKLMNOPQRSTUV
WXYZ$12344567890(.,""''-;:!)?&

abcdefghijklmnopqrstuvwxyzABCDEFGHIJKL
MNOPQRSTUVWXYZ$12344567890(.,""''-;:!)?&

72 Point

abcdefghijklmnopqr
stuvwxyzABCDEFGH
IJKLMNOPQRSTUV
WXYZ$1234567890
(.,'""-;:!)?&

abcdefghijklmnopqrstuvw
xyzABCDEFGHIJKLMNOPQRS
TUVWXYZ$12344567890
(.,'""-;:!)?&

abcdefghijklmnopqrstuvwxyz

ABCDEFGHIJKLMNOPQRSTUVWXYZ

$12344567890 (.,'""-;:!)?&

abcdefghijklmnopqrstuvwxyz
ABCDEFGHIJKLMNOPQRSTUVWXYZ
$12344567890 (.,'""-;:!)?&

72 Point

abcdefghijklmnopq
rstuvwxyz ABCDE
FGHIJKLMNOPQRS
TUVWXYZ$12345
67890 (,""–;:!)?&

abcdefghijklmnopqrstuvw
xyz ABCDEFGHIJKLMNOPQ
RSTUVWXYZ $12345678
90 (.,""''-;:!)?&

abcdefghijklmnopqrstuvwxyz
ABCDEFGHIJKLMNOPQRSTUVWXYZ
$12344567890 (.,""''-;:!)?&

abcdefghijklmnopqrstuvwxyz
ABCDEFGHIJKLMNOPQRSTUVWXYZ
$12344567890 (.,""''-;:!)?&

72 Point

abcdefghijklmn
opqrstuvwxyz
ABCDEFGHIJKLM
NOPQRSTUVWX
YZ$12344567890
(.,'""",-;:!)?&

abcdefghijklmnopqrstu
vwxyz ABCDEFGHIJKLMN
OPQRSTUVWXYZ $12344
567890 (.,'""-;:!)?&

abcdefghijklmnopqrstuvwxyz
ABCDEFGHIJKLMNOPQRSTUVWXYZ
$12344567890 (.,'""-;:!)?&

abcdefghijklmnopqrstuvwxyz
ABCDEFGHIJKLMNOPQRSTUVWXYZ
$12344567890 (.,'""-;:!)?&

72 Point

abcdefghijklmnop
qrstuvwxyzABCD
EFGHIJKLMNOPQ
RSTUVWXYZ$1234
567890

abcdefghijklmnopqrstuv
wxyzABCDEFGHIJKLMNOP
QRSTUVWXYZ$12345678
90(.,'""''-;:!)?&

abcdefghijklmnopqrstuvwxyz
ABCDEFGHIJKLMNOPQRSTUVWXYZ
$12344567890(.,'""''-;:!)?&

abcdefghijklmnopqrstuvwxyz
ABCDEFGHIJKLMNOPQRSTUVWXYZ
$12344567890(.,'""''-;:!)?&

abcdefghijklmnopqrstuvwxyz
ABCDEFGHIJKLMNOPQRSTUVWXYZ
$1234567890(.,'"-;:!)?&

abcdefghijklmnopqrstuvwxyz
ABCDEFGHIJKLMNOPQRSTUVWXYZ
$1234567890(.,'"-;:!)?&

abcdefghijklmnopqrstuvwxyz
ABCDEFGHIJKLMNOPQRSTUVWXYZ
$1234567890(.,'"-;:!)?&

abcdefghijklmnopqrstuvwxyz
ABCDEFGHIJKLMNOPQRSTUVWXYZ
$1234567890(.,'"-;:!)?&

ITC Garamond Light

The whole duty of Typography, as of Calligraphy, is to communicate to the imagination, without loss by the way, the thought or image intended to be communicated by the Author. And the whole duty of beautiful typography is not to substitute for the beauty or interest of the thing thought and intended to be conveyed by the symbol, a beauty or interest of its own, but, on the one hand, to win access for that communication by the clearness and beauty of the vehicle, and on the other hand, to take advantage of every pause or stage in that communication to interpose some characteristic & restful beauty in its own art. We thus have a reason for the clearness and beauty of the text as a whole, for the especial beauty of the first or introductory page and of the title, and for the especial beauty of the headings of chapters, capital or initial letters, and so on, and an opening for the illustrator as we shall see by and by. Further, in the case of Poetry, verse, in my opinion, appeals by its form to the eye, as well as to
the ear, and should be placed on the page so that its structure
8/9

The whole duty of Typography, as of Calligraphy, is to communicate to the imagination, without loss by the way, the thought or image intended to be communicated by the Author. And the whole duty of beautiful typography is not to substitute for the beauty or interest of the thing thought and intended to be conveyed by the symbol, a beauty or interest of its own, but, on the one hand, to win access for that communication by the clearness and beauty of the vehicle, and on the other hand, to take advantage of every pause or stage in that communication to interpose some characteristic & restful beauty in its own art. We thus have a reason for the clearness and beauty of the text as a whole, for the especial beauty of the first or introductory page and of the title, and for the especial beauty of the headings of chapters, capital or initial letters, and so on, and an opening for the illustrator as we shall see by and by. Further, in the case of Poetry,
verse, in my opinion, appeals by its form to the eye, as well as to
8/10

The whole duty of Typography, as of Calligraphy, is to communicate to the imagination, without loss by the way, the thought or image intended to be communicated by the Author. And the whole duty of beautiful typography is not to substitute for the beauty or interest of the thing thought and intended to be conveyed by the symbol, a beauty or interest of its own, but, on the one hand, to win access for that communication by the clearness and beauty of the vehicle, and on the other hand, to take advantage of every pause or stage in that communication to interpose some characteristic & restful beauty in its own art. We thus have a reason for the clearness and beauty of the text as a whole, for the especial beauty of the first or introductory page and of the title, and for the especial beauty of the headings of chapters,
capital or initial letters, and so on, and an opening for the illus-
8/11

The whole duty of Typography, as of Calligraphy, is to communicate to the imagination, without loss by the way, the thought or image intended to be communicated by the Author. And the whole duty of beautiful typography is not to substitute for the beauty or interest of the thing thought and intended to be conveyed by the symbol, a beauty or interest of its own, but, on the one hand, to win access for that communication by the clearness and beauty of the vehicle, and on the other hand, to take advantage of every pause or stage in that communication to interpose some characteristic & restful beauty in its own art. We thus have a reason for the clearness and beauty of the text as a whole, for the especial beauty of the first or introductory page and of the title, and for the especial beauty of the headings of chapters, capital or
initial letters, and so on, and an opening for the illustrator
9/10

The whole duty of Typography, as of Calligraphy, is to communicate to the imagination, without loss by the way, the thought or image intended to be communicated by the Author. And the whole duty of beautiful typography is not to substitute for the beauty or interest of the thing thought and intended to be conveyed by the symbol, a beauty or interest of its own, but, on the one hand, to win access for that communication by the clearness and beauty of the vehicle, and on the other hand, to take advantage of every pause or stage in that communication to interpose some characteristic & restful beauty in its own art. We thus have a reason for the clearness and beauty of the text as a whole, for the especial beauty of
the first or introductory page and of the title, and for the
9/11

The whole duty of Typography, as of Calligraphy, is to communicate to the imagination, without loss by the way, the thought or image intended to be communicated by the Author. And the whole duty of beautiful typography is not to substitute for the beauty or interest of the thing thought and intended to be conveyed by the symbol, a beauty or interest of its own, but, on the one hand, to win access for that communication by the clearness and beauty of the vehicle, and on the other hand, to take advantage of every pause or stage in that communication to interpose some characteristic & restful beauty in its own art. We thus have a reason for the clearness and
beauty of the text as a whole, for the especial beauty of
9/12

abcdefghijklmnopqrstuvwxyz
ABCDEFGHIJKLMNOPQRSTUVWXYZ
$1234567890(.,'"-;:!)?&

abcdefghijklmnopqrstuvwxyz
ABCDEFGHIJKLMNOPQRSTUVWXYZ
$1234567890(.,'"-;:!)?&

abcdefghijklmnopqrstuvwxyz
ABCDEFGHIJKLMNOPQRSTUVWXYZ
$1234567890(.,'"-;:!)?&

abcdefghijklmnopqrstuvwxyz
ABCDEFGHIJKLMNOPQRSTUVWXYZ
$1234567890(.,'"-;:!)?&

The whole duty of Typography, as of Calligraphy, is to communicate to the imagination, without loss by the way, the thought or image intended to be communicated by the Author. And the whole duty of beautiful typography is not to substitute for the beauty or interest of the thing thought and intended to be conveyed by the symbol, a beauty or interest of its own, but, on the one hand, to win access for that communication by the clearness and beauty of the vehicle, and on the other hand, to take advantage of every pause or stage in that communication to interpose some characteristic & restful beauty in its own art. We thus have a reason for the clearness *and beauty of the text as a whole, for the especial*
10/11

The whole duty of Typography, as of Calligraphy, is to communicate to the imagination, without loss by the way, the thought or image intended to be communicated by the Author. And the whole duty of beautiful typography is not to substitute for the beauty or interest of the thing thought and intended to be conveyed by the symbol, a beauty or interest of its own, but, on the one hand, to win access for that communication by the clearness and beauty of the vehicle, and on the other hand, to take advantage of every pause or stage in that communication to interpose some characteristic & restful beauty in *its own art. We thus have a reason for the clearness*
10/12

The whole duty of Typography, as of Calligraphy, is to communicate to the imagination, without loss by the way, the thought or image intended to be communicated by the Author. And the whole duty of beautiful typography is not to substitute for the beauty or interest of the thing thought and intended to be conveyed by the symbol, a beauty or interest of its own, but, on the one hand, to win access for that communication by the clearness and beauty of the vehicle, and on the other hand, to take advantage of every pause or stage in that communication *to interpose some characteristic & restful beauty in*
10/13

The whole duty of Typography, as of Calligraphy, is to communicate to the imagination, without loss by the way, the thought or image intended to be communicated by the Author. And the whole duty of beautiful typography is not to substitute for the beauty or interest of the thing thought and intended to be conveyed by the symbol, a beauty or interest of its own, but, on the one hand, to win access for that communication by the clearness and beauty of the *vehicle, and on the other hand, to take ad-*
12/13

The whole duty of Typography, as of Calligraphy, is to communicate to the imagination, without loss by the way, the thought or image intended to be communicated by the Author. And the whole duty of beautiful typography is not to substitute for the beauty or interest of the thing thought and intended to be conveyed by the symbol, a beauty or interest of its own, but, on the one hand, to win access for that communi-*cation by the clearness and beauty of the*
12/14

The whole duty of Typography, as of Calligraphy, is to communicate to the imagination, without loss by the way, the thought or image intended to be communicated by the Author. And the whole duty of beautiful typography is not to substitute for the beauty or interest of the thing thought and intended to be conveyed by the symbol, a beauty or interest of its own, but, on the *one hand, to win access for that communi-*
12/15

abcdefghijklmnopqrstuvwxyz
ABCDEFGHIJKLMNOPQRSTUVWXYZ
$1234567890(.,'"-;:!)?&

abcdefghijklmnopqrstuvwxyz
ABCDEFGHIJKLMNOPQRSTUVWXYZ
$1234567890(.,'"-;:!)?&

abcdefghijklmnopqrstuvwxyz
ABCDEFGHIJKLMNOPQRSTUVWXYZ
$1234567890(.,'"-;:!)?&

abcdefghijklmnopqrstuvwxyz
ABCDEFGHIJKLMNOPQRSTUVWXYZ
$1234567890(.,'"-;:!)?&

ITC Garamond Book

The whole duty of Typography, as of Calligraphy, is to communicate to the imagination, without loss by the way, the thought or image intended to be communicated by the Author. And the whole duty of beautiful typography is not to substitute for the beauty or interest of the thing thought and intended to be conveyed by the symbol, a beauty or interest of its own, but, on the one hand, to win access for that communication by the clearness and beauty of the vehicle, and on the other hand, to take advantage of every pause or stage in that communication to interpose some characteristic & restful beauty in its own art. We thus have a reason for the clearness and beauty of the text as a whole, for the especial beauty of the first or introductory page and of the title, and for the especial beauty of the headings of chapters, capital or initial letters, and so on, and an opening for the illustrator as we shall see by and by. Further, in the case of Poetry, verse, *in my opinion, appeals by its form to the eye, as well as to the*
8/9

The whole duty of Typography, as of Calligraphy, is to communicate to the imagination, without loss by the way, the thought or image intended to be communicated by the Author. And the whole duty of beautiful typography is not to substitute for the beauty or interest of the thing thought and intended to be conveyed by the symbol, a beauty or interest of its own, but, on the one hand, to win access for that communication by the clearness and beauty of the vehicle, and on the other hand, to take advantage of every pause or stage in that communication to interpose some characteristic & restful beauty in its own art. We thus have a reason for the clearness and beauty of the text as a whole, for the especial beauty of the first or introductory page and of the title, and for the especial beauty of the headings of chapters, capital or initial letters, and so on, and an opening for the illustrator *as we shall see by and by. Further, in the case of Poetry, verse,*
8/10

The whole duty of Typography, as of Calligraphy, is to communicate to the imagination, without loss by the way, the thought or image intended to be communicated by the Author. And the whole duty of beautiful typography is not to substitute for the beauty or interest of the thing thought and intended to be conveyed by the symbol, a beauty or interest of its own, but, on the one hand, to win access for that communication by the clearness and beauty of the vehicle, and on the other hand, to take advantage of every pause or stage in that communication to interpose some characteristic & restful beauty in its own art. We thus have a reason for the clearness and beauty of the text as a whole, for the especial beauty of the first or introductory page and of the title, and *for the especial beauty of the headings of chapters, capital*
8/11

The whole duty of Typography, as of Calligraphy, is to communicate to the imagination, without loss by the way, the thought or image intended to be communicated by the Author. And the whole duty of beautiful typography is not to substitute for the beauty or interest of the thing thought and intended to be conveyed by the symbol, a beauty or interest of its own, but, on the one hand, to win access for that communication by the clearness and beauty of the vehicle, and on the other hand, to take advantage of every pause or stage in that communication to interpose some characteristic & restful beauty in its own art. We thus have a reason for the clearness and beauty of the text as a whole, for the especial beauty of the first or introductory page and of the title, and for the especial beauty of the headings *of chapters, capital or initial letters, and so on, and*
9/10

The whole duty of Typography, as of Calligraphy, is to communicate to the imagination, without loss by the way, the thought or image intended to be communicated by the Author. And the whole duty of beautiful typography is not to substitute for the beauty or interest of the thing thought and intended to be conveyed by the symbol, a beauty or interest of its own, but, on the one hand, to win access for that communication by the clearness and beauty of the vehicle, and on the other hand, to take advantage of every pause or stage in that communication to interpose some characteristic & restful beauty in its own art. We thus have a reason for the clearness and beauty of the text as a whole, for the *especial beauty of the first or introductory page and*
9/11

The whole duty of Typography, as of Calligraphy, is to communicate to the imagination, without loss by the way, the thought or image intended to be communicated by the Author. And the whole duty of beautiful typography is not to substitute for the beauty or interest of the thing thought and intended to be conveyed by the symbol, a beauty or interest of its own, but, on the one hand, to win access for that communication by the clearness and beauty of the vehicle, and on the other hand, to take advantage of every pause or stage in that communication to interpose some characteristic & restful beauty in its own art. We thus have a reason for the *clearness and beauty of the text as a whole, for*
9/12

abcdefghijklmnopqrstuvwxyz
ABCDEFGHIJKLMNOPQRSTUVWXYZ
$1234567890(.,'"-;:!)?&

abcdefghijklmnopqrstuvwxyz
ABCDEFGHIJKLMNOPQRSTUVWXYZ
$1234567890(.,'"-;:!)?&

abcdefghijklmnopqrstuvwxyz
ABCDEFGHIJKLMNOPQRSTUVWXYZ
$1234567890(.,'"-;:!)?&

abcdefghijklmnopqrstuvwxyz
ABCDEFGHIJKLMNOPQRSTUVWXYZ
$1234567890(.,'"-;:!)?&

The whole duty of Typography, as of Calligraphy, is to communicate to the imagination, without loss by the way, the thought or image intended to be communicated by the Author. And the whole duty of beautiful typography is not to substitute for the beauty or interest of the thing thought and intended to be conveyed by the symbol, a beauty or interest of its own, but, on the one hand, to win access for that communication by the clearness and beauty of the vehicle, and on the other hand, to take advantage of every pause or stage in that communication to interpose some characteristic & restful beauty in its own art. We thus have *a reason for the clearness and beauty of the text*

10/11

The whole duty of Typography, as of Calligraphy, is to communicate to the imagination, without loss by the way, the thought or image intended to be communicated by the Author. And the whole duty of beautiful typography is not to substitute for the beauty or interest of the thing thought and intended to be conveyed by the symbol, a beauty or interest of its own, but, on the one hand, to win access for that communication by the clearness and beauty of the vehicle, and on the other hand, to take advantage of every pause or stage in that communication to interpose some character-*istic & restful beauty in its own art. We thus have*

10/12

The whole duty of Typography, as of Calligraphy, is to communicate to the imagination, without loss by the way, the thought or image intended to be communicated by the Author. And the whole duty of beautiful typography is not to substitute for the beauty or interest of the thing thought and intended to be conveyed by the symbol, a beauty or interest of its own, but, on the one hand, to win access for that communication by the clearness and beauty of the vehicle, and on the other hand, to take advantage of every pause or stage in *that communication to interpose some char-*

10/13

The whole duty of Typography, as of Calligraphy, is to communicate to the imagination, without loss by the way, the thought or image intended to be communicated by the Author. And the whole duty of beautiful typography is not to substitute for the beauty or interest of the thing thought and intended to be conveyed by the symbol, a beauty or interest of its own, but, on the one hand, to win access for that communication by the *clearness and beauty of the vehicle, and*

12/13

The whole duty of Typography, as of Calligraphy, is to communicate to the imagination, without loss by the way, the thought or image intended to be communicated by the Author. And the whole duty of beautiful typography is not to substitute for the beauty or interest of the thing thought and intended to be conveyed by the symbol, a beauty or interest of its own, but, on the one hand, to win *access for that communication by the*

12/14

The whole duty of Typography, as of Calligraphy, is to communicate to the imagination, without loss by the way, the thought or image intended to be communicated by the Author. And the whole duty of beautiful typography is not to substitute for the beauty or interest of the thing thought and intended to be conveyed by the symbol, a beauty or interest *of its own, but, on the one hand, to win*

12/15

abcdefghijklmnopqrstuvwxyz
ABCDEFGHIJKLMNOPQRSTUVWXYZ
$1234567890(.,'"-;:!)?&

abcdefghijklmnopqrstuvwxyz
ABCDEFGHIJKLMNOPQRSTUVWXYZ
$1234567890(.,'"-;:!)?&

abcdefghijklmnopqrstuvwxyz
ABCDEFGHIJKLMNOPQRSTUVWXYZ
$1234567890(.,'"-;:!)?&

abcdefghijklmnopqrstuvwxyz
ABCDEFGHIJKLMNOPQRSTUVWXYZ
$1234567890(.,'"-;:!)?&

ITC Garamond Bold

The whole duty of Typography, as of Calligraphy, is to communicate to the imagination, without loss by the way, the thought or image intended to be communicated by the Author. And the whole duty of beautiful typography is not to substitute for the beauty or interest of the thing thought and intended to be conveyed by the symbol, a beauty or interest of its own, but, on the one hand, to win access for that communication by the clearness and beauty of the vehicle, and on the other hand, to take advantage of every pause or stage in that communication to interpose some characteristic & restful beauty in its own art. We thus have a reason for the clearness and beauty of the text as a whole, for the especial beauty of the first or introductory page and of the title, and for the especial beauty of the headings of chapters, capital or initial *letters, and so on, and an opening for the illustrator*
8/9

The whole duty of Typography, as of Calligraphy, is to communicate to the imagination, without loss by the way, the thought or image intended to be communicated by the Author. And the whole duty of beautiful typography is not to substitute for the beauty or interest of the thing thought and intended to be conveyed by the symbol, a beauty or interest of its own, but, on the one hand, to win access for that communication by the clearness and beauty of the vehicle, and on the other hand, to take advantage of every pause or stage in that communication to interpose some characteristic & restful beauty in its own art. We thus have a reason for the clearness and beauty of the text as a whole, for the especial beauty of the first or introductory page and of the title, and for the especial *beauty of the headings of chapters, capital or initial*
8/10

The whole duty of Typography, as of Calligraphy, is to communicate to the imagination, without loss by the way, the thought or image intended to be communicated by the Author. And the whole duty of beautiful typography is not to substitute for the beauty or interest of the thing thought and intended to be conveyed by the symbol, a beauty or interest of its own, but, on the one hand, to win access for that communication by the clearness and beauty of the vehicle, and on the other hand, to take advantage of every pause or stage in that communication to interpose some characteristic & restful beauty in its own art. We thus have a reason for the clearness and beauty of the text as a *whole, for the especial beauty of the first or intro-*
8/11

The whole duty of Typography, as of Calligraphy, is to communicate to the imagination, without loss by the way, the thought or image intended to be communicated by the Author. And the whole duty of beautiful typography is not to substitute for the beauty or interest of the thing thought and intended to be conveyed by the symbol, a beauty or interest of its own, but, on the one hand, to win access for that communication by the clearness and beauty of the vehicle, and on the other hand, to take advantage of every pause or stage in that communication to interpose some characteristic & restful beauty in its own art. We thus have a reason for the clearness and beauty of the text as a whole, for *the especial beauty of the first or introductory*
9/10

The whole duty of Typography, as of Calligraphy, is to communicate to the imagination, without loss by the way, the thought or image intended to be communicated by the Author. And the whole duty of beautiful typography is not to substitute for the beauty or interest of the thing thought and intended to be conveyed by the symbol, a beauty or interest of its own, but, on the one hand, to win access for that communication by the clearness and beauty of the vehicle, and on the other hand, to take advantage of every pause or stage in that communication to interpose some characteristic & restful beauty *in its own art. We thus have a reason for the*
9/11

The whole duty of Typography, as of Calligraphy, is to communicate to the imagination, without loss by the way, the thought or image intended to be communicated by the Author. And the whole duty of beautiful typography is not to substitute for the beauty or interest of the thing thought and intended to be conveyed by the symbol, a beauty or interest of its own, but, on the one hand, to win access for that communication by the clearness and beauty of the vehicle, and on the other hand, to take advantage of every pause or stage in that communication to *interpose some characteristic & restful beauty*
9/12

abcdefghijklmnopqrstuvwxyz
ABCDEFGHIJKLMNOPQRSTUVWXYZ
$1234567890(.,'"-;:!)?&

abcdefghijklmnopqrstuvwxyz
ABCDEFGHIJKLMNOPQRSTUVWXYZ
$1234567890(.,'"-;:!)?&

abcdefghijklmnopqrstuvwxyz
ABCDEFGHIJKLMNOPQRSTUVWXYZ
$1234567890(.,'"-;:!)?&

abcdefghijklmnopqrstuvwxyz
ABCDEFGHIJKLMNOPQRSTUVWXYZ
$1234567890(.,'"-;:!)?&

The whole duty of Typography, as of Calligraphy, is to communicate to the imagination, without loss by the way, the thought or image intended to be communicated by the Author. And the whole duty of beautiful typography is not to substitute for the beauty or interest of the thing thought and intended to be conveyed by the symbol, a beauty or interest of its own, but, on the one hand, to win access for that communication by the clearness and beauty of the vehicle, and on the other hand, to take advantage of every pause or stage in that com*munication to interpose some characteris-*
10/11

The whole duty of Typography, as of Calligraphy, is to communicate to the imagination, without loss by the way, the thought or image intended to be communicated by the Author. And the whole duty of beautiful typography is not to substitute for the beauty or interest of the thing thought and intended to be conveyed by the symbol, a beauty or interest of its own, but, on the one hand, to win access for that communication by the clearness and beauty of the *vantage of every pause or stage in that com-*
10/12

The whole duty of Typography, as of Calligraphy, is to communicate to the imagination, without loss by the way, the thought or image intended to be communicated by the Author. And the whole duty of beautiful typography is not to substitute for the beauty or interest of the thing thought and intended to be conveyed by the symbol, a beauty or interest of its own, but, on the one hand, to win access for that communication by the clearness and beauty of the *vehicle, and on the other hand, to take ad-*
10/13

The whole duty of Typography, as of Calligraphy, is to communicate to the imagination, without loss by the way, the thought or image intended to be communicated by the Author. And the whole duty of beautiful typography is not to substitute for the beauty or interest of the thing thought and intended to be conveyed by the symbol, a beauty or interest of its own, but, on the one *hand, to win access for that com-*
12/13

The whole duty of Typography, as of Calligraphy, is to communicate to the imagination, without loss by the way, the thought or image intended to be communicated by the Author. And the whole duty of beautiful typography is not to substitute for the beauty or interest of the thing thought and intended to be conveyed by the symbol, a beauty or in*terest of its own, but, on the one*
12/14

The whole duty of Typography, as of Calligraphy, is to communicate to the imagination, without loss by the way, the thought or image intended to be communicated by the Author. And the whole duty of beautiful typography is not to substitute for the beauty or interest of the thing thought and intended to be con*veyed by the symbol, a beauty or in-*
12/15

Im VERLAG DES BILDUNGSVERBANDES der Deutschen Buchdrucker,
Berlin SW 61, Dreibundstr. 5, erscheint demnächst:

JAN TSCHICHOLD
Lehrer an der Meisterschule für Deutschlands Buchdrucker in München

DIE NEUE TYPOGRAPHIE

**Handbuch für die gesamte Fachwelt
und die drucksachenverbrauchenden Kreise**

Das Problem der neuen gestaltenden Typographie hat eine lebhafte
Diskussion bei allen Beteiligten hervorgerufen. Wir glauben dem Bedürf-
nis, die aufgeworfenen Fragen ausführlich behandelt zu sehen, zu ent-
sprechen, wenn wir jetzt ein Handbuch der **NEUEN TYPOGRAPHIE**
herausbringen.

Es kam dem Verfasser, einem ihrer bekanntesten Vertreter, in diesem
Buche zunächst darauf an, den engen Zusammenhang der neuen
Typographie mit dem **Gesamtkomplex heutigen Lebens** aufzuzei-
gen und zu beweisen, daß die neue Typographie ein ebenso notwendi-
ger Ausdruck einer neuen Gesinnung ist wie die neue Baukunst und
alles Neue, das mit unserer Zeit anbricht. Diese geschichtliche Notwen-
digkeit der neuen Typographie belegt weiterhin eine kritische Dar-
stellung der **alten Typographie**. Die Entwicklung der **neuen Male-
rei,** die für alles Neue unserer Zeit geistig bahnbrechend gewesen ist,
wird in einem reich illustrierten Aufsatz des Buches leicht faßlich dar-
gestellt. Ein kurzer Abschnitt „**Zur Geschichte der neuen Typographie**" leitet zu dem wichtigsten Teile des Buches, den **Grundbegriffen
der neuen Typographie** über. Diese werden klar herausgeschält,
richtige und falsche Beispiele einander gegenübergestellt. Zwei wei-
tere Artikel behandeln „**Photographie und Typographie**" und
„**Neue Typographie und Normung**".

Der Hauptwert des Buches für den Praktiker besteht in dem zweiten
Teil „**Typographische Hauptformen**" (siehe das nebenstehende
Inhaltsverzeichnis). Es fehlte bisher an einem Werke, das wie dieses Buch
die schon bei einfachen Satzaufgaben auftauchenden gestalterischen
Fragen in gebührender Ausführlichkeit behandelte. Jeder Teilabschnitt
enthält neben **allgemeinen typographischen Regeln** vor allem die
Abbildungen aller in Betracht kommenden **Normblätter** des Deutschen
Normenausschusses, alle andern (z. B. postalischen) **Vorschriften** und
zahlreiche Beispiele, Gegenbeispiele und Schemen.

Für jeden Buchdrucker, insbesondere jeden Akzidenzsetzer, wird „Die
neue Typographie" ein **unentbehrliches Handbuch** sein. Von nicht
geringerer Bedeutung ist es für Reklamefachleute, Gebrauchsgraphiker,
Kaufleute, Photographen, Architekten, Ingenieure und Schriftsteller,
also für alle, die mit dem Buchdruck in Berührung kommen.

typ. tschichold

Das Buch enthält über 125 Abbildungen, von
denen etwa ein Viertel **zweifarbig** gedruckt ist,
und umfaßt gegen **200** Seiten auf gutem Kunst-
druckpapier. Es erscheint im Format DIN A5 (148×
210 mm) und ist biegsam in Ganzleinen gebunden.

Preis bei Vorbestellung bis 1. Juni 1928: **5.00** RM
durch den Buchhandel nur zum Preise von **6.50** RM

Bestellschein umstehend ➡

Sans Serif

Univers

2.

Prospectus designed by Jan Tschichold for his book, *Die Neue Typographie,* 1928.

Sans Serif typefaces have elemental letterforms stripped of serifs and decorations. Although sans serifs first appeared early in the nineteenth century, their use accelerated during the l920s. "Form follows function" became the design dictum, and the functional simplicity of sans serif typefaces led many designers to look upon them as the ideal typographic expression of a scientific and technological century.

In Jan Tschichold's influential book *Die Neue Typographie,* he advocated a new functional style for a rational era. In the prospectus for the book, he used sans serif type as an expression of the age (Fig. **2**). The page also demonstrates asymmetrical balancing of elements on a grid system, visual

contrasts of type size and weight, and the importance of spatial intervals and white space as design elements.

During the l950s, Univers and Helvetica were both designed as more contemporary versions of Akzidenz Grotesque, a German turn-of-the-century sans serif. Compare the text setting and the display specimens of Helvetica with their Univers counterparts. There are subtle differences in the drawing of many letterforms. The Univers family (shown here) is renowned for its remarkable graphic unity, which enables the typographic designer to use all twenty-one fonts together as a flexible, integrated typographic system.

abcdefghi
jklmnopq
rstuvwx
yz $1234
567890!?

ABCDEF
GHIJKLM
NOPQRS
TUVWX
YZ&(.,""::)

abcdefghijklmnop
qrstuvwxyz AB
CDEFGHIJKLMN
OPQRSTUVW
XYZ$12345678
90(.,""""-;:!)?&

(.,"'""\"'"-;:!])?&

abcdefghijklmn
opqrstuvwxyz
ABCDEFGHIJKL
MNOPQRSTU
VWXYZ$1234
567890

abcdefghijklmnopqr
stuvwxyzABCDEF
GHIJKLMNOPQRST
UVWXYZ$123456
7890(.,""''-;:!)?&

abcdefghijklmnopqrstuv
wxyzABCDEFGHIJKLMN
OPQRSTUVWXYZ$123
4567890(.,""''-;:!)?&

abcdefghijklmnopq
rstuvwxyzABCD
EFGHIJKLMNOPQ
RSTUVWXYZ$123
4567890(.,""""-;:!)?&

abcdefghijklmnopqrstuv
wxyzABCDEFGHIJKL
MNOPQRSTUVWXYZ
$1234567890(.,""""-;:!)?&

abcdefghijklmnopqrstuvwxyz
ABCDEFGHIJKLMNOPQRSTUVW
XYZ$1234567890(.,""''-;:!)?&

abcdefghijklmnopqrstuvwxyz
ABCDEFGHIJKLMNOPQRSTUVWXYZ
$1234567890(.,""''-;:!)?&

abcdefghijklmnopqrstuvwxyz
ABCDEFGHIJKLMNOPQRSTUVWXYZ
$1234567890(.,""''-;:!)?&

abcdefghijklmnopqrstuvwxyz
ABCDEFGHIJKLMNOPQRSTUVWXYZ
$1234567890(.,""''-;:!)?&

36 Point

abcdefghijklmnopqrstuvwxyz
ABCDEFGHIJKLMNOPQRSTUV
WXYZ$1234567890(.,""""-;:!)?&

30 Point

abcdefghijklmnopqrstuvwxyz
ABCDEFGHIJKLMNOPQRSTUVWXYZ
$1234567890(.,""""-;:!)?&

24 Point

abcdefghijklmnopqrstuvwxyz
ABCDEFGHIJKLMNOPQRSTUVWXYZ
$1234567890(.,""""-;:!)?&

18 Point

abcdefghijklmnopqrstuvwxyz
ABCDEFGHIJKLMNOPQRSTUVWXYZ
$1234567890(.,""""-;:!)?&

72 Point

abcdefghijklmnop

qrstuvwxyzAB

CDEFGHIJKLMN

OPQRSTUVW

XYZ$12345678

90 (.,""''-;:!)?&

72 Point

abcdefghijklmn

opqrstuvwxyz

ABCDEFGHIJKL

MNOPQRSTU

VWXYZ$12345

67890

---

48 Point

abcdefghijklmnopqrstuvw
xyzABCDEFGHIJKLMNOP
QRSTUVWXYZ$123456
7890 (.,""""-;:!)?&

---

30 Point

abcdefghijklmnopqrstuvwxyz
ABCDEFGHIJKLMNOPQRSTUVWXYZ
$1234567890 (.,""""-;:!)?&

---

18 Point

abcdefghijklmnopqrstuvwxyz
ABCDEFGHIJKLMNOPQRSTUVWXYZ
$1234567890 (.,""""-;:!)?&

___
48 Point

abcdefghijklmnopqrst
uvwxyzABCDEFGHIJKL
MNOPQRSTUVWXYZ
$1234567890(.,'"""-;:!)?&

___
30 Point

abcdefghijklmnopqrstuvwxyz
ABCDEFGHIJKLMNOPQRSTUVWXYZ
$1234567890(.,'"""-;:!)?&

___
18 Point

abcdefghijklmnopqrstuvwxyz
ABCDEFGHIJKLMNOPQRSTUVWXYZ
$1234567890(.,'"""-;:!)?&

Univers 47

abcdefghijklmnopqrstuvwxyz
ABCDEFGHIJKLMNOPQRSTUVWXYZ
$1234567890(.,'"-;.:!)?&

abcdefghijklmnopqrstu
vwxyzABCDEFGHIJKLM
NOPQRSTUVWXYZ$12
34567890(.,'"-;.:!)?&

abcdefghijklmnopqrstuvwxyz
ABCDEFGHIJKLMNOPQRSTUVWXYZ
$1234567890 (.,""''-;:.!/?&

72 Point

abcdefghijklmnopqrstuvw

xyz ABCDEFGHIJKLM

NOPQRSTUVWXYZ $123

4567890 (.,""''-;:.!/)?&

18 Point

abcdefghijklmnopqrstuvwxyz
ABCDEFGHIJKLMNOPQRSTUVWXYZ
$1234567890 (.,""''-;:!)?&

72 Point

abcdefghijklmno
pqrstuvwxyzABC
DEFGHIJKLMNO
PQRSTUVWX
YZ$1234567890
(.,""''-;:!)?&

Univers 46

abcdefghijklmnopqrstuvwxyz
ABCDEFGGHIJKLMNOPQRSTUVWXYZ
$11234567890(.,""''-;:!)?&&

abcdefghijklmno
pqrstuvwxyzAB
CDEFGGHIJKL
MNOPQRSTUV
WXYZ$112345
67890(.,""""-;:!)?&&

Univers 57

abcdefghijklmnopqrstuvwxyz
ABCDEFGGHIJKLMNOPQRSTUVWXYZ
$1234567890 (.,'''':;:!)?&

abcdefghijklmnopq
rstuvwxyzABCDEFGG
HIJKLMNOPQRSTU
VWXYZ$123
4567890(.,''''-;:!)?&

204

Univers 58

18 Point

abcdefghijklmnopqrstuvwxyz
ABCDEFGHIJKLMNOPQRSTUVWXYZ
$1234567890(.,""''-;:!)?&

72 Point

abcdefghijklmnopqr

stuvwxyzABCDEFGH

IJKLMNOPQRSTU

VWXYZ$12345678

90(.,""''-;:!)?&

18 Point

abcdefghijklmnopqrstuvwxyz
ABCDEFGHIJKLMNOPQRSTUVWXYZ
$11234567890(.,"'''-;:!)?&

72 Point

abcdefghijklmnop
qrstuvwxyzABCDE
FGHIJKLMNOPQR
STUVWXYZ$11234
567890(.,"'''-;:!)?&

Univers 68

abcdefghijklmnopqrstuvwxyz
ABCDEFGHIJKLMNOPQRSTUVWXYZ
$1234567890 (.,"''"-;:!)?&

abcdefghijklmnop

qrstuvwxyzABCDE

FGHIJKLMNOPQ

RSTUVWXYZ$123

4567890(.,"''"-;:!)?&

abcdefghijklmnopqrstuvwxyz
ABCDEFGHIJKLMNOPQRSTUVW
XYZ $1234567890 (.,'"-;:!)?&

72 Point

abcdefghijklm
nopqrstuvwx
yzABCDEFGHI
JKLMNOPQR
STUVWXYZ
$1234 (.,'"-;:!)?&

Univers 76

abcdefghijklmnopqrstuvwxyz
ABCDEFGHIJKLMNOPQRSTUVWX
YZ$1234567890 (.,"'-;:!)?&

abcdefghijklm
nopqrstuvwx
yzABCDEFGHI
JKLMNOPQR
STUVWXYZ
$1234(.,""'-;:!)?&

209

abcdefghijklmnopqrstuvw
xyz ABCDEFGHIJKLMNOPQ
RSTUVWXYZ $1234567890
(.,""''-;:!)?&&

72 Point

abcdefghijk
lmnopqrstu
vwxyz ABC
DEFGHIJKL
MNOPQRST
UVWXYZ $

Univers 83   **Univers 39**

24 Point

abcdefghijklmnopqrstuvwxyz
ABCDEFGGHIJKLMNOPQRSTUVWXYZ
$1234567890 (.,'""-;:!)?&

72 Point

1234567890

(.,'""-;:!)?&&

72 Point

abcdefghijklmnopqrstuvwxyz

ABCDEFGGHIJKLMNOPQRSTUVWXYZ

$1234567890 (.,'""-;:!)?&

abcdefghijklmnopqrstuvwxyz
ABCDEFGHIJKLMNOPQRSTUVWXYZ
$1234567890(.,'''-;:!)?&

abcdefghijklmnopqrstuvwxyz
ABCDEFGHIJKLMNOPQRSTUVWXYZ
$1234567890(.,'''-;:!)?&

abcdefghijklmnopqrstuvwxyz
ABCDEFGHIJKLMNOPQRSTUVWXYZ
$1234567890(.,'''-;:!)?&

abcdefghijklmnopqrstuvwxyz
ABCDEFGHIJKLMNOPQRSTUVWXYZ
$1234567890(.,'''-;:!)?&

Univers 45

The whole duty of Typography, as of Calligraphy, is to communicate to the imagination, without loss by the way, the thought or image intended to be communicated by the Author. And the whole duty of beautiful typography is not to substitute for the beauty or interest of the thing thought and intended to be conveyed by the symbol, a beauty or interest of its own, but, on the one hand, to win access for that communication by the clearness and beauty of the vehicle, and on the other hand, to take advantage of every pause or stage in that communication to interpose some characteristic & restful beauty in its own art. We thus have a reason for the clearness and beauty of the text as a whole, for the especial beauty of the first or introductory page and of the title, and for the especial beauty of the headings of chapters, capital or initial letters, and so on, and an opening for the illustrator as we shall see by and *by. Further, in the case of Poetry, verse, in my opinion,*
8/9

The whole duty of Typography, as of Calligraphy, is to communicate to the imagination, without loss by the way, the thought or image intended to be communicated by the Author. And the whole duty of beautiful typography is not to substitute for the beauty or interest of the thing thought and intended to be conveyed by the symbol, a beauty or interest of its own, but, on the one hand, to win access for that communication by the clearness and beauty of the vehicle, and on the other hand, to take advantage of every pause or stage in that communication to interpose some characteristic & restful beauty in its own art. We thus have a reason for the clearness and beauty of the text as a whole, for the especial beauty of the first or introductory page and of the title, and for the especial beauty of the *and an opening for the illustrator as we shall see by and*
8/10

The whole duty of Typography, as of Calligraphy, is to communicate to the imagination, without loss by the way, the thought or image intended to be communicated by the Author. And the whole duty of beautiful typography is not to substitute for the beauty or interest of the thing thought and intended to be conveyed by the symbol, a beauty or interest of its own, but, on the one hand, to win access for that communication by the clearness and beauty of the vehicle, and on the other hand, to take advantage of every pause or stage in that communication to interpose some characteristic & restful beauty in its own art. We thus have a reason for the clearness and beauty of the text as a whole, for the especial beauty of the first or introductory *page and of the title, and for the especial beauty of the*
8/11

The whole duty of Typography, as of Calligraphy, is to communicate to the imagination, without loss by the way, the thought or image intended to be communicated by the Author. And the whole duty of beautiful typography is not to substitute for the beauty or interest of the thing thought and intended to be conveyed by the symbol, a beauty or interest of its own, but, on the one hand, to win access for that communication by the clearness and beauty of the vehicle, and on the other hand, to take advantage of every pause or stage in that communication to interpose some characteristic & restful beauty in its own art. We thus have a reason for the clearness and beauty of the text as a whole, for the especial *title, and for the especial beauty of the headings of*
9/10

The whole duty of Typography, as of Calligraphy, is to communicate to the imagination, without loss by the way, the thought or image intended to be communicated by the Author. And the whole duty of beautiful typography is not to substitute for the beauty or interest of the thing thought and intended to be conveyed by the symbol, a beauty or interest of its own, but, on the one hand, to win access for that communication by the clearness and beauty of the vehicle, and on the other hand, to take advantage of every pause or stage in that communication to interpose some characteristic & restful beauty in its own art. We thus have a reason for the clearness *and beauty of the text as a whole, for the especial*
9/11

The whole duty of Typography, as of Calligraphy, is to communicate to the imagination, without loss by the way, the thought or image intended to be communicated by the Author. And the whole duty of beautiful typography is not to substitute for the beauty or interest of the thing thought and intended to be conveyed by the symbol, a beauty or interest of its own, but, on the one hand, to win access for that communication by the clearness and beauty of the vehicle, and on the other hand, to take advantage of every pause or stage in that communication to interpose some characteristic & restful beauty in its *own art. We thus have a reason for the clearness*
9/12

abcdefghijklmnopqrstuvwxyz
ABCDEFGHIJKLMNOPQRSTUVWXYZ
$1234567890(.,'"-;:!)?&

abcdefghijklmnopqrstuvwxyz
ABCDEFGHIJKLMNOPQRSTUVWXYZ
$1234567890(.,'"-;:!)?&

abcdefghijklmnopqrstuvwxyz
ABCDEFGHIJKLMNOPQRSTUVWXYZ
$1234567890(.,'"-;:!)?&

abcdefghijklmnopqrstuvwxyz
ABCDEFGHIJKLMNOPQRSTUVWXYZ
$1234567890(.,'"-;:!)?&

The whole duty of Typography, as of Calligraphy, is to communicate to the imagination, without loss by the way, the thought or image intended to be communicated by the Author. And the whole duty of beautiful typography is not to substitute for the beauty or interest of the thing thought and intended to be conveyed by the symbol, a beauty or interest of its own, but, on the one hand, to win access for that communication by the clearness and beauty of the vehicle, and on the other hand, to take advantage of every pause or stage in that communication to interpose some characteristic *& restful beauty in its own art. We thus have a*

10/11

The whole duty of Typography, as of Calligraphy, is to communicate to the imagination, without loss by the way, the thought or image intended to be communicated by the Author. And the whole duty of beautiful typography is not to substitute for the beauty or interest of the thing thought and intended to be conveyed by the symbol, a beauty or interest of its own, but, on the one hand, to win access for that communication by the clearness and beauty of the vehicle, and on the other hand, to take advantage of every pause or stage in that com*munication to interpose some characteristic*

10/12

The whole duty of Typography, as of Calligraphy, is to communicate to the imagination, without loss by the way, the thought or image intended to be communicated by the Author. And the whole duty of beautiful typography is not to substitute for the beauty or interest of the thing thought and intended to be conveyed by the symbol, a beauty or interest of its own, but, on the one hand, to win access for that communication by the clearness and beauty of the vehicle, and on the other hand, to take *advantage of every pause or stage in that*

10/13

The whole duty of Typography, as of Calligraphy, is to communicate to the imagination, without loss by the way, the thought or image intended to be communicated by the Author. And the whole duty of beautiful typography is not to substitute for the beauty or interest of the thing thought and intended to be conveyed by the symbol, a beauty or interest of its own, but, on the one hand, to win access for that *communication by the clearness and*

12/13

The whole duty of Typography, as of Calligraphy, is to communicate to the imagination, without loss by the way, the thought or image intended to be communicated by the Author. And the whole duty of beautiful typography is not to substitute for the beauty or interest of the thing thought and intended to be conveyed by the symbol, a beauty or interest of its own, but, on *the one hand, to win access for that*

12/14

The whole duty of Typography, as of Calligraphy, is to communicate to the imagination, without loss by the way, the thought or image intended to be communicated by the Author. And the whole duty of beautiful typography is not to substitute for the beauty or interest of the thing thought and intended to be conveyed by the symbol, a *beauty or interest of its own, but, on*

12/15

abcdefghijklmnopqrstuvwxyz
ABCDEFGHIJKLMNOPQRSTUVWXYZ
$1234567890(.,'"-;:!)?&

abcdefghijklmnopqrstuvwxyz
ABCDEFGHIJKLMNOPQRSTUVWXYZ
$1234567890(.,'"-;:!)?&

abcdefghijklmnopqrstuvwxyz
ABCDEFGHIJKLMNOPQRSTUVWXYZ
$1234567890(.,'"-;:!)?&

abcdefghijklmnopqrstuvwxyz
ABCDEFGHIJKLMNOPQRSTUVWXYZ
$1234567890(.,'"-;:!)?&

Univers 55

The whole duty of Typography, as of Calligraphy, is to communicate to the imagination, without loss by the way, the thought or image intended to be communicated by the Author. And the whole duty of beautiful typography is not to substitute for the beauty or interest of the thing thought and intended to be conveyed by the symbol, a beauty or interest of its own, but, on the one hand, to win access for that communication by the clearness and beauty of the vehicle, and on the other hand, to take advantage of every pause or stage in that communication to interpose some characteristic & restful beauty in its own art. We thus have a reason for the clearness and beauty of the text as a whole, for the especial beauty of the first or introductory page and of the title, and for the especial beauty of the headings of chapters, capital or initial letters, and so on, and an *opening for the illustrator as we shall see by and by.*
8/9

The whole duty of Typography, as of Calligraphy, is to communicate to the imagination, without loss by the way, the thought or image intended to be communicated by the Author. And the whole duty of beautiful typography is not to substitute for the beauty or interest of the thing thought and intended to be conveyed by the symbol, a beauty or interest of its own, but, on the one hand, to win access for that communication by the clearness and beauty of the vehicle, and on the other hand, to take advantage of every pause or stage in that communication to interpose some characteristic & restful beauty in its own art. We thus have a reason for the clearness and beauty of the text as a whole, for the especial beauty of the first or introductory page and of the title, and for the especial beauty of the headings *of chapters, capital or initial letters, and so on, and an*
8/10

The whole duty of Typography, as of Calligraphy, is to communicate to the imagination, without loss by the way, the thought or image intended to be communicated by the Author. And the whole duty of beautiful typography is not to substitute for the beauty or interest of the thing thought and intended to be conveyed by the symbol, a beauty or interest of its own, but, on the one hand, to win access for that communication by the clearness and beauty of the vehicle, and on the other hand, to take advantage of every pause or stage in that communication to interpose some characteristic & restful beauty in its own art. We thus have a reason for the clearness and beauty of the text as a whole, for the *especial beauty of the first or introductory page and*
8/11

The whole duty of Typography, as of Calligraphy, is to communicate to the imagination, without loss by the way, the thought or image intended to be communicated by the Author. And the whole duty of beautiful typography is not to substitute for the beauty or interest of the thing thought and intended to be conveyed by the symbol, a beauty or interest of its own, but, on the one hand, to win access for that communication by the clearness and beauty of the vehicle, and on the other hand, to take advantage of every pause or stage in that communication to interpose some characteristic & restful beauty in its own art. We thus have a reason for the clearness and beauty of the text as a whole, for the especial beauty of the first or introductory page and of the title, and for the es-
9/10

The whole duty of Typography, as of Calligraphy, is to communicate to the imagination, without loss by the way, the thought or image intended to be communicated by the Author. And the whole duty of beautiful typography is not to substitute for the beauty or interest of the thing thought and intended to be conveyed by the symbol, a beauty or interest of its own, but, on the one hand, to win access for that communication by the clearness and beauty of the vehicle, and on the other hand, to take advantage of every pause or stage in that communication to interpose some characteristic & restful beauty in its own art. We thus have a *reason for the clearness and beauty of the text as*
9/11

The whole duty of Typography, as of Calligraphy, is to communicate to the imagination, without loss by the way, the thought or image intended to be communicated by the Author. And the whole duty of beautiful typography is not to substitute for the beauty or interest of the thing thought and intended to be conveyed by the symbol, a beauty or interest of its own, but, on the one hand, to win access for that communication by the clearness and beauty of the vehicle, and on the other hand, to take advantage of every pause or stage in that communication to interpose some characteristic *& restful beauty in its own art. We thus have a*
9/12

abcdefghijklmnopqrstuvwxyz
ABCDEFGHIJKLMNOPQRSTUVWXYZ
$1234567890(.,'"-;:!)?&

abcdefghijklmnopqrstuvwxyz
ABCDEFGHIJKLMNOPQRSTUVWXYZ
$1234567890(.,'"-;:!)?&

abcdefghijklmnopqrstuvwxyz
ABCDEFGHIJKLMNOPQRSTUVWXYZ
$1234567890(.,'"-;:!)?&

abcdefghijklmnopqrstuvwxyz
ABCDEFGHIJKLMNOPQRSTUVWXYZ
$1234567890(.,'"-;:!)?&

The whole duty of Typography, as of Callig-raphy, is to communicate to the imagination, without loss by the way, the thought or image intended to be communicated by the Author. And the whole duty of beautiful typography is not to substitute for the beauty or interest of the thing thought and intended to be con-veyed by the symbol, a beauty or interest of its own, but, on the one hand, to win access for that communication by the clearness and beauty of the vehicle, and on the other hand, to take advantage of every pause or stage in that communication to interpose some char-*acteristic & restful beauty in its own art. We*

10/11

The whole duty of Typography, as of Callig-raphy, is to communicate to the imagination, without loss by the way, the thought or image intended to be communicated by the Author. And the whole duty of beautiful typography is not to substitute for the beauty or interest of the thing thought and intended to be con-veyed by the symbol, a beauty or interest of its own, but, on the one hand, to win access for that communication by the clearness and beauty of the vehicle, and on the other hand, to take advantage of every pause or stage in *that communication to interpose some char-*

10/12

The whole duty of Typography, as of Callig-raphy, is to communicate to the imagination, without loss by the way, the thought or image intended to be communicated by the Author. And the whole duty of beautiful typography is not to substitute for the beauty or interest of the thing thought and intended to be con-veyed by the symbol, a beauty or interest of its own, but, on the one hand, to win access for that communication by the clearness and beauty of the vehicle, and on the other hand, *to take advantage of every pause or stage in*

10/13

The whole duty of Typography, as of Calligraphy, is to communicate to the imagination, without loss by the way, the thought or image intended to be communicated by the Author. And the whole duty of beautiful typography is not to substitute for the beauty or in-terest of the thing thought and in-tended to be conveyed by the symbol, a beauty or interest of its own, but, on the one hand, to win access for that *communication by the clearness and*

12/13

The whole duty of Typography, as of Calligraphy, is to communicate to the imagination, without loss by the way, the thought or image intended to be communicated by the Author. And the whole duty of beautiful typography is not to substitute for the beauty or in-terest of the thing thought and in-tended to be conveyed by the symbol, a beauty or interest of its own, but, on *the one hand, to win access for that*

12/14

The whole duty of Typography, as of Calligraphy, is to communicate to the imagination, without loss by the way, the thought or image intended to be communicated by the Author. And the whole duty of beautiful typography is not to substitute for the beauty or in-terest of the thing thought and in-tended to be conveyed by the symbol, *a beauty or interest of its own, but, on*

12/15

abcdefghijklmnopqrstuvwxyz
ABCDEFGHIJKLMNOPQRSTUVWXYZ
$1234567890(.,'"-;:!)?&

abcdefghijklmnopqrstuvwxyz
ABCDEFGHIJKLMNOPQRSTUVWXYZ
$1234567890(.,'"-;:!)?&

abcdefghijklmnopqrstuvwxyz
ABCDEFGHIJKLMNOPQRSTUVWXYZ
$1234567890(.,'"-;:!)?&

abcdefghijklmnopqrstuvwxyz
ABCDEFGHIJKLMNOPQRSTUVWXYZ
$1234567890(.,'"-;:!)?&

Univers 65

The whole duty of Typography, as of Calligraphy, is to communicate to the imagination, without loss by the way, the thought or image intended to be communicated by the Author. And the whole duty of beautiful typography is not to substitute for the beauty or interest of the thing thought and intended to be conveyed by the symbol, a beauty or interest of its own, but, on the one hand, to win access for that communication by the clearness and beauty of the vehicle, and on the other hand, to take advantage of every pause or stage in that communication to interpose some characteristic & restful beauty in its own art. We thus have a reason for the clearness and beauty of the text as a whole, for the especial beauty of the first or introductory page and of the title, and for the especial *beauty of the headings of chapters, capital or*
8/9

The whole duty of Typography, as of Calligraphy, is to communicate to the imagination, without loss by the way, the thought or image intended to be communicated by the Author. And the whole duty of beautiful typography is not to substitute for the beauty or interest of the thing thought and intended to be conveyed by the symbol, a beauty or interest of its own, but, on the one hand, to win access for that communication by the clearness and beauty of the vehicle, and on the other hand, to take advantage of every pause or stage in that communication to interpose some characteristic & restful beauty in its own art. We thus have a reason for the clearness and beauty of the text as a whole, for the especial beauty of the first or introductory page and of the title, and for the especial
ductory page and of the title, and for the especial
8/10

The whole duty of Typography, as of Calligraphy, is to communicate to the imagination, without loss by the way, the thought or image intended to be communicated by the Author. And the whole duty of beautiful typography is not to substitute for the beauty or interest of the thing thought and intended to be conveyed by the symbol, a beauty or interest of its own, but, on the one hand, to win access for that communication by the clearness and beauty of the vehicle, and on the other hand, to take advantage of every pause or stage in that communication to interpose some characteristic & restful beauty in its own art. We thus have a reason for the clearness and beauty of the text as a
son for the clearness and beauty of the text as a
8/11

The whole duty of Typography, as of Calligraphy, is to communicate to the imagination, without loss by the way, the thought or image intended to be communicated by the Author. And the whole duty of beautiful typography is not to substitute for the beauty or interest of the thing thought and intended to be conveyed by the symbol, a beauty or interest of its own, but, on the one hand, to win access for that communication by the clearness and beauty of the vehicle, and on the other hand, to take advantage of every pause or stage in that communication to interpose some characteristic & restful beauty in its own art. We
beauty of the text as a whole, for the especial
9/10

The whole duty of Typography, as of Calligraphy, is to communicate to the imagination, without loss by the way, the thought or image intended to be communicated by the Author. And the whole duty of beautiful typography is not to substitute for the beauty or interest of the thing thought and intended to be conveyed by the symbol, a beauty or interest of its own, but, on the one hand, to win access for that communication by the clearness and beauty of the vehicle, and on the other hand, to take advantage of every pause or stage in that communication to interpose some char-*acteristic & restful beauty in its own art. We*
9/11

The whole duty of Typography, as of Calligraphy, is to communicate to the imagination, without loss by the way, the thought or image intended to be communicated by the Author. And the whole duty of beautiful typography is not to substitute for the beauty or interest of the thing thought and intended to be conveyed by the symbol, a beauty or interest of its own, but, on the one hand, to win access for that communication by the clearness and beauty of the vehicle, and on the other hand, to take advantage of every pause or stage in *that communication to interpose some char-*
9/12

abcdefghijklmnopqrstuvwxyz
ABCDEFGHIJKLMNOPQRSTUVWXYZ
$1234567890(.,'"-;:!)?&

abcdefghijklmnopqrstuvwxyz
ABCDEFGHIJKLMNOPQRSTUVWXYZ
$1234567890(.,'"-;:!)?&

abcdefghijklmnopqrstuvwxyz
ABCDEFGHIJKLMNOPQRSTUVWXYZ
$1234567890(.,'"-;:!)?&

abcdefghijklmnopqrstuvwxyz
ABCDEFGHIJKLMNOPQRSTUVWXYZ
$1234567890(.,'"-;:!)?&

The whole duty of Typography, as of Calligraphy, is to communicate to the imagination, without loss by the way, the
thought or image intended to be communicated by the Author. And the whole
duty of beautiful typography is not to
substitute for the beauty or interest of
the thing thought and intended to be conveyed by the symbol, a beauty or interest
of its own, but, on the one hand, to win
access for that communication by the
clearness and beauty of the vehicle, and
on the other hand, to take advantage of
every pause or stage in that communica-
10/11

The whole duty of Typography, as of Calligraphy, is to communicate to the imagination, without loss by the way, the
thought or image intended to be communicated by the Author. And the whole
duty of beautiful typography is not to
substitute for the beauty or interest of
the thing thought and intended to be conveyed by the symbol, a beauty or interest
of its own, but, on the one hand, to win
access for that communication by the
clearness and beauty of the vehicle, and
on the other hand, to take advantage of
10/12

The whole duty of Typography, as of Calligraphy, is to communicate to the imagination, without loss by the way, the
thought or image intended to be communicated by the Author. And the whole
duty of beautiful typography is not to
substitute for the beauty or interest of
the thing thought and intended to be conveyed by the symbol, a beauty or interest
of its own, but, on the one hand, to win
access for that communication by the
clearness and beauty of the vehicle, and
10/13

The whole duty of Typography, as
of Calligraphy, is to communicate
to the imagination, without loss by
the way, the thought or image intended to be communicated by the
Author. And the whole duty of
beautiful typography is not to substitute for the beauty or interest of
the thing thought and intended to
be conveyed by the symbol, a
beauty or interest of its own, but,
on the one hand, to win access for
12/13

The whole duty of Typography, as
of Calligraphy, is to communicate
to the imagination, without loss by
the way, the thought or image intended to be communicated by the
Author. And the whole duty of
beautiful typography is not to substitute for the beauty or interest of
the thing thought and intended to
be conveyed by the symbol, a
beauty or interest of its own, but,
12/14

The whole duty of Typography, as
of Calligraphy, is to communicate
to the imagination, without loss by
the way, the thought or image intended to be communicated by the
Author. And the whole duty of
beautiful typography is not to substitute for the beauty or interest of
the thing thought and intended to
be conveyed by the symbol, a
12/15

HACTENUS arvorum cultus, et sidera cœli:
Nunc te, Bacche, canam, nec non silvestria tecum
Virgulta, et prolem tarde crescentis olivæ.
Huc, pater o Lenæe; (tuis hic omnia plena
5 Muneribus: tibi pampineo gravidus autumno
Floret ager; spumat plenis vindemia labris)
Huc, pater o Lenæe, veni; nudataque musto
Tinge novo mecum direptis crura cothurnis.
  Principio arboribus varia est natura creandis:
10 Namque aliæ, nullis hominum cogentibus, ipsæ
Sponte sua veniunt, camposque et flumina late
Curva tenent: ut molle siler, lentæque genistæ,
Populus, et glauca canentia fronde salicta.
Pars autem posito surgunt de semine: ut altæ
15 Castaneæ, nemorumque Jovi quæ maxima frondet
Aesculus, atque habitæ Graiis oracula quercus.
Pullulat ab radice aliis densissima silva:
Ut cerasis, ulmisque: etiam Parnassia laurus
Parva sub ingenti matris se subjicit umbra.
20 Hos natura modos primum dedit: his genus omne
Silvarum, fruticumque viret, nemorumque sacrorum.
Sunt alii, quos ipse via sibi repperit usus.
Hic plantas tenero abscindens de corpore matrum

Deposuit

Transitional

Baskerville

3.

Title page for the second book of Virgil's *Georgics,* designed and printed by John Baskerville, 1757.

Transitional typefaces appeared during the eighteenth century, a period of typographic evolution. Designers gradually increased the contrast between thick and thin strokes, made serifs sharper and more horizontal, and increased the vertical stress of rounded letterforms. By the century's end, Old Style typefaces had evolved into the Modern styles with hairline serifs and geometric proportions: typefaces designed in the middle of this period of change were *transitional.*

Simplicity and understated elegance were achieved through the use of John Baskerville's masterful Transitional typefaces, seen in the title page of Virgil's *Georgics* (Fig. **3**). Generous

margins, letterspaced display type, and thoughtfully considered interline and word spacing are present. The great Roman poet is presented to the reader with clarity and dignity in a book that "went forth to astonish all the librarians of Europe."

If the words *Transitional* and *Baskerville* have become interwoven in the lexicon of typography, it is because the Transitional typefaces produced by John Baskerville of Birmingham, England, have an unsurpassed beauty and harmony. Many Transitional typefaces in use today, including the specimens shown, are closely modeled after Baskerville's work.

abcdefghijklmnop

qrstuvwxyzAB

CDEFGHIJKLM

NOPQRSTUV

WXYZ$1234567

890(.,""''-;:!)?&

72 Point

abcdefghijklmnopq
rstuvwxyzABC
DEFGHIJKLMN
OPQRSTUVW
XYZ$1234567890
(.,""''-;:.!)?&

Baskerville

abcdefghijklmnopqrstuvwxyz
ABCDEFGHIJKLMNOPQRSTUVW
XYZ$1234567890(.,""'-;:!)?&

abcdefghijklmnopqrstuvw
xyzABCDEFGHIJKLMN
OPQRSTUVWXYZ$12
34567890(.,""'-;:!)?&

abcdefghijklmnopqrstuvwxyz
ABCDEFGHIJKLMNOPQRSTU
VWXYZ$1234567890(.,""'-;:!)?&

abcdefghijklmnopqrstuvwxyz
ABCDEFGHIJKLMNOPQRSTUVW
XYZ$1234567890(.,""'-;:!)?&

222

Baskerville Italic

abcdefghijklmnopqrstuvwxyz
ABCDEFGHIJKLMNOPQRSTUVWXYZ
$1234567890(.,""''-,:!)?&

abcdefghijklmnopqrstuvw
xyzABCDEFGHIJKLMNO
PQRSTUVWXYZ$12345
67890(.,""''-,:!)?&

abcdefghijklmnopqrstuvwxyz
ABCDEFGHIJKLMNOPQRSTUV
WXYZ$1234567890(.,""''-,:!)?&

abcdefghijklmnopqrstuvwxyz
ABCDEFGHIJKLMNOPQRSTUVWXYZ
$1234567890(.,""''-,:!)?&

abcdefghijklmnopqrstuvwxyz
ABCDEFGHIJKLMNOPQRSTUVWXYZ
$1234567890(.,'"-;:!)?&

abcdefghijklmnopqrstuvwxyz
ABCDEFGHIJKLMNOPQRSTUVWXYZ
$1234567890(.,'"-;:!)?&

abcdefghijklmnopqrstuvwxyz
ABCDEFGHIJKLMNOPQRSTUVWXYZ
$1234567890(.,'"-;:!)?&

abcdefghijklmnopqrstuvwxyz
ABCDEFGHIJKLMNOPQRSTUVWXYZ
$1234567890(.,'"-;:!)?&

Baskerville

The whole duty of Typography, as of Calligraphy, is to communicate to the imagination, without loss by the way, the thought or image intended to be communicated by the Author. And the whole duty of beautiful typography is not to substitute for the beauty or interest of the thing thought and intended to be conveyed by the symbol, a beauty or interest of its own, but, on the one hand, to win access for that communication by the clearness and beauty of the vehicle, and on the other hand, to take advantage of every pause or stage in that communication to interpose some characteristic & restful beauty in its own art. We thus have a reason for the clearness and beauty of the text as a whole, for the especial beauty of the first or introductory page and of the title, and for the especial beauty of the headings of chapters, capital or initial letters, and so on, and an opening for the illustrator as we shall see by and by. Further, in the case of Poetry, verse, in my opinion, appeals by its form to the eye, as well as to *the ear, and should be placed on the page so that its structure may be*
8/9

The whole duty of Typography, as of Calligraphy, is to communicate to the imagination, without loss by the way, the thought or image intended to be communicated by the Author. And the whole duty of beautiful typography is not to substitute for the beauty or interest of the thing thought and intended to be conveyed by the symbol, a beauty or interest of its own, but, on the one hand, to win access for that communication by the clearness and beauty of the vehicle, and on the other hand, to take advantage of every pause or stage in that communication to interpose some characteristic & restful beauty in its own art. We thus have a reason for the clearness and beauty of the text as a whole, for the especial beauty of the first or introductory page and of the title, and for the especial beauty of the headings of chapters, capital or initial letters, and so on, and an opening for the illustrator as we shall see by and by. Further, in the case of Poetry, *verse, in my opinion, appeals by its form to the eye, as well as to the ear,*
8/10

The whole duty of Typography, as of Calligraphy, is to communicate to the imagination, without loss by the way, the thought or image intended to be communicated by the Author. And the whole duty of beautiful typography is not to substitute for the beauty or interest of the thing thought and intended to be conveyed by the symbol, a beauty or interest of its own, but, on the one hand, to win access for that communication by the clearness and beauty of the vehicle, and on the other hand, to take advantage of every pause or stage in that communication to interpose some characteristic & restful beauty in its own art. We thus have a reason for the clearness and beauty of the text as a whole, for the especial beauty of the first or introductory page and of the title, and for the especial beauty of the headings of chapters, *capital or initial letters, and so on, and an opening for the illustrator as*
8/11

The whole duty of Typography, as of Calligraphy, is to communicate to the imagination, without loss by the way, the thought or image intended to be communicated by the Author. And the whole duty of beautiful typography is not to substitute for the beauty or interest of the thing thought and intended to be conveyed by the symbol, a beauty or interest of its own, but, on the one hand, to win access for that communication by the clearness and beauty of the vehicle, and on the other hand, to take advantage of every pause or stage in that communication to interpose some characteristic & restful beauty in its own art. We thus have a reason for the clearness and beauty of the text as a whole, for the especial beauty of the first or introductory page and of the title, and for the especial beauty of the headings of chapters, capital or initial letters, and so on, and an opening for the illustrator as we shall *ters, and so on, and an opening for the illustrator as we shall*
9/10

The whole duty of Typography, as of Calligraphy, is to communicate to the imagination, without loss by the way, the thought or image intended to be communicated by the Author. And the whole duty of beautiful typography is not to substitute for the beauty or interest of the thing thought and intended to be conveyed by the symbol, a beauty or interest of its own, but, on the one hand, to win access for that communication by the clearness and beauty of the vehicle, and on the other hand, to take advantage of every pause or stage in that communication to interpose some characteristic & restful beauty in its own art. We thus have a reason for the clearness and beauty of the text as a whole, for the especial beauty of the first or introductory page and of the title, and for the especial beauty of *troductory page and of the title, and for the especial beauty of*
9/11

The whole duty of Typography, as of Calligraphy, is to communicate to the imagination, without loss by the way, the thought or image intended to be communicated by the Author. And the whole duty of beautiful typography is not to substitute for the beauty or interest of the thing thought and intended to be conveyed by the symbol, a beauty or interest of its own, but, on the one hand, to win access for that communication by the clearness and beauty of the vehicle, and on the other hand, to take advantage of every pause or stage in that communication to interpose some characteristic & restful beauty in its own art. We thus have a reason for the clearness and beauty of the *text as a whole, for the especial beauty of the first or introductory*
9/12

abcdefghijklmnopqrstuvwxyz
ABCDEFGHIJKLMNOPQRSTUVWXYZ
$1234567890(.,'"-;:!)?&

abcdefghijklmnopqrstuvwxyz
ABCDEFGHIJKLMNOPQRSTUVWXYZ
$1234567890(.,'"-;:!)?&

abcdefghijklmnopqrstuvwxyz
ABCDEFGHIJKLMNOPQRSTUVWXYZ
$1234567890(.,'"-;:!)?&

abcdefghijklmnopqrstuvwxyz
ABCDEFGHIJKLMNOPQRSTUVWXYZ
$1234567890(.,'"-;:!)?&

The whole duty of Typography, as of Calligraphy, is to communicate to the imagination, without loss by the way, the thought or image intended to be communicated by the Author. And the whole duty of beautiful typography is not to substitute for the beauty or interest of the thing thought and intended to be conveyed by the symbol, a beauty or interest of its own, but, on the one hand, to win access for that communication by the clearness and beauty of the vehicle, and on the other hand, to take advantage of every pause or stage in that communication to interpose some characteristic & restful beauty in its own art. We thus have a reason for *the clearness and beauty of the text as a whole, for the*
10/11

The whole duty of Typography, as of Calligraphy, is to communicate to the imagination, without loss by the way, the thought or image intended to be communicated by the Author. And the whole duty of beautiful typography is not to substitute for the beauty or interest of the thing thought and intended to be conveyed by the symbol, a beauty or interest of its own, but, on the one hand, to win access for that communication by the clearness and beauty of the vehicle, and on the other hand, to take advantage of every pause or stage in that communication to interpose some characteristic & rest*ful beauty in its own art. We thus have a reason for the*
10/12

The whole duty of Typography, as of Calligraphy, is to communicate to the imagination, without loss by the way, the thought or image intended to be communicated by the Author. And the whole duty of beautiful typography is not to substitute for the beauty or interest of the thing thought and intended to be conveyed by the symbol, a beauty or interest of its own, but, on the one hand, to win access for that communication by the clearness and beauty of the vehicle, and on the other hand, to take advantage of every pause or stage in that com*munication to interpose some characteristic & restful*
10/13

The whole duty of Typography, as of Calligraphy, is to communicate to the imagination, without loss by the way, the thought or image intended to be communicated by the Author. And the whole duty of beautiful typography is not to substitute for the beauty or interest of the thing thought and intended to be conveyed by the symbol, a beauty or interest of its own, but, on the one hand, to win access for that communication by the clearness and beauty of the vehicle, and on *the other hand, to take advantage of every pause*
12/13

The whole duty of Typography, as of Calligraphy, is to communicate to the imagination, without loss by the way, the thought or image intended to be communicated by the Author. And the whole duty of beautiful typography is not to substitute for the beauty or interest of the thing thought and intended to be conveyed by the symbol, a beauty or interest of its own, but, on the one hand, to win access for that communication by the *clearness and beauty of the vehicle, and on the*
12/14

The whole duty of Typography, as of Calligraphy, is to communicate to the imagination, without loss by the way, the thought or image intended to be communicated by the Author. And the whole duty of beautiful typography is not to substitute for the beauty or interest of the thing thought and intended to be conveyed by the symbol, a beauty or interest of its own, but, on the one hand, to *win access for that communication by the clear-*
12/15

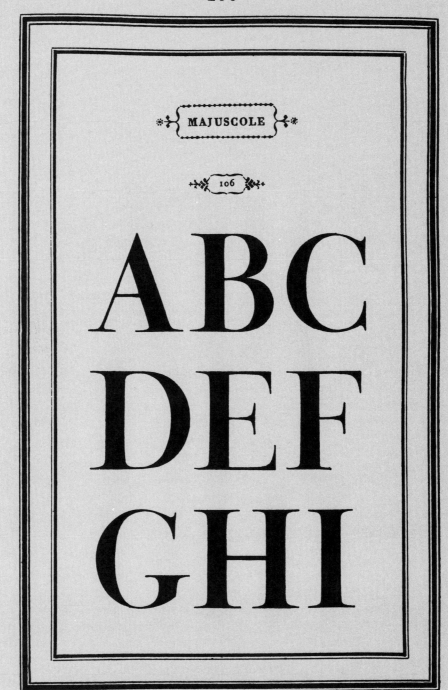

MAJUSCOLE

106

ABC
DEF
GHI

Modern **Bodoni**

Page 250 from the *Manuale Tipographico,* 1818.

The word *modern* is a relative term. Often, we use it interchangeably with the term *contemporary;* sometimes it is used to identify movements or periods in the arts representing a radical break with tradition. In typographic design, Modern identifies typefaces of the late 1700s with flat, unbracketed serifs, extreme contrast between thick-and-thin strokes, and geometric construction. The influence of writing and calligraphy was replaced by mathematical measurement and the use of mechanical instruments to construct letterforms.

After the death of type designer and printer Giambattista Bodoni, his widow and foreman published the *Manuale Tipographico,* displaying specimens of the approximately three hundred type fonts designed by Bodoni. The page reproduced here in

its actual size shows the dazzling contrasts and vigorous proportions of modern-style typography (Fig. **4**). The thick-and-thin scotch rules (See Fig. **17**, Syntax and Communication) echo and complement the thick-and-thin stroke weights.

Modern-style typefaces dominated nineteenth-century book typography and have enjoyed continued acceptance during the twentieth century. Numerous variations—from extreme hairline versions to ultrabolds; and from narrow, condensed fonts to wide, expanded forms—have been designed. Many contemporary fonts bear the names of eighteenth-century designers: Bodoni, Didot, and Walbaum.

72 Point

abcdefghijklmnopq
rstuvwxyzABCDEFG
HIJKLMNOPQRST
UVWXYZ$12345678
90(.,""''"-;:!)?&

72 Point

abcdefghijklmnopq
rstuvvwxyz ABCDE
FGHIJKLMNOPQ
RSTUVWXYZ$123
4567890(.,""''-;:!)?&

Bodoni

abcdefghijklmnopqrstuvwxyz
ABCDEFGHIJKLMNOPQRSTUVWXYZ
$1234567890 (.,""''-;:!)?&

abcdefghijklmnopqrstuvwxyz
ABCDEFGHIJKLMNOPQRSTU
VWXYZ$1234567890 (.,""''-;:!)?&

abcdefghijklmnopqrstuvwxyz
ABCDEFGHIJKLMNOPQRSTUVWXYZ
$1234567890 (.,""''-;:!)?&

abcdefghijklmnopqrstuvwxyz
ABCDEFGHIJKLMNOPQRSTUVWXYZ
$1234567890 (.,""''-;:!)?&

Bodoni Italic

abcdefghijklmnopqrstuvvwxyz
ABCDEFGHIJKLMNOPQRSTUVWXYZ
$1234567890 (.,""''-;:!)?&

abcdefghijklmnopqrstuvvwxyz
ABCDEFGHIJKLMNOPQRSTU
VWXYZ$1234567890(.,""''-;:!)?&

abcdefghijklmnopqrstuvvwxyz
ABCDEFGHIJKLMNOPQRSTUVWXYZ
$1234567890 (.,""''-;:!)?&

abcdefghijklmnopqrstuvvwxyz
ABCDEFGHIJKLMNOPQRSTUVWXYZ
$1234567890 (.,""''-;:!)?&

abcdefghijklmnopqrstuvwxyz
ABCDEFGHIJKLMNOPQRSTUVWXYZ
$1234567890(.,""-;:!)?&

abcdefghijklmnopqrstuvwxyz
ABCDEFGHIJKLMNOPQRSTUVWXYZ
$1234567890(.,""-;:!)?&

abcdefghijklmnopqrstuvwxyz
ABCDEFGHIJKLMNOPQRSTUVWXYZ
$1234567890(.,""-;:!)?&

abcdefghijklmnopqrstuvwxyz
ABCDEFGHIJKLMNOPQRSTUVWXYZ
$1234567890(.,""-;:!)?&

Bodoni

The whole duty of Typography, as of Calligraphy, is to communicate to the imagination, without loss by the way, the thought or image intended to be communicated by the Author. And the whole duty of beautiful typography is not to substitute for the beauty or interest of the thing thought and intended to be conveyed by the symbol, a beauty or interest of its own, but, on the one hand, to win access for that communication by the clearness and beauty of the vehicle, and on the other hand, to take advantage of every pause or stage in that communication to interpose some characteristic & restful beauty in its own art. We thus have a reason for the clearness and beauty of the text as a whole, for the especial beauty of the first or introductory page and of the title, and for the especial beauty of the headings of chapters, capital or initial letters, and so on, and an opening for the illustrator as we shall see by and by. Further, in the case of Poetry, verse, in my opinion, appeals by its form to the eye, as well as to the ear, and should be placed on the page so that its structure may be *taken in at a glance and distinctively appreciated, & anything*
8/9

The whole duty of Typography, as of Calligraphy, is to communicate to the imagination, without loss by the way, the thought or image intended to be communicated by the Author. And the whole duty of beautiful typography is not to substitute for the beauty or interest of the thing thought and intended to be conveyed by the symbol, a beauty or interest of its own, but, on the one hand, to win access for that communication by the clearness and beauty of the vehicle, and on the other hand, to take advantage of every pause or stage in that communication to interpose some characteristic & restful beauty in its own art. We thus have a reason for the clearness and beauty of the text as a whole, for the especial beauty of the first or introductory page and of the title, and for the especial beauty of the headings of chapters, capital or initial letters, and so on, and an opening for the *illustrator as we shall see by and by. Further, in the case of Poetry,*
8/10

The whole duty of Typography, as of Calligraphy, is to communicate to the imagination, without loss by the way, the thought or image intended to be communicated by the Author. And the whole duty of beautiful typography is not to substitute for the beauty or interest of the thing thought and intended to be conveyed by the symbol, a beauty or interest of its own, but, on the one hand, to win access for that communication by the clearness and beauty of the vehicle, and on the other hand, to take advantage of every pause or stage in that communication to interpose some characteristic & restful beauty in its own art. We thus have a reason for the clearness and beauty of the text as a whole, for the especial beauty of the first or introductory page and of the title, and for the especial beauty of the headings of chapters, capital or initial letters, and so on, and an opening for the illustrator as we shall see by and by. Further, in the case of Poetry, *ear, and should be placed on the page so that its structure may be*
8/11

The whole duty of Typography, as of Calligraphy, is to communicate to the imagination, without loss by the way, the thought or image intended to be communicated by the Author. And the whole duty of beautiful typography is not to substitute for the beauty or interest of the thing thought and intended to be conveyed by the symbol, a beauty or interest of its own, but, on the one hand, to win access for that communication by the clearness and beauty of the vehicle, and on the other hand, to take advantage of every pause or stage in that communication to interpose some characteristic & restful beauty in its own art. We thus have a reason for the clearness and beauty of the text as a whole, for the especial beauty of the first or introductory page and of the title, and for the especial beauty of the headings of chapters, capital or initial letters, and so on, and an opening *case of Poetry, verse, in my opinion, appeals by its form to the*
9/10

The whole duty of Typography, as of Calligraphy, is to communicate to the imagination, without loss by the way, the thought or image intended to be communicated by the Author. And the whole duty of beautiful typography is not to substitute for the beauty or interest of the thing thought and intended to be conveyed by the symbol, a beauty or interest of its own, but, on the one hand, to win access for that communication by the clearness and beauty of the vehicle, and on the other hand, to take advantage of every pause or stage in that communication to interpose some characteristic & restful beauty in its own art. We thus have a reason for the clearness and beauty of the text as a whole, for the especial beauty of the first or introductory page and of the title, and for the especial beauty of the headings *of chapters, capital or initial letters, and so on, and an opening*
9/11

The whole duty of Typography, as of Calligraphy, is to communicate to the imagination, without loss by the way, the thought or image intended to be communicated by the Author. And the whole duty of beautiful typography is not to substitute for the beauty or interest of the thing thought and intended to be conveyed by the symbol, a beauty or interest of its own, but, on the one hand, to win access for that communication by the clearness and beauty of the vehicle, and on the other hand, to take advantage of every pause or stage in that communication to interpose some characteristic & restful beauty in its own art. We thus have a reason for the clearness and beauty of the text as a whole, for the especial beauty of the first or introductory *for the illustrator as we shall see by and by. Further, in the*
9/12

abcdefghijklmnopqrstuvwxyz
ABCDEFGHIJKLMNOPQRSTUVWXYZ
$1234567890(.,"‘-;:!)?&

abcdefghijklmnopqrstuvwxyz
ABCDEFGHIJKLMNOPQRSTUVWXYZ
$1234567890(.,"‘-;:!)?&

abcdefghijklmnopqrstuvwxyz
ABCDEFGHIJKLMNOPQRSTUVWXYZ
$1234567890(.,"‘-;:!)?&

abcdefghijklmnopqrstuvwxyz
ABCDEFGHIJKLMNOPQRSTUVWXYZ
$1234567890(.,"‘-;:!)?&

The whole duty of Typography, as of Calligraphy, is to communicate to the imagination, without loss by the way, the thought or image intended to be communicated by the Author. And the whole duty of beautiful typography is not to substitute for the beauty or interest of the thing thought and intended to be conveyed by the symbol, a beauty or interest of its own, but, on the one hand, to win access for that communication by the clearness and beauty of the vehicle, and on the other hand, to take advantage of every pause or stage in that communication to interpose some characteristic & restful beauty in its own art. We thus have a reason for the clearness and beauty of the text as a whole, for the especial beauty of the first *or introductory page and of the title, and for the especial*

10/11

The whole duty of Typography, as of Calligraphy, is to communicate to the imagination, without loss by the way, the thought or image intended to be communicated by the Author. And the whole duty of beautiful typography is not to substitute for the beauty or interest of the thing thought and intended to be conveyed by the symbol, a beauty or interest of its own, but, on the one hand, to win access for that communication by the clearness and beauty of the vehicle, and on the other hand, to take advantage of every pause or stage in that communication to interpose some characteristic & restful beauty in its own art. We thus have a reason for the clearness and beauty of *the text as a whole, for the especial beauty of the first*

10/12

The whole duty of Typography, as of Calligraphy, is to communicate to the imagination, without loss by the way, the thought or image intended to be communicated by the Author. And the whole duty of beautiful typography is not to substitute for the beauty or interest of the thing thought and intended to be conveyed by the symbol, a beauty or interest of its own, but, on the one hand, to win access for that communication by the clearness and beauty of the vehicle, and on the other hand, to take advantage of every pause or stage in that communication to interpose some characteristic & restful beauty in its own art. *We thus have a reason for the clearness and beauty of*

10/13

The whole duty of Typography, as of Calligraphy, is to communicate to the imagination, without loss by the way, the thought or image intended to be communicated by the Author. And the whole duty of beautiful typography is not to substitute for the beauty or interest of the thing thought and intended to be conveyed by the symbol, a beauty or interest of its own, but, on the one hand, to win access for that communication by the clearness and beauty of the vehicle, and on the other hand, to take ad-*vantage of every pause or stage in that com-*

12/13

The whole duty of Typography, as of Calligraphy, is to communicate to the imagination, without loss by the way, the thought or image intended to be communicated by the Author. And the whole duty of beautiful typography is not to substitute for the beauty or interest of the thing thought and intended to be conveyed by the symbol, a beauty or interest of its own, but, on the one hand, to win access for that communication by the clearness and beauty of *the vehicle, and on the other hand, to take ad-*

12/14

The whole duty of Typography, as of Calligraphy, is to communicate to the imagination, without loss by the way, the thought or image intended to be communicated by the Author. And the whole duty of beautiful typography is not to substitute for the beauty or interest of the thing thought and intended to be conveyed by the symbol, a beauty or interest of its own, but, on the one hand, to win access for that *communication by the clearness and beauty of*

12/15

NEW LINE BETWEEN
ALBANY & NEWBURG

LANDING AT

Hamburgh, Marlborough, Milton, Poughkeepsie, Hyde Park, Kingston, Rhinebeck, Barrytown, Redhook, Bristol, Westcamp Catskill, Hudson, Coxsackie, Stuyvesant, Baltimore & Coeymans.

On and after *MONDAY*, October 15th,

The Superior Low Pressure Steame

ST. NICHOLAS

CAPTAIN WILSON,

Will run as a Passage and Freight Boat between Newburgh and Albany, leaving Newburgh

MONDAYS, WEDNESDAYS & FRIDAYS

AT SEVEN O'CLOCK A.M.,

And ALBANY on Tuesdays, Thursdays & Saturdays, at half-past 9 o'clock A.M.

Albany, Oct. 9th, 1849.

Egyptian

ITC Lubalin Graph

5.
Broadsheet, 1849. This slab-serif display type has been lightly inked, and the textured grain of the wooden type is clearly visible, as in the words St. Nicolas.

Egyptian or slab-serif typefaces first appeared in the early nineteenth century and enjoyed great popularity. Their bold, machinelike qualities offered a dynamic expression of the industrial age. During the Industrial Revolution, letterpress printers delighted in using bold slab-serif display fonts to give their messages graphic impact (Fig. **5**). Rectangular serifs, uniform or almost unform stroke weight, and geometric letterform construction give Egyptian typefaces a bold, abstract design quality. Egyptian styles whose abrupt right-angle joinery is tempered by curved bracketing include the Clarendon, Century, and Cheltenham type families.

ITC Lubalin Graph is a contemporary Egyptian typeface designed by Herb Lubalin. It is available in five weights: light, book, demi, medium, and bold. Typographic historians have speculated that the first sans serif typefaces may have been created by removing the serifs from slab-serif designs. ITC Lubalin Graph was designed by adding serifs to the geometric sans-serif type family Avant Garde Gothic.

abcdefghijkl
mnopqrstuvwx
yzABCDEFGHI
JKLMNOPQRST
UVWXYZ$123
4567890(,'""-;:!)?&

(., '""-,:!)?&

abcdefghijkl
mnopqrstuv
wxyzABCDEF
GHIJKLMNOP
QRSTUVWX
YZ$123456789

48 Point

abcdeefghijklmnopq
rstuvwxyzABCDEFGHI
JKLMNOPQRSTUVW
XYZ$1234567890(.,'""-;:!)?&

30 Point

abcdeefghijklmnopqrstuvwxyz
ABCDEFGHIJKLMNOPQRSTUVWXYZ
$1234567890(.,'""-;:!)?&

18 Point

abcdeefghijklmnopqrstuvwxyz
ABCDEFGHIJKLMNOPQRSTUVWXYZ
$1234567890(.,'""-;:!)?&

---
48 Point

abcdefghijklmnop
qrstuvwxyzABCDEF
GHIJKLMNOPQRST
UVWXYZ$1234567890

---
30 Point

abcdefghijklmnopqrstuvwxyz
ABCDEFGHIJKLMNOPQRSTUVW
XYZ$1234567890(.,""''-;:!)?&

---
18 Point

abcdefghijklmnopqrstuvwxyz
ABCDEFGHIJKLMNOPQRSTUVWXYZ
$1234567890(.,""''-;:!)?&

abcdefghijklmnopqrstuvwxyz
ABCDEFGHIJKLMNOPQRSTUVWXYZ
$1234567890(.,'"-;:!)?&

abcdefghijklmnopqrstuvwxyz
ABCDEFGHIJKLMNOPQRSTUVWXYZ
$1234567890(.,'"-;:!)?&

abcdefghijklmnopqrstuvwxyz
ABCDEFGHIJKLMNOPQRSTUVWXYZ
$1234567890(.,'"-;:!)?&

abcdefghijklmnopqrstuvwxyz
ABCDEFGHIJKLMNOPQRSTUVWXYZ
$1234567890(.,'"-;:!)?&

ITC Lubalin Graph
Book

The whole duty of Typography, as of Calligraphy, is to communicate to the imagination, without loss by the way, the thought or image intended to be communicated by the Author. And the whole duty of beautiful typography is not to substitute for the beauty or interest of the thing thought and intended to be conveyed by the symbol, a beauty or interest of its own, but, on the one hand, to win access for that communication by the clearness and beauty of the vehicle, and on the other hand, to take advantage of every pause or stage in that communication to interpose some characteristic & restful beauty in its own art. We thus have a reason for the clearness and beauty of the text as a whole, for the especial beauty of the first or introductory page and of the title, and for the especial beauty *of the headings of chapters, capital or initial let-*
8/9

The whole duty of Typography, as of Calligraphy, is to communicate to the imagination, without loss by the way, the thought or image intended to be communicated by the Author. And the whole duty of beautiful typography is not to substitute for the beauty or interest of the thing thought and intended to be conveyed by the symbol, a beauty or interest of its own, but, on the one hand, to win access for that communication by the clearness and beauty of the vehicle, and on the other hand, to take advantage of every pause or stage in that communication to interpose some characteristic & restful beauty in its own art. We thus have a reason for the clearness and beauty of the text as a whole, *page and of the title, and for the especial beauty*
8/10

The whole duty of Typography, as of Calligraphy, is to communicate to the imagination, without loss by the way, the thought or image intended to be communicated by the Author. And the whole duty of beautiful typography is not to substitute for the beauty or interest of the thing thought and intended to be conveyed by the symbol, a beauty or interest of its own, but, on the one hand, to win access for that communication by the clearness and beauty of the vehicle, and on the other hand, to take advantage of every pause or stage in that communication to interpose some characteristic & restful beauty in its own art. We thus have a reason *for the especial beauty of the first or introductory*
8/11

The whole duty of Typography, as of Calligraphy, is to communicate to the imagination, without loss by the way, the thought or image intended to be communicated by the Author. And the whole duty of beautiful typography is not to substitute for the beauty or interest of the thing thought and intended to be conveyed by the symbol, a beauty or interest of its own, but, on the one hand, to win access for that communication by the clearness and beauty of the vehicle, and on the other hand, to take advantage of every pause or stage in that communication to interpose some characteristic & restful beauty in its own art. We *beauty of the text as a whole, for the especial*
9/10

The whole duty of Typography, as of Calligraphy, is to communicate to the imagination, without loss by the way, the thought or image intended to be communicated by the Author. And the whole duty of beautiful typography is not to substitute for the beauty or interest of the thing thought and intended to be conveyed by the symbol, a beauty or interest of its own, but, on the one hand, to win access for that communication by the clearness and beauty of the vehicle, and on the other hand, to take advantage of every pause or stage in that communication to interpose some char*acteristic & restful beauty in its own art. We*
9/11

The whole duty of Typography, as of Calligraphy, is to communicate to the imagination, without loss by the way, the thought or image intended to be communicated by the Author. And the whole duty of beautiful typography is not to substitute for the beauty or interest of the thing thought and intended to be conveyed by the symbol, a beauty or interest of its own, but, on the one hand, to win access for that communication by the clearness and beauty of the vehicle, and on the other hand, to take advantage of every pause or stage in *that communication to interpose some char-*
9/12

abcdefghijklmnopqrstuvwxyz
ABCDEFGHIJKLMNOPQRSTUVWXYZ
$1234567890(.,'"-;:!)?&

abcdefghijklmnopqrstuvwxyz
ABCDEFGHIJKLMNOPQRSTUVWXYZ
$1234567890(.,'"-;:!)?&

abcdefghijklmnopqrstuvwxyz
ABCDEFGHIJKLMNOPQRSTUVWXYZ
$1234567890(.,'"-;:!)?&

abcdefghijklmnopqrstuvwxyz
ABCDEFGHIJKLMNOPQRSTUVWXYZ
$1234567890(.,'"-;:!)?&

The whole duty of Typography, as of Calligraphy, is to communicate to the imagination, without loss by the way, the thought or image intended to be communicated by the Author. And the whole duty of beautiful typography is not to substitute for the beauty or interest of the thing thought and intended to be conveyed by the symbol, a beauty or interest of its own, but, on the one hand, to win access for that communication by the clearness and beauty of the vehicle, and on the other hand, to take advantage of *every pause or stage in that communica-*

10/11

The whole duty of Typography, as of Calligraphy, is to communicate to the imagination, without loss by the way, the thought or image intended to be communicated by the Author. And the whole duty of beautiful typography is not to substitute for the beauty or interest of the thing thought and intended to be conveyed by the symbol, a beauty or interest of its own, but, on the one hand, to win access for that communication by the clearness and beauty of the vehicle, and *on the other hand, to take advantage of*

10/12

The whole duty of Typography, as of Calligraphy, is to communicate to the imagination, without loss by the way, the thought or image intended to be communicated by the Author. And the whole duty of beautiful typography is not to substitute for the beauty or interest of the thing thought and intended to be conveyed by the symbol, a beauty or interest of its own, but, on the one hand, to win access for that communication by the *clearness and beauty of the vehicle, and*

10/13

The whole duty of Typography, as of Calligraphy, is to communicate to the imagination, without loss by the way, the thought or image intended to be communicated by the Author. And the whole duty of beautiful typography is not to substitute for the beauty or interest of the thing thought and intended to be conveyed by the symbol, a beauty or interest of its own, but, *on the one hand, to win access for*

12/13

The whole duty of Typography, as of Calligraphy, is to communicate to the imagination, without loss by the way, the thought or image intended to be communicated by the Author. And the whole duty of beautiful typography is not to substitute for the beauty or interest of the thing thought and intended to be conveyed by the symbol, a *beauty or interest of its own, but,*

12/14

The whole duty of Typography, as of Calligraphy, is to communicate to the imagination, without loss by the way, the thought or image intended to be communicated by the Author. And the whole duty of beautiful typography is not to substitute for the beauty or interest of the thing thought and intended to *be conveyed by the symbol, a*

12/15

Avant Garde X-light

abcdefghijklmnopqrstuvwxyz
ABCDEFGHIJKLMNOPQRSTUVWXYZ
$1234567890(.,'""–‚;,;!)?&

Avant Garde Book

abcdefghijklmnopqrstuvwxyz
ABCDEFGHIJKLMNOPQRSTUVWXYZ
$1234567890(.,'""–,;,!)?&

Avant Garde Medium

abcdefghijklmnopqrstuvwxyz
ABCDEFGHIJKLMNOPQRSTUVWXYZ
$1234567890(.,""""-;,;!)?&

Avant Garde Bold

abcdefghijklmnopqrstuvwxyz
ABCDEFGHIJKLMNOPQRSTUVWX
YZ$1234567890O(.,'""''-;,;!)?&

Bembo

abcdefghijklmnopqrstuvwxyz
ABCDEFGHIJKLMNOPQRSTUVWX
YZ$1234567890(.,'""''–;:!)?&

Bembo Italic

abcdefghijklmnopqrstuvwxyz
ABCDEFGHIJKLMNOPQRSTUVWX
YZ$1234567890(.,'""-;:!)?&

Bembo Bold

abcdefghijklmnopqrstuvwxyz
ABCDEFGHIJKLMNOPQRSTU
VWXYZ$1234567890(.,'""-;:!)?&

Benguiat Book

abcdefghijklmnopqrstuvwxyz
ABCDEFGHIJKLMNOPQRSTUVWX
YZ$1234567890(.,'""-;:!)?&

Benguiat Italic

abcdefghijklmnopqrstuvwxyz
ABCDEFGHIJKLMMNOPQRSTUVW
XYZ$1234567890(.,'""-;:!)?&

Benguiat Bold

abcdefghijklmnopqrstuvwxyz
ABCDEFGHIJKLMMNOPQRSTU
VWXYZ$1234567890(.,'""-;:!)?&

abcdefghijklmnopqrstuvwxyz
ABCDEFGHIJKLMNOPQRSTUV
WXYZ$1234567890(.,'"\"\"-;:!)?&

abcdefghijklmnopqrstuvwxyz
ABCDEFGHIJKLMNOPQRSTUVW
XYZ $1234567890(.,""""-;:!)?&

abcdefghijklmnopqrstuvwxyz
ABCDEFGHIJKLMNOPQRSTUV
WXYZ$1234567890(.,'"""-;:!)?&

abcdefghijklmnopqrstuvwxyz
ABCDEFGHIJKLMNOPQRSTUVWXYZ
$1234567890(.,""""-;:!)?&

abcdefghijklmnopqrstuvwxyz
ABCDEFGHIJKLMNOPQRSTUVWXYZ
$1234567890(.,""""-;:!)?&

abcdefghijklmnopqrstuvwxyz
ABCDEFGHIJKLMNOPQRSTUV
WXYZ$1234567890 .,""""-;:!?&

abcdefghijklmnopqrstuvwxyz
ABCDEFGHIJKLMNOPQRSTUV
WXYZ$1234567890(.,""""-;:!)?&

abcdefghijklmnopqrstuvwxyz
ABCDEFGHIJKLMNOPQRSTUVWX
YZ$1234567890(.,""""-;:!)?&

abcdefghijklmnopqrstuvwxyz
ABCDEFGHIJKLMNOPQRSTUVWX
YZ$1234567890(.,""""-;:!)?&

abcdefghijklmnopqrstuvwxyz
ABCDEFGHIJKLMNOPQRSTUVWX
YZ$1234567890(.,""""-;:!)?&

abcdefghijklmnopqrstuvwxyz
ABCDEFGHIJKLMNOPQRSTUVWXYZ
$1234567890(.,""""-;:!)?&

abcdefghijklmnopqrstuvwxyz
ABCDEFGHIJKLMNOPQRSTUVWXYZ
$1234567890(.,""""-;:!)?&

abcdefghijklmnopqrstuvwxyz
ABCDEFGHIJKLMNOPQRSTUVW
XYZ$1234567890(.,""""-;:!)?&

abcdefghijklmnopqrstuvwxyz
ABCDEFGHIJKLMNOPQRSTUV
WXYZ$1234567890(.,""""-;:!)?&

abcdefghijklmnopqrstuvwxyz
ABCDEFGHIJKLMNOPQRSTUVWXYZ
$1234567890 (.,""""-;:!)?&

abcdefghijklmnopqrstuvwxyz
ABCDEFGHIJKLMNOPQRSTUVWX
YZ$1234567890(.,""''-;:!)?&

abcdefghijklmnopqrstuvwxyz
ABCDEFGHIJKLMNOPQRSTUVWXYZ
$1234567890(.,""''-;:!)?&

abcdefghijklmnopqrstuvwxyz
ABCDEFGHIJKLMNOPQRSTUVWXYZ
$1234567890(.,''''''-;:!)?&

abcdefghijklmnopqrstuvwxyz
ABCDEFGHIJKLMNOPQRSTUVWXYZ
$1234567890(.,""''-;:!)?&

abcdefghijklmnopqrstuvwxyz
ABCDEFGHIJKLMNOPQRSTUVWXYZ
$1234567890(.,'""''-;:!)?&

Gill Sans Medium

abcdefghijklmnopqrstuvwxyz
ABCDEFGHIJKLMNOPQRSTUVWXYZ
$1234567890(.,'""-;:!)?&

Goudy Old Style

abcdefghijklmnopqrstuvwxyz
ABCDEFGHIJKLMNOPQRSTUVWX
YZ$1234567890(.,'""-;:!)?&

Goudy Bold

abcdefghijklmnopqrstuvwxyz
ABCDEFGHIJKLMNOPQRSTUVWX
YZ$1234567890(.,'""-;:!)?&

Helvetica Light

abcdefghijklmnopqrstuvwxyz
ABCDEFGHIJKLMNOPQRSTUVWXYZ
$1234567890(.,'""-;:!)?&

Helvetica

abcdefghijklmnopqrstuvwxyz
ABCDEFGHIJKLMNOPQRSTUVWX
YZ$1234567890(.,'""-;:!)?&

Helvetica Medium

abcdefghijklmnopqrstuvwxyz
ABCDEFGHIJKLMNOPQRSTUVW
XYZ$1234567890(.,'"""-;:!)?&

Helvetica Bold

abcdefghijklmnopqrstuvwxyz
ABCDEFGHIJKLMNOPQRSTUV
WXYZ$1234567890(.,'"""-;:!)?&

Helvetica Extra Bold Condensed

abcdefghijklmnopqrstuvwxyz
ABCDEFGHIJKLMNOPQRSTUVWXYZ
$1234567890(.,'"""-;:!)?&

Kabel Medium

abcdefghijklmnopqrstuvwxyz
ABCDEFGHIJKLMNOPQRSTUVWXYZ
$1234567890(.,'"""-;:!)?&

Kabel Bold

abcdefghijklmnopqrstuvwxyz
ABCDEFGHIJKLMNOPQRSTUVWXYZ
$1234567890(.,'"""-;:!)?&

abcdefghijklmnopqrstuvwxyz
ABCDEFGHIJKLMNOPQRSTUVWX
YZ$1234567890(.,'""!-;:!)?&

abcdefghijklmnopqrstuvwxyz
ABCDEFGHIJKLMNOPQRSTUVWXYZ
$1234567890(.,'""-;:!)?&

**abcdefghijklmnopqrstuvwxyz
ABCDEFGHIJKLMNOPQRSTUVWXYZ
$1234567890(.,'""-;:!)?&**

abcdefghijklmnopqrstuvwxyz
ABCDEFGHIJKLMNOPQRSTUVW
XYZ$1234567890(.,'""-:;!)?&

*abcdefghijklmnopqrstuvwxyz
ABCDEFGHIJKLMNOPQRSTUVWXYZ
$1234567890(.,'`'"-;:!)?&*

abcdefghijklmnopqrstuvwxyz
ABCDEFGHIJKLMNOPQRSTUVWX
YZ$1234567890(.,""''-;:!)?&

abcdefghijklmnopqrstuvwxyz
ABCDEFGHIJKLMNOPQRSTUVWX
YZ$1234567890(.,"'-;:!)?&

abcdefghijklmnopqrstuvwxyz
ABCDEFGHIJKLMNOPQRSTUVWX
YZ$1234567890(.,""-;:!)?&

abcdefghijklmnopqrstuvwxyz
ABCDEFGHIJKLMNOPQRSTUVW
XYZ$1234567890(.,""''-;:!)?&

abcdefghijklmnopqrstuvwxyz
ABCDEFGHIJKLMNOPQRSTUVWXYZ
$1234567890(.,'""''-;:!)?&

The text settings shown are presented for comparative analysis of typeface texture, tone, and legibility. They can be photostated or photocopied for use in layouts. Different column structures with varying line length, paragraph indications, and justification are shown. These factors influence the visual appearance and readability of the specimens.

Of all the achievements of the human mind, the birth of the alphabet is the most momentous. "Letters, like men, have now an ancestry, and the ancestry of words, as of men, is often a very noble possession, making them capable of great things": indeed, it has been said that the invention of writing is more important than all the victories ever won or constitutions devised by man. The history of writing is, in a way, the history of the human race, since in it are bound up, severally and together, the development of thought, of expression, of art, of intercommunication, and of mechanical invention.

When and to whom in the dim past the idea came that man's speech could be better represented by fewer symbols (to denote certain unvarying sounds) selected from the confused mass of picture ideographs, phonograms, and their like, which constituted the first methods of representing human speech, we have no certain means of knowing. But whatever the source, the development did come; and we must deal with it. To present briefly the early history of the alphabet requires that much collateral matter must be disregarded and a great deal that is omitted here must necessarily be taken for granted; the writer desires, however, to present what seems to him to be a logical and probable story of the alphabet's beginnings.

Although it has not yet been proved conclusively, it is quite possible, and altogether probable, that the traders of Phoenicia and the Aegean adopted both the use of papyrus and Egyptian hieratic writing, from which developed the Phoenician alphabet. Whether all the earliest writing systems of different countries sprang from one common stock of picture writing, we shall, perhaps, never surely know; we do know that the picture writing of Egypt exercised a very great influence, and it seems quite safe for us to assume that crude attempts by those ancient Nile-dwellers to express thought visible or to record facts by a series of pictures – or by diagrams sufficiently pictorial, at least, to connect them with well-known objects (disregarding the earlier mnemonic stage or use of memory aids like the quipu or knotted cord, of which the rosary is a modern example) – constitute the origin of the abstract and arbitrary signs or symbols which we call "letters."

Let us assume, as logically we may, that picture writing in which a drawing depicting or suggesting the object itself came first; next must have come the ideograph, the sign suggesting the name of the object represented instead of representing the thing itself; & next the phonogram, or sign that suggests a sound only.

In the first class just named belong the wedge-

10/12 ITC Garamond Book

Of all the achievements of the human mind, the birth of the alphabet is the most momentous. "Letters, like men, have now an ancestry, and the ancestry of words, as of men, is often a very noble possession, making them capable of great things": indeed, it has been said that the invention of writing is more important than all the victories ever won or constitutions devised by man. The history of writing is, in a way, the history of the human race, since in it are bound up, severally and together, the development of thought, of expression, of art, of intercommunication, and of mechanical invention.

When and to whom in the dim past the idea came that man's speech could be better represented by fewer symbols (to denote certain unvarying sounds) selected from the confused mass of picture ideographs, phonograms, and their like, which constituted the first methods of representing human speech, we have no certain means of knowing. But whatever the source, the development did come; and we must deal with it. To present briefly the early history of the alphabet requires that much collateral matter must be disregarded and a great deal that is omitted here must necessarily be taken for granted; the writer desires, however, to present what seems to him to be a logical and probable story of the alphabet's beginnings.

Although it has not yet been proved conclusively, it is quite possible, and altogether probable, that the traders of Phoenicia and the Aegean adopted both the use of papyrus and Egyptian hieratic writing, from which developed the Phoenician alphabet. Whether all the earliest writing systems of different countries sprang from one common stock of picture writing, we shall, perhaps, never surely know; we do know that the picture writing of Egypt exercised a very great influence, and it seems quite safe for us to assume that crude attempts by those ancient Nile-dwellers to express thought visible or to record facts by a series of pictures — or by diagrams sufficiently pictorial, at least, to connect them with well-known objects (disregarding the earlier mnemonic stage or use of memory aids like the quipu or knotted cord, of which the rosary is a modern example) — constitute the origin of the abstract and arbitrary signs or symbols which we call "letters."

Let us assume, as logically we may, that picture writing in which a drawing depicting or suggesting the object itself came first; next must have come the ideograph, the sign suggesting the name of the object represented instead of representing the thing itself; & next the phonogram, or sign that suggests a sound only.

In the first class just named belong the wedge-shaped, or cuneiform, characters inscribed in the clay tablets, cylinders, and monuments of Assyria, Babylonia, &

10/12 Futura Medium

Of all the achievements of the human mind, the birth of the alphabet is the most momentous. "Letters, like men, have now an ancestry, and the ancestry of words, as of men, is often a very noble possession, making them capable of great things": indeed, it has been said that the invention of writing is more important than all the victories ever won or constitutions devised by man. The history of writing is, in a way, the history of the human race, since in it are bound up, severally and together, the development of thought, of expression, of art, of intercommunication, and of mechanical invention.

When and to whom in the dim past the idea came that man's speech could be better represented by fewer symbols (to denote certain unvarying sounds) selected from the confused mass of picture ideographs, phonograms, and their like, which constituted the first methods of representing human speech, we have no certain means of knowing. But whatever the source, the development did come; and we must deal with it. To present briefly the early history of the alphabet requires that much collateral matter must be disregarded and a great deal that is omitted here must necessarily be taken for granted; the writer desires, however, to present what seems to him to be a logical and probable story of the alphabet's beginnings.

Although it has not yet been proved conclusively, it is quite possible, and altogether probable, that the traders of Phoenicia and the Aegean adopted both the use of papyrus and Egyptian hieratic writing, from which developed the Phoenician alphabet. Whether all the earliest writing systems of different countries sprang from one common stock of picture writing, we shall, perhaps, never surely know; we do know that the picture writing of Egypt exercised a very great influence, and it seems quite safe for us to assume that crude attempts by those ancient Nile-dwellers to express thought visible or to record facts by a series of pictures—or by diagrams sufficiently pictorial, at least, to connect them with well-known objects (disregarding the earlier mnemonic stage or use of memory aids like the quipu or knotted cord, of which the rosary is a modern example)—constitute the origin of the abstract and arbitrary signs or symbols which we call "letters."

Let us assume, as logically we may, that picture writing in which a drawing depicting or suggesting the object itself came first; next must have come the ideograph, the sign suggesting the name of the object represented instead of representing the thing itself; & next the phonogram, or sign that suggests a sound only.

In the first class just named belong the wedge-shaped, or cuneiform, characters inscribed in the clay tablets, cylinders, and monuments of Assyria, Babylonia, & other Near Eastern countries—characters the very existence of which was overlooked or forgotten for some sixteen hundred years. They were almost purely pictorial—were drawings only, really not writing at all, and, as far as we now know, have little direct bearing on the derivation of our present alphabet.

To this first class also belong the hieroglyphs of Egypt, highly elaborated types of picture writing which changed so little over a long period that "it is like a language which has never forgotten the derivation of its words, or corrupted their etymological forms, however much it may have altered its meaning." Developed at least five thousand years B.C., the purely pictorial character was preserved by its Egyptian users until the end. Sir Edw. Maunde Thompson asserts that "we may without exaggeration...carry back the invention of Egyptian writing to six or seven thousand years B.C." Most of the material available goes back not farther than the First Dynasty (3300 B.C.).

Possibly the earliest method of recording the payment of taxes indicates, too, the earliest stage in the process of learning to write. The

Of all the achievements of the human mind, the birth of the alphabet is the most momentous. "Letters, like men, have now an ancestry, and the ancestry of words, as of men, is often a very noble possession, making them capable of great things": indeed, it has been said that the invention of writing is more important than all the victories ever won or constitutions devised by man. The history of writing is, in a way, the history of the human race, since in it are bound up, severally and together, the development of thought, of expression, of art, of intercommunication, and of mechanical invention.

When and to whom in the dim past the idea came that man's speech could be better represented by fewer symbols (to denote certain unvarying sounds) selected from the confused mass of picture ideographs, phonograms, and their like, which constituted the first methods of representing human speech, we have no certain means of knowing. But whatever the source, the development did come; and we must deal with it. To present briefly the early history of the alphabet requires that much collateral matter must be disregarded and a great deal that is omitted here must necessarily be taken for granted; the writer desires, however, to present what seems to him to be a logical and probable story of the alphabet's beginnings.

Although it has not yet been proved conclusively, it is quite possible, and altogether probable, that the traders of Phoenicia and the Aegean adopted both the use of papyrus and Egyptian hieratic writing, from which developed the Phoenician alphabet. Whether all the earliest writing systems of different countries sprang from one common stock of picture writing, we shall, perhaps, never surely know; we do know that the picture writing of Egypt exercised a very great influence, and it seems quite safe for us to assume that crude attempts by those ancient Nile-dwellers to express thought visible or to record facts by a series of pictures – or by diagrams sufficiently pictorial, at least, to connect them with well-known objects (disregarding the earlier mnemonic stage or use of memory aids like the quipu or knotted cord, of which the rosary is a modern example) – constitute the origin of the abstract and arbitrary signs or symbols which we call "letters."

Let us assume, as logically we may, that picture writing in which a drawing depict-

Of all the achievements of the human mind, the birth of the alphabet is the most momentous. "Letters, like men, have now an ancestry, and the ancestry of words, as of men, is often a very noble possession, making them capable of great things": indeed, it has been said that the invention of writing is more important than all the victories ever won or constitutions devised by man. The history of writing is, in a way, the history of the human race, since in it are bound up, severally and together, the development of thought, of expression, of art, of intercommunication, and of mechanical invention.

When and to whom in the dim past the idea came that man's speech could be better represented by fewer symbols (to denote certain unvarying sounds) selected from the confused mass of picture ideographs, phonograms, and their like, which constituted the first methods of representing human speech, we have no certain means of knowing. But whatever the source, the development did come; and we must deal with it. To present briefly the early history of the alphabet requires that much collateral matter must be disregarded and a great deal that is omitted here must necessarily be taken for granted; the writer desires, however, to present what seems to him to be a logical and probable story of the alphabet's beginnings.

Although it has not yet been proved conclusively, it is quite possible, and altogether probable, that the traders of Phoenicia and the Aegean adopted both the use of papyrus and Egyptian hieratic writing, from which developed the Phoenician alphabet. Whether all the earliest writing systems of different countries sprang from one common stock of picture writing, we shall, perhaps, never surely know; we do know that the picture writing of Egypt exercised a very great influence, and it seems quite safe for us to assume that crude attempts by those ancient Nile-dwellers to express thought visible or to record facts by a series of pictures—or by diagrams sufficiently pictorial, at least, to connect them with well-known objects (disregarding the earlier mnemonic stage or use of memory aids like the quipu or knotted cord, of which the rosary is a modern example)—constitute the origin of the abstract and arbitrary signs or symbols which we call "letters."

Let us assume, as logically we may, that picture writing in which a drawing depicting or suggesting the object itself came first; next must have come the ideograph, the sign suggesting the name of the object represented instead of representing the thing itself; & next the phonogram, or

Of all the achievements of the human mind, the birth of the alphabet is the most momentous. "Letters, like men, have now an ancestry, and the ancestry of words, as of men, is often a very noble possession, making them capable of great things": indeed, it has been said that the invention of writing is more important than all the victories ever won or constitutions devised by man. The history of writing is, in a way, the history of the human race, since in it are bound up, severally and together, the development of thought, of expression, of art, of intercommunication, and of mechanical invention.

When and to whom in the dim past the idea came that man's speech could be better represented by fewer symbols (to denote certain unvarying sounds) selected from the confused mass of picture ideographs, phonograms, and their like, which constituted the first methods of representing human speech, we have no certain means of knowing. But whatever the source, the development did come; and we must deal with it. To present briefly the early history of the alphabet requires that much collateral matter must be disregarded and a great deal that is omitted here must necessarily be taken for granted; the writer desires, however, to present what seems to him to be a logical and probable story of the alphabet's beginnings.

Although it has not yet been proved conclusively, it is quite possible, and altogether probable, that the traders of Phoenicia and the Aegean adopted both the use of papyrus and Egyptian hieratic writing, from which developed the Phoenician alphabet. Whether all the earliest writing systems of different countries sprang from one common stock of picture writing, we shall, perhaps, never surely know; we do know that the picture writing of Egypt exercised a very great influence, and it seems quite safe for us to assume that crude attempts by those ancient Nile-dwellers to express thought visible or to record facts by a series of pictures — or by diagrams sufficiently pictorial, at least, to connect them with well-known objects (disregarding the earlier mnemonic stage or use of memory aids like the quipu or knotted cord,

Of all the achievements of the human mind, the birth of the alphabet is the most momentous. "Letters, like men, have now an ancestry, and the ancestry of words, as of men, is often a very noble possession, making them capable of great things": indeed, it has been said that the invention of writing is more important than all the victories ever won or constitutions devised by man. The history of writing is, in a way, the history of the human race, since in it are bound up, severally and together, the development of thought, of expression, of art, of intercommunication, and of mechanical invention.

When and to whom in the dim past the idea came that man's speech could be better represented by fewer symbols (to denote certain unvarying sounds) selected from the confused mass of picture ideographs, phonograms, and their like, which constituted the first methods of representing human speech, we have no certain means of knowing. But whatever the source, the development did come; and we must deal with it. To present briefly the early history of the alphabet requires that much collateral matter must be disregarded and a great deal that is omitted here must necessarily be taken for granted; the writer desires, however, to present what seems to him to be a logical and probable story of the alphabet's beginnings.

Although it has not yet been proved conclusively, it is quite possible, and altogether probable, that the traders of Phoenicia and the Aegean adopted both the use of papyrus and Egyptian hieratic writing, from which developed the Phoenician alphabet. Whether all the earliest writing systems of different countries sprang from one common stock of picture writing, we shall, perhaps, never surely know; we do know that the picture writing of Egypt exercised a very great influence, and it seems quite safe for us to assume that crude attempts by those ancient Nile-dwellers to express thought visible or to record facts by a series of pictures — or by diagrams sufficiently pictorial, at least, to connect them with well-known objects (disregarding the earlier mnemonic stage or use of memory aids like the quipu or knotted cord, of which the rosary is a modern example) — constitute the origin of the abstract and arbitrary signs or symbols which we call "letters."

Let us assume, as logically we may, that picture writing in which a drawing depicting or suggesting the object itself came first; next must have come the ideograph, the sign suggesting the name of the object represented instead of representing the thing itself; & next the phonogram, or sign that suggests a sound only.

In the first class just named belong the wedge-shaped, or cuneiform, characters inscribed in the clay tablets, cylinders, and monuments of Assyria, Babylonia, & other Near Eastern countries — characters the very existence of which was overlooked or forgotten for some sixteen hundred years. They were almost purely pictorial — were drawings only, really not writing at all, and, as far as we now know, have little direct bearing on the derivation of our present alphabet.

To this first class also belong the hieroglyphs of Egypt, highly elaborated types of picture writing which changed so little over a long period that "it is like a language which has never forgotten the derivation of its words, or corrupted their etymological forms, however much it may have altered its meaning." Developed at least five thousand years B.C., the purely pictorial

Of all the achievements of the human mind, the birth of the alphabet is the most momentous. "Letters, like men, have now an ancestry, and the ancestry of words, as of men, is often a very noble possession, making them capable of great things": indeed, it has been said that the invention of writing is more important than all the victories ever won or constitutions devised by man. The history of writing is, in a way, the history of the human race, since in it are bound up, severally and together, the development of thought, of expression, of art, of intercommunication, and of mechanical invention.

When and to whom in the dim past the idea came that man's speech could be better represented by fewer symbols (to denote certain unvarying sounds) selected from the confused mass of picture ideographs, phonograms, and their like, which constituted the first methods of representing human speech, we have no certain means of knowing. But whatever the source, the development did come; and we must deal with it. To present briefly the early history of the alphabet requires that much collateral matter must be disregarded and a great deal that is omitted here must necessarily be taken for granted; the writer desires, however, to present what seems to him to be a logical and probable story of the alphabet's beginnings.

Although it has not yet been proved conclusively, it is quite possible, and altogether probable, that the traders of Phoenicia and the Aegean adopted both the use of papyrus and Egyptian hieratic writing, from which developed the Phoenician alphabet. Whether all the earliest writing systems of different countries sprang from one common stock of picture writing, we shall, perhaps, never surely know; we do know that the picture writing of Egypt exercised a very great influence, and it seems quite safe for us to assume that crude attempts by those ancient Nile-dwellers to express thought visible or to record facts by a series of pictures — or by diagrams sufficiently pictorial, at least, to connect them with well-known objects (disregarding the earlier mnemonic stage or use of memory aids like the quipu or knotted cord, of which the

A.A. Abbreviation for Author's Alteration, used to flag errors or corrections by the author.

ABA form. Design principle of form interrelationships, involving repetition and contrast.

Accents. Small marks over, under, or through a letterform, indicating specific punctuation or changes in stress.

Agate. Vertical unit used to measure space in newspaper columns, originally five-and-one-half point type. Fourteen agate lines equal approximately one inch.

Alert box. A message box that appears on a computer screen with information for the user, for example, a "bomb message" when a computer crashes.

Alignment. Precise arrangement of letterforms upon an imaginary horizontal or vertical line.

Alphabet length. Horizontal measure of the lowercase alphabet in a type font, used to approximate the horizontal measure of type set in that font.

Ampersand. Typographic character (&) representing the word *and.*

Anti-aliasing. The blurring of a jagged line or edge on a screen or output device to give the appearance of a smooth line.

Application program. Computer software used to create and modify documents.

Area composition. The organization of typographic and other graphic elements into their final positions by electronic means (keyboard, graphics tablets and electronic pens, etc.), eliminating the need for hand assembly or pasteup.

Ascender. Stroke on a lowercase letter that rises above the meanline.

ASCII code. Abbreviation for American Standard Code of Information Interchange. The numbers 0 through 127 represent the alphanumeric characters and functions on the keyboard.

Aspect ratio. The ratio of an image, screen, or other medium's height to its width. Images will become distorted if forced into a different aspect ratio during enlargement, reduction, or transfer.

Autoflow. A page-layout program setting for placing blocks of text from page to page without operator intervention.

Autopaging, Automatic pagination. A capability in computer typesetting for dividing text into pages. Advanced autopaging can add page numbers and running heads, and avoid awkward widows and orphans.

Auto-runaround, Automatic runaround. A page-layout program feature that flows text smoothly around graphics or headlines placed within the normal text area.

Base alignment. A typesetter or printer specification that the baseline for all letters should be horizontal, even in a line of mixed sizes or styles; also called baseline alignment.

Baseline. An imaginary horizontal line upon which the base of each capital letter rests.

Baud rate. The number of bits per second, often used as a measure of data transmission; for example, by a modem.

Bezier curve. A type of curve with nonuniform arcs, as opposed to curves with uniform curvature, which are called arcs. A Bezier curve is defined by specifying control points that set the shape of the curve and are used to create letter shapes and other computer graphics.

Binary code. Number system using two digits: 0 and 1.

Bit. Contraction of binary digit, which is the smallest unit of information that a computer can hold. The value of a bit (1 or 0) represents a two-way choice, such as yes or no, on or off, positive or negative.

Bit-map. A computerized image made up of dots. These are "mapped" onto the screen directly from corresponding bits in memory (hence the name). Also referred to as paint format.

Bit-mapped font. A font whose letters are composed of dots, such as fonts designed for dot matrix printers. Compare *Outline font.*

Body size. Depth of a piece of metal type, usually measured in points.

Body type. Text material, usually set in sizes from six to twelve point. Also called text type.

Boldface. Type with thicker, heavier strokes than the regular font. Indicated as BF in type specifications.

Boot. A computer's start-up procedures; coined from "pulling yourself up by your bootstraps."

Bounding box. In drawing or page-description languages, an imaginary box within which an image is located. It represents the rectangular area needed to create the image.

Byte. Unit of computer information. The number of bits used to represent a character. For personal computers, a byte is usually eight bits.

Backslant. Letterforms having a diagonal slant to the left.

C. and l. c. Used in marking copy, to instruct the typesetter to use capitals and lowercase.

C. and s. c. Used in marking copy, to instruct the typesetter to use capitals and small capitals.

Camera ready (or camera-ready copy). Copy and/or artwork that is ready to be photographed to make negatives, which are exposed to printing plates.

Cap height. Height of the capital letters, measured from the baseline to the capline.

Capline. Imaginary horizontal line defined by the height of the capital letters.

Capitals. Letters larger than—and often differing from—the corresponding lowercase letters. Also called uppercase.

Caps. See *Capitals.*

Caption. Title, explanation, or description accompanying an illustration or photograph.

Casting off. Determining the length of manuscript copy, enabling a calculation of the area that type will occupy when set in a given size and style of type.

Cathode -ray tube (CRT). An electronic tube with a phosphorescent surface that produces a glowing image when activated by an electronic beam.

CD-ROM. An optical data storage device; initials for compact disk read-only memory.

Central processing unit (CPU). Computer component that controls all other parts, performs logical operations, and stores information.

Character. Symbol, sign, or mark in a language system.

Character count. The number of characters in a block of text. In typography, spaces are counted but other non-printing characters usually are not. In data processing, both printing and non-printing characters are usually counted.

Chase. Heavy metal frame into which metal type is locked for proofing or printing.

Chip. A small piece of silicon impregnated with impurities that form miniaturized computer circuits.

Chooser. Software that tells a computer which output device and connection port to use.

Cicero. European typographic unit of measure, approximately equal to the American pica.

Clipboard. A computer's "holding place," a buffer area in memory for the last material to be cut or copied from a document. Information on the clipboard can be inserted (pasted) into documents.

Cold type. Type that is set by means other than casting molten metal. The term is most frequently used to indicate strike-on composition rather than photo or digital typesetting.

Colophon. Inscription, frequently placed at the end of a book, that contains facts about its production.

Column guide. Non-printing lines that define the location of columns of type.

Command. The generic name for an order or instruction to a computer.

Command character. The combination of a command key plus character(s) used to instruct a computer to take an action.

Comp. See *Comprehensive layout.*

Compensation. In visual organization, the counterbalancing of elements.

Composing stick. Adjustable hand-held metal tray, used to hold handset type as it is being composed.

Composition. Alternate term for typesetting.

Compositor. Person who sets type.

Comprehensive layout (Comp). An accurate representation of a printed piece showing all type and pictures in their size and position. Comps are used to evaluate a design before producing final type and artwork.

Computer. Electronic device that performs predefined (programmed) high-speed mathematical or logical calculations.
Condensed. Letterforms whose horizontal width has been compressed.

Consonance. In design, harmonious interaction between elements.

Copyfitting. Calculating the area that will be occupied by a given manuscript when set in a specified size and style of type.

Counter. Space enclosed by the strokes of a letterform.

Counterform. "Negative" spatial areas defined and shaped by letterforms, including both interior counters and spaces between characters.

CPS. Characters per inch.

CPU. See *Central processing unit.*

CRT. See *Cathode-ray tube.*

Cursive. Type styles that imitate handwriting, often with letters that do not connect.

Cursor. The pointer or insertion point on a computer screen.

Cut and paste. To move material from one location to another within a document, or from one document to another. This is a computer's electronic equivalent to clipping something with scissors, then using glue to paste the clipping in another location.

Cutoff rules. Rules used to separate pages into various units, such as advertisements or news stories.

Daisy wheel. Strike-on printing wheel containing relief characters on spokes, radiating from a central disk. As the wheel spins, a hammer impacts the characters against an inked ribbon.

Data. Information, particularly that upon which a computer program is based.

Data bank. Mass storage of large quantities of information, indexed for rapid retrieval.

Data processing. The storing and handling of information by a computer.

Data transmission. Rapid electronic transfer of coded data via telephone or other communication links.

Dazzle. Visual effect caused by extreme contrast in the strokes of letterforms.

Default. A value, action, or setting that a computer system assumes, unless the user gives an explicit instruction to the contrary; for example, a certain size and typeface will be used by a page-layout program unless the user selects another size and font.

Descender. Stroke on a lowercase letterform that falls below the baseline.

Desktop. Refers to the desktop metaphor depicted on the computer screen, with a menu bar across the top, icons for applications and disk drives, and other icons, such as a trash basket that can be used to throw away unwanted material.

Desktop publishing. The popular use of this term is incorrect, because publishing encompasses writing, editing, designing, printing, and distribution activities, not just makeup and production. See *Electronic page design.*

Dialog box. A box displayed on a computer screen requesting information or a decision by the user.

Digital type. Type stored electronically as digital dot or stroke patterns, rather than as photographic images.

Digitizer. A computer peripheral device that converts images or sound into a digital signal.

Directory. The contents of a computer disk or folder. Directory contents can be arranged and displayed on a screen by name, icon, date created, size, kind, and so on.

Digital computer. A device that translates data into a discrete number system to facilitate electronic processing.

Disk. Thin, flat, circular plate with a magnetic surface upon which data may be stored. See *Floppy disk* and *Hard disk.* Also, a circular grid containing the master font in some typesetting systems.

Display Postscript. A technology by Adobe Systems that allows PostScript commands (for special graphic effects) to be displayed on the screen.

Display type. Type sizes 14 point and above, used primarily for headlines and titles.

Dissonance. In design, visual tension and contrast between typographic elements.

Dithering. A technique for alternating the value of adjacent dots or pixels to create the effect of an intermediate value. When printing color images or displaying color on a computer screen, dithering refers to the technique of making different colors for adjacent dots or pixels to give the illusion of a third color; for example, a printed field of alternating cyan and yellow dots appears to be green. Dithering gives the effect of shades of gray on a black-and-white display or the effect of more colors on a color display.

Dot-matrix printer. A printer that forms characters out of a pattern of dots; many have pins that strike against an inked ribbon to transfer the pattern of dots making up each character onto paper.

Dots per inch (dpi). A measure of the resolution of a screen image or printed page. Dots are also known as pixels. Some computer screens display 72 dpi; many laser printers print 300 dpi; and imagesetters often print 1270 or 2540 dpi.

Downloadable font. A font can be downloaded into a printer or computerized typesetter, which means that tables telling how to construct the type characters are sent from the computer to the output device. By accepting additional character sets—downloadable fonts—an output device can print many typefaces. To be able to accept downloadable fonts, a printer or typesetter must have sufficient computer memory and processing power to receive and store the images.

Downloading. Transferring information from one computer to another and storing it there.

DRAM. Abbreviation for dynamic random access memory chip; dynamic refers to the loss of data in its memory when a computer is shut off.

Draw program. Computer applications for drawing graphics that are object-oriented; that is, it produces graphics from arc and line segments that are mathematically defined by points located on the horizontal and vertical axes on the screen. Compare *Paint program.*

Drop initial. Display letterform set into the text.

E.A. Abbreviation for Editor's Alteration, used to flag errors or corrections made by the editor.

Editing terminal. Workstation consisting of a keyboard and visual display device, used to input and edit copy prior to typesetting.

Egyptian. Typefaces characterized by slablike serifs similar in weight to the main strokes.

Electronic page design. The layout and typesetting of complete pages using a computer with input and output devices.

Elite. Size of typewriter type approximately equal to 10 point typography.

Ellipses. Three dots used to indicate an omission in quoted material.

Em. The square of the body size of any type, used as a unit of measure. In some expanded or condensed faces, the em is also expanded or condensed from the square proportion.

Em dash. A dash one em long. Also called a long dash.

Em leader. Horizontal dots or dashes with one em between their centers.

Em space. Space equal to the width of an em quad.

En. One-half of an em (see *Em*).

En dash. A dash one en long. Also called a short dash.

En leader. Horizontal dots or dashes with one en between their centers.

En space. Space equal to the width of an en quad.

Encapsulated PostScript (ESP). A computer format for encoding pictures. These can be stored, edited, transferred, and output in the form of structured PostScript code.

ESP. See *Encapsulated PostScript.*

Exception dictionary. See *Hyphenation.*

Expanded. Letterforms whose horizontal width has been extended.

Export. To send text, graphics, or layouts created in one program from the computer memory in a form suitable for use with other programs.

Face. The part of metal type that is inked for printing. Also, another word for typeface.

Family. See *Type family.*

FAX machine. An electronic device that scans documents and transmits them over telephone lines. Documents are received and output by another FAX machine.

Film font. A photographic film master used in some typesetting machines. Characters from a film font are exposed through lenses of different sizes onto paper or film. Unlike digital typesetting, typesetting systems using film fonts cannot set an entire page complete with graphics.

Finder. A computer program that generates the desktop and is used to access and manage files and disks. See *Multifinder.*

Firmware. Software that has been written into nonchangeable memory that does not need to be loaded into the system for each use. Most printers and output devices store their software in this form.

Fit. The spatial relationships between letters after they are set into words and lines.

Floppy disk. Portable, flexible disk housed in a 3.5-inch hard plastic case and inserted into a disk drive, which reads the information on it.

Flush left (or right). The even vertical alignment of lines of type at the left (or right) edge of a column.

Folio. Page number.

Font. A complete set of characters in one design, size, and style. In traditional metal type, a font meant a particular size and style; in digital typography a font can output multiple sizes and even altered styles of a typeface design.

Font/DA Mover. An application that allows a user to add and/or remove fonts and desk accessories from a file on a disk.

Font substitution. During output of a page, the replacement of a requested but unavailable font by another (usually similar) available font.

Footer. An identifying line, such as a page number and/or a chapter title, appearing in the bottom margin of a document. Footers repeated throughout a document are called running footers or running feet.

Footprint. The amount of space a machine such as a computer takes up on a surface such as a desktop.

Format. The overall typographic and spatial schema established for a publication or any other application.

Formatting. In digital typesetting and phototypesetting, the process of issuing specific commands that establish the typographic format.

Foundry type. Metal type used in hand composition.

Furniture. Rectangular pieces of wood, metal, or plastic used to fill in excess space when locking up a form for letterpress printing.

Galley. A three-sided, shallow metal tray used to hold metal type forms before printing.

Galley proof. Originally, a type proof pulled from metal type assembled in a galley. Frequently used today to indicate any first proof, regardless of the type system.

"Golf" ball. An interchangeable metal ball approximately one inch in diameter with raised characters on its surface, used as the printing element in some typewriters.

Greeking. Type set using random or Greek characters to simulate typeset text in a layout or comp.

Grid. Underlying structure composed of a linear framework used by designers to organize typographic and pictorial elements.

Also, a film or glass master font, containing characters in a predetermined configuration and used in phototypesetting.

Grotesque. Name for sans serif typefaces.

Gutter. The interval separating two facing pages in a publication.

Gutter margin. Inner margin of a page in a publication.

Hairline. Thinnest strokes on a typeface having strokes of varying weight.

Hand composition. Method of setting type by placing individual pieces of metal type from a type case into a composing stick.

Hanging indent. In composition, a column format in which the first line of type is set to a full measure while all additional lines are indented.

Hanging punctuation. Punctuation set outside the column measure to achieve an optical alignment.

Hard copy. Computer output printed on paper.

Hard disk. Large rigid disk having large storage capacity, fast operating speed, and permanent installation within the computer or a separate case.

Hardware. The physical equipment of a computer system, such as the CPU, input/output devices, and peripherals.

Header. An identifying line at the top margin of a document. A header can appear on every page and can include text, pictures, page numbers, the date, and the time. Headers repeated throughout a document are called running headers or running heads.

Heading. Copy that is given emphasis over the body of text, through changes in size, weight, or spatial interval.

Headline. The most significant type in the visual hierarchy of a printed communication.

Hertz. One cycle per second. See *Megahertz*.

Hot type. Type produced by casting molten metal.

Hyphenation. The syllabic division of words when they must be broken at the end of a line. In electronic textsetting, hyphenation can be done by the operator, or automatically by the computer.

I-beam pointer. The shape the pointer or cursor on a computer screen usually takes when working with text.

Icon. A pictorial representation. The elemental pictures on a computer screen used to represent disk drives, files, applications, tools, and so on are called icons.

Import. To transfer text, graphics, or layouts into a program in a form suitable for its use.

Imposition. The arrangement of pages in a printed signature to achieve the proper sequencing after the sheets are folded and trimmed.

Incunabula. European printing during the first half-century of typography, from Gutenberg's invention of movable type until the year 1500.

Indent. An interval of space at the beginning of a line to indicate a new paragraph.

Inferior characters. Small characters, usually slightly smaller than the x-height, positioned on or below the baseline and used for footnotes or fractions.

Initial. A large letter used at the beginning of a column; for example, at the beginning of a chapter.

Initialize. Electronically formatting a disk to prepare it to record data from a computer.

Input. Raw data, text, or commands entered into a computer memory from a peripheral device, such as a keyboard.

Interletter spacing. The spatial interval between letters, also called letterspacing.

Insertion point. The location in a document where the next text or graphics will be placed, represented by a blinking vertical cursor. A user selects the insertion point by clicking where he or she wishes to work.

Interline spacing. The spatial interval between lines, also called leading.

Interword spacing. The spatial interval between words, also called wordspacing.

Italic. Letterforms having a pronounced diagonal slant to the right.

Jaggies. The jagged "staircase" edges formed on raster-scan displays when displaying diagonal and curved lines. See *Anti-aliasing*.

Justified setting. A column of type with even vertical edges on both the left and the right, achieved by adjusting interword spacing. Also called flush left, flush right.

Justified text. Copy in which all the lines of text—regardless of the words they contain—have been made exactly the same length, so that they align vertically at both the left and right margins.

K. Computer term for 1,024 bytes of memory.

Kerning. In typesetting, the process of subtracting space between specific pairs of characters so that the overall letterspacing appears to be even. Compare *Tracking*.

Keyboard. A device having keys or buttons used to enter data into typesetting and computer systems.

Laser. A concentrated light source that can be optically manipulated. Coined from "Light Amplification by Stimulated Emission of Radiation."

Laser printer. A computer printer that creates the image by drawing it on a metal drum with a laser. The latent image becomes visible after dry ink particles are electrostatically attracted to it.

Latin. Type styles characterized by triangular, pointed serifs.

Leader. Typographic dots or periods that are repeated to connect other elements.

Lead-in. Introductory copy set in a contrasting typeface.

Leading (Pronounced "LED-ing"). In early typesetting, strips of lead were placed between lines of type for spacing, hence the term. See *Linespacing, Interline spacing*.

Letterpress. The process of printing from a raised, inked surface.

Letterspacing. See *Interletter spacing*.

Ligature. A typographic character produced by combining two or more letters.

Line breaks. The relationships of line endings in a ragged-right or ragged-left setting. Rhythmic line breaks are achieved by adjusting the length of individual lines of type.

Line length. The measure of the length of a line of type, usually expressed in picas.

Line spacing. The vertical distance between two lines of type measured from baseline to baseline. For example, "10/12" indicates 10-point type with 12 points base-to-base (that is, with 2 points of leading). See *Leading, Interline spacing*.

Lining figures. Numerals identical in size to the capitals and aligned on the baseline: 1 2 3 4 5 6 7 8 9 10.

Linotype. A machine that casts an entire line of raised type on a single metal slug.

Local area network (LAN). A network of computers and peripherals, usually in the same office or building, connected by dedicated electrical cables rather than telephone lines.

Logotype. Two or more type characters that are combined as a sign or trademark.

Lowercase. The alphabet set of small letters, as opposed to capitals.

LPM. Lines per minute, a unit of measure expressing the speed of a typesetting system.

Ludlow. A typecasting machine that produces individual letters from hand-assembled matrices.

Machine composition. General term for the mechanical casting of metal type.

Makeup. The assembly of typographic matter into a page, or a sequence of pages, ready for printing.

Margin. The unprinted space surrounding type matter on a page.

Mark up. The marking of typesetting specifications upon manuscript copy.

Marquee. A rectangular area, often surrounded by blinking dashed or dotted lines, used to select objects or regions in a application programs.

Master page. In a page-layout program, a template providing standard columns, margins, and typographic elements that appear on a publication's individual pages.

Masthead. The visual identification of a magazine or newspaper, usually a logotype.

Matrix. In typesetting, the master image from which type is produced. The matrix is a brass mold in linecasting and a glass plate bearing the font negative in phototypesetting.

Meanline. An imaginary line marking the tops of lowercase letters, not including the ascenders.

Measure. See *Line length*.

Mechanical. A camera-ready pasteup of artwork including type, images showing position of color and halftone matter, line art, and so on, all on one piece of artboard.

Megabyte (MB). A unit of measurement equal to 1024 kilobytes, or 1,048,576 bytes.

Megahertz (MHz). A million cycles per second; describes the speed of computer chips; used to measure how rapidly a computer processes information.

Menu. A list of choices in a computer application, from which the user selects a desired action. In a computer's desktop interface, menus appear when you point to and click on menu titles in the menu bar. Dragging through a menu and releasing the mouse button while a command is highlighted chooses that command.

Menu bar. A horizontal band on a computer screen that contains menu titles.

Message box. A box that appears on a computer screen to give the user information.

Microprocessor. A single silicon chip containing thousands of electronic components for processing information; the "brains" of a personal computer.

Minuscules. An early term for small, or lowercase, letters.

Minus spacing. A reduction of interline spacing, resulting in a baseline-to-baseline measurement that is smaller than the point size of the type.

Mixing. The alignment of more than one type style or typeface on a single baseline.

Modern. Term used to describe typefaces designed at the end of the eighteenth century. Characteristics include vertical stress, hairline serifs, and pronounced contrasts between thick and thin strokes.

Monotype. A trade name for a keyboard-operated typesetting machine that casts individual letters from matrices.

Modem. Contraction of modulator/demodulator; a peripheral device to send data over telephone lines from a computer to other computers, service bureaus, information services, and so on.

Monospacing. Spacing in a font with characters that all have the same set width or horizontal measure; often found in typewriter and screen fonts. See *Proportional spacing*.

Mouse. A small computer device that controls an on-screen pointer or tool when moved around on a flat surface by hand. The mouse-controlled pointer can select operations, move data, and draw images.

Multifinder. A computer program permitting several applications to be open at the same time, permitting a designer to work back and forth between page-layout and drawing programs, for example, without having to repeatedly open and close programs.

Negative. The reversal of a positive photographic image.

Network. A system connecting multiple computers so they can share printers, information, and so on.

Object-oriented. A method in drawing and other computer programs that produces graphics from arc and line segments that are mathematically defined by points located on the horizontal and vertical axes on the screen.

Oblique. A slanted roman character. Unlike many italics, oblique characters do not have cursive design properties.

Offset lithography. A printing method using flat photo-mechanical plates, in which the inked image is transferred or offset from the printing plate onto a rubber blanket, then onto the paper.

Old Style. Typeface styles derived from fifteenth- to eighteenth-century designs, and characterized by moderate thick-and-thin contrasts, bracketed serifs, and a handwriting influence.

Old Style figures. Numerals that exhibit a variation in size, including characters aligning with the lowercase x-height, and others with ascenders or descenders: 1234567890.

Operating system. A computer program that controls a computer's operation, directing information to and from different components.

Optical adjustment. The precise visual alignment and spacing of typographic elements. In interletter spacing, the adjustment of individual characters to achieve consistent spacing.

Outline font. A font designed, not as a bit-map, but as an outline of the letter shapes that can be scaled to any size. Laser printers and imagesetters use outline fonts. See *Bit-mapped font*.

Outline type. Letterforms described by a contour line that encloses the entire character on all sides. The interior usually remains open.

Output. The product of a computer operation. In computerized typesetting, output is reproduction proofs of composition.

Page preview. A mode on many word-processing and page-layout programs that shows a full-page view of what the page will look like when printed, including added elements such as headers, footers, and margins.

Pagination. The sequential numbering of pages.

Paint program. A computer application that creates images as a series of bit-mapped dots, which can be erased and manipulated by turning the pixels on and off. Compare *Draw program*.

Pantone Matching System (PMS). The trademarked name of a system for specifying colors and inks that is a standard in the printing industry.

Paragraph mark. Typographic element that signals the beginning of a paragraph. For example, ¶.

Parallel construction. In typography, the use of similar typographic elements or arrangements to create a visual unity or to convey a relationship in content.

Paste. To place a copy of saved material into a computer-generated document or layout.

P.E. Abbreviation for Printer's Error, used to flag a mistake made by the compositor rather than by the author.

Pen plotter. A printer that draws using ink-filled pens that are moved along a bar that also moves back and forth. Many plotters have very high resolutions, but have slow operation, poor text quality, and poor handling of raster images.

Peripheral. An electronic device that connects to a computer, such as a disk drive, scanner, or printer.

Photocomposition. The process of setting type by projecting light onto a light-sensitive film or paper.

Photodisplay typesetting. The process of setting headline type on film or paper by photographic means.

Phototype. Type matter set on film or paper by photographic projection of type characters.

Photounit. Output component of a photocomposition system, which sets the type and exposes it to light-sensitive film or paper.

Pica. Typographic unit of measurement: 12 points equal 1 pica. Six picas equal approximately one inch. Line lengths and column widths are measured in picas.

PICT. A computer format for encoding pictures. PICT data can be created, displayed on the screen, and printed, thus applications without graphics-processing routines can incorporate PICT data generated by other software.

Pixel. Stands for picture element; the smallest dot that can be displayed on a screen.

Point. A measure of size used principally in typesetting. One point is equal to 1/12 of a pica, or approximately 1/72 of an inch. It is most often used to indicate the size of type or amount of leading added between lines.

Pointer. A graphic form that moves on a computer screen and is controlled by a pointing device; usually a symbolic icon such as an arrow, I-beam, or clock.

Pointing device. An computer input device, such as a mouse, tablet, or joystick, used to indicate when an onscreen pointer or tool should be placed or moved.

Port. An electrical socket where cables are inserted to connect computers, peripheral devices, or networks. Ports are named for the type of signals they carry, such as printer port, serial port, or SCSI port.

PostScript.™ A page-description programming language created by Adobe Systems that handles text and the graphics, placing them on the page with mathematical precision.

Preview. To view the final output on a computer screen before printing. Because most screens have lower resolution than an imagesetter or laser printer, fine details are often different from the final output.

Processor. In a computer system, the general term for any device capable of carrying out operations upon data. In phototypography, the unit that automatically develops the light-sensitive paper or film.

Program. A sequence of instructions that directs the operations of a computer to execute a given task.

Proof. Traditionally, an impression from metal type for examination and correction; now applies to initial output for examination and correction before final output.

Proportional spacing. Spacing in a font adjusted to give wide letters (M) a larger set width than narrow letters (I).

Quad. In metal type, pieces of type metal shorter than type-high, which are used as spacing matter to separate elements and fill out lines.

Quoins. Wedges use to lock up metal type in the chase. These devices are tightened and loosened by a quoin key.

Ragged. See *Unjustified type.*

RAM. Abbreviation for random access memory, the area of a computer's memory that temporarily stores applications and documents while they are being used.

RAM cache. An area of the computer's memory set aside to hold information from a disk until it is needed again. Data can be accessed much more quickly from a RAM cache than from a disk.

Raster display. A raster image is divided into scan lines, each consisting of a series of dots from a thin section of the final image. This dot pattern corresponds exactly to a bit pattern in the computer memory.

Raster image file format (RIFF). A file format for paint-style color graphics, developed by Letraset USA.

Raster image processor (RIP). A device or program that translates an image or page into the actual pattern of dots received by a printing or display system.

Raster scan. The generation of an image upon a cathode-ray tube made by refreshing the display area line by line.

Recto. In publication design, the right-hand page. Page one (and all odd-numbered pages) always appears on a recto. The left-hand page is called the verso.

Resolution. The degree of detail and clarity of a display; usually specified in dots per inch (dpi). The higher the resolution, or the greater the number of dpi, the sharper the image.

Reverse. Type or image that is dropped out of a printed area, revealing the paper surface.

Reverse leading. A reduction in the amount of interline space, making it less than normal for the point size. For example, 12 point type set on an 11 point body size becomes reverse leading of 1 point.

RIFF. See *Raster image file format.*

River. In text type, a series of interword spaces that accidentally align vertically or diagonally, creating an objectionable flow of white space within the column.

ROM. Abbreviation for read only memory, which is permanently installed on a computer chip and can be read but cannot accept new or changed data; for example, some laser printers have basic fonts permanently installed in a ROM chip.

Roman. Upright letterforms, as distinguished from italics. More specifically, letters in an alphabet style based on the upright, serifed letterforms of Roman inscriptions.

Rule. In handset metal type, a strip of metal that prints as a line. Generally, any line used as an element in typographic design, whether handset, photographic, digital, or hand-drawn.

Run-around. Type that is set with a shortened line measure to fit around a photograph, drawing, or other visual element inserted into the running text.

Run in. To set type without a paragraph indentation or other break. Also, to insert additional matter into the running text as part of an existing paragraph.

Running head. Type at the head of sequential pages, providing a title or publication name.

Sans serif. Typefaces without serifs.

Saving. Transferring information—such as an electronic page design—from a computer's memory to a storage device.

Scanner. A computer peripheral device that scans pictures and converts them to digital form so they can be stored, manipulated, and output.

Scrapbook. A computer's "holding place" for permanent storage of images, text, and so on.

Screen font. A bit-mapped version of an outline font that is used to represent the outline font on a computer screen.

Script. Typefaces based on handwriting, usually having connecting strokes between the letters.

Scroll bar. A rectangular bar that may appear along the right or bottom of a window on a computer screen. By clicking or dragging in the scroll bar, the user can move through the document.

Scrolling. In typesetting and computer-assisted design, moving through a document to bring onto the screen portions of the document not currently displayed.

SCSI. Abbreviation for Small Computer System Interface; pronounced scuzzy. SCSI is a computer-industry standard interface allowing very fast transfer of data.

Semantics. The science of meaning in linguistics; the study of the relationships between signs and symbols, and what they represent.

Serifs. Small elements added to the ends of the main strokes of a letterform in serifed type styles.

Set width. In metal type, the width of the body upon which a letter is cast. In phototype and digital type, the horizontal width of a letterform measured in units, including the normal space before and after the character. This interletter space can be increased or decreased to control the tightness or looseness of the fit.

Shoulder. In metal type, the flat top of the type body that surrounds the raised printing surface of the letterform.

Side head. A title or other heading material placed to the side of a type column.

Slab serifs. Square or rectangular serifs that align horizontally and vertically to the baseline and are usually the same (or heavier) weight as the main strokes of the letterform.

Slug. A line of metal type cast on a linecasting machine, such as the Linotype. Also, strips of metal spacing material in thicknesses of 6 points or more.

Small capitals. A set of capital letters having the same height as the lowercase x-height, frequently used for cross references and abbreviations. Also called small caps, and often abbreviated s.c.

Smoothing. The electronic process of eliminating jaggies (the uneven staircase effect on diagonal or curved lines).

Software. The programs or instructions of a comuter system that control the behavior of the computer hardware.

Solid. Lines of type that are set without additional interline space. Also called set solid.

Sorts. In metal type, material that is not part of a regular font, such as symbols, piece fractions, and spaces. Also, individual characters used to replace worn-out type in a font.

Stand-alone typesetting system. A typesetting system that is completely self-contained, including editing terminal, memory, and character generation.

Startup disk. The computer disk drive containing the system software used to operate the computer.

Stet. A proofreader's mark meaning that copy marked for correction should not be changed; rather, it should be left as originally set.

Storage. In computer typesetting, a device (such as a disk, drum, or tape) that can receive information and retain it for future use.

Straight matter. Text material set in continuous columns with limited deviation from the basic typographic specifications.

Style sheets. In several word-processing and page-layout programs, style sheets are special files containing formatting instructions for creating standardized documents.

Subscript. A small character beneath (or adjacent to and slightly below) another character.

Superscript. A small character above (or adjacent to and slightly above) another character.

Swash letters. Letters ornamented with flourishes or flowing tails.

Syntax. In grammar, the way in which words or phrases are put together to form sentences. In design, the connecting or ordering of typographic elements into a visual unity.

System. A related group of interdependent design elements forming a whole. In computer science, a complete computing operation including software and hardware (Central Processing

Unit, memory, input/output devices, and peripherals or devices required for the intended functions).

System software. Computer files containing the operating system program and its supporting programs needed to make the computer work, interface with peripherals, and run applications.

Tag Image File Format (TIFF). A computer format for encoding pictures as high-resolution bit-mapped images, such as those created by scanners.

Telecommunications. Sending messages to distant locations; usually refers to communicating by telephone lines.

Terminal. See Video display terminal.

Text. The main body of written or printed material, as opposed to display matter, footnotes, appendices, and so on.

Text type. See Body type.

Thumbnail. A miniature image of a page, either a small planning sketch made by a designer, or a reduction in a page-layout program.

TIFF. See Tag Image File Format.

Tracking. The overall tightness or looseness of the spacing between all characters in a line or block of text. Sometimes used interchangeably with kerning, which more precisely is the reduction in spacing between a specific pair of letters.

Transitional. Classification of type styles combining aspects of both Old Style and Modern typefaces; for example, Baskerville.

Typeface. The design of alphabetical and numerical characters unified by consistent visual properties.

Type family. The complete range of variations of a typeface design, including roman, italic, bold, expanded, condensed, and other versions.

Type-high. The standard foot-to-face height of metal types; 0.9186 inches in English-speaking countries.

Typescript. Typewritten manuscript material used as copy for typesetting.

Typesetting. The composing of type by any method or process, also called composition.

Type specimen. A typeset sample produced to show the visual properties of a typeface.

Typo. See Typographical error.

Typographer. A firm specializing in typesetting. Sometimes used to denote a compositor or typesetter.

Typographical error. A mistake in typesetting, typing, or writing.

Typography. Originally the composition of printed matter from movable type. Now the art and process of typesetting by any system or method.

U. and l.c. Abbreviation for uppercase and lowercase, used to specify typesetting that combines capitals with lowercase letters.

Undo. A standard computer command that undoes the last command or operation executed.

Unit. A subdivision of the em, used in measuring and counting characters in photo- and digital-typesetting systems.

Unitization. The process of designing a typeface so that the individual character widths conform to a typesetter's unit system.

Unitized font. A font with character widths conforming to a typesetter's unit system.

Unit system. A counting system first developed for Monotype, used by most typesetting machines. The width of characters and spaces is measured in units. There data are used to control line breaks, justification, and interword and interletter spacing.

Unit value. The established width, in units, of a typographic character.

Unjustified type. Lines of type set with equal interword spacing, resulting in irregular line lengths. Also called ragged.

Uploading. Sending information from your computer to a distant computer. See Downloading.

Uppercase. See Capitals.

User interface. The way a computer system communicates with its user; the "look and feel" of the machine as experienced by the user.

Virus. A computer program that invades computers and modifies data, usually in a destructive manner.

Verso. In publication design, the left-hand page. Page two (and all even-numbered pages) always appear on a verso. The right-hand page is called the recto.

Visual display terminal. A computer input/output device utilizing a cathode-ray tube to display data on a screen. Information from memory, storage, or a keyboard can be displayed.

Weight. The lightness or heaviness of a typeface, which is determined by ratio of the stroke thickness to character height.

White space. The "negative" area surrounding a letterform. See Counter and Counterform.

White space reduction. A decrease in the amount of interletter space, achieved in typesetting by reducing the unit value of typeset characters. See Tracking.

Widow. A very short line that appears at the end of a paragraph, column, or page, or at the top of a column or page. These awkward typographic configurations should be corrected editorially.

Width tables. Collections of information about how much horizontal room each character in a font should occupy, often accompanied by information about special kerning pairs or other exceptions.

Windows. An area of a computer screen where a single document is displayed.

Woodtype. Hand-set types cut from wood by a mechanical router. Formerly used for large display sizes that were not practical for metal casting, woodtype has been virtually eliminated by display photographic typesetting.

Word. In computer systems, a logical unit of information, composed of a predetermined number of bits.

Word-processing program. A computer application used to type in text, then edit, correct, move or remove it.

Wordspacing. In typesetting, adding space between words to extend each line to achieve a justified setting. See Interword spacing.

WYSIWGY. Abbreviation for "what you see is what you get"; pronounced Wizzywig. This means the image on the screen is identical to the image that will be produced as final output.

x-height. The height of lowercase letters, excluding ascenders and descenders. This is most easily measured on the lowercase x.

Copyfitting

Copyfitting is the process of converting a typewritten manuscript into text type that will accurately fit a typographic layout. Copyfitting often occurs at a computer workstation; however, designers are sometimes asked to copyfit manuscripts using these traditional procedures. Throughout this process, a designer should carefully consider legibility factors, visual characteristics, and spatial requirements. Understanding copyfitting enables the designer to control the details of typesetting, which can contribute to a typographic design of clarity and distinction. A suggested method for proper copyfitting follows.

1. Count all the characters in the typewritten manuscript.
This manuscript should be as clean and orderly as possible to increase accuracy while keeping costs to a minimum. Copy should be double-spaced in a single column. Although the size of manuscript type varies with different output devices, traditionally there are two sizes: elite, with twelve characters to an inch, and pica, with ten characters to an inch. To begin, determine the number of characters in an average line length of the author's manuscript by counting the number of characters in four typical lines (including all spaces and punctuation), adding the number of characters in these lines, and dividing this total by four. Then, multiply this average by the number of lines in the whole manuscript to get the total number of characters.

When manuscript copy is provided on a computer disk, use the character and word count feature of a word processor software program to determine the number of characters when a character count is needed.

2. Fit the copy to the layout.
After choosing a specific typeface and size, refer to the layout, and measure the line length in picas. Determine how many characters of the chosen typeface will fit on a line. This can easily be determined by referring to a characters-per-pica or characters-per-line table (Appendix B) often found in specimen books or provided by typographers. If a characters-per-pica figure is given, multiply the number of characters per pica by the number of picas in a line. If a characters-per-line table is provided, simply find the line length which indicates the number of characters in the average typeset line. Divide the number of characters per line into the total number of characters in the typewritten manuscript to determine the total number of typeset lines. Compare the vertical column depth of this number of typeset lines to the vertical column depth on the layout. (Remember to consider the effect of paragraph indication, particularly if you are using additional interline space between paragraphs.) Will the depth of the typeset lines correspond to the depth of the area allowed on the layout? If the typesetting will run too long, or if it will be too short to fill the space, adjustments can be made. These adjustments might include changing the type size, interline spacing, or typeface.

3. Mark the manuscript.
After fitting the copy to the layout, it is important to clearly mark specifications for the typographer on the manuscript. Specifications should always include: type size and interline spacing (leading) in points; complete name of the typeface, including weight and width (Garamond Bold Condensed); line length in picas; line alignment (justified, flush left/ragged right, or centered); paragraph indication (indent one pica, or one line space between paragraphs); variations and special instructions (italics, underlining, changes in size, weight, or typeface).

Line length in picas

	1	10	12	14	16	18	20	22	24	26	28	30
8 point Baskerville	3.25	33	39	46	52	59	65	72	78	85	91	98
9 point Baskerville	2.90	29	35	41	46	52	58	64	70	75	81	87
10 point Baskerville	2.60	26	31	36	42	47	52	57	62	68	73	78
12 point Baskerville	2.30	23	28	32	37	41	46	51	55	60	64	69
8 point Bodoni	3.40	34	41	48	54	61	68	75	82	88	95	102
9 point Bodoni	3.10	31	37	43	50	56	62	68	74	81	87	93
10 point Bodoni	2.80	28	34	39	45	50	56	62	67	73	78	84
12 point Bodoni	2.40	24	29	34	38	43	48	53	58	62	67	72
10 point Helvetica	2.40	24	29	34	38	43	48	53	58	62	67	72
8 point ITC Garamond Light	3.35	34	40	47	54	60	67	74	80	87	94	101
9 point ITC Garamond Light	3.05	31	37	43	49	55	61	67	73	79	85	92
10 point ITC Garamond Light	2.75	28	33	39	44	50	55	61	66	72	77	83
12 point ITC Garamond Light	2.35	24	28	33	38	42	47	52	56	61	66	71
8 point ITC Garamond Book	3.25	33	39	46	52	59	65	72	78	85	91	98
9 point ITC Garamond Book	2.95	30	35	41	47	53	59	65	71	77	83	89
10 point ITC Garamond Book	2.65	27	32	37	42	48	53	58	64	69	74	80
12 point ITC Garamond Book	2.25	23	27	32	36	41	45	50	54	59	63	68
8 point ITC Garamond Bold	3.00	30	36	42	48	54	60	66	72	78	84	90
9 point ITC Garamond Bold	2.65	27	32	37	42	48	53	58	64	69	74	80
10 point ITC Garamond Bold	2.40	24	29	34	38	43	48	53	58	62	67	72
12 point ITC Garamond Bold	2.05	21	25	29	33	37	41	45	49	53	57	62
8 point Lubalin Graph Med.	2.80	28	34	39	45	50	56	62	67	73	78	84
9 point Lubalin Graph Med.	2.45	25	29	34	39	44	49	54	59	64	69	74
10 point Lubalin Graph Med.	2.30	23	28	32	37	41	46	51	55	60	64	69
12 point Lubalin Graph Med.	1.95	20	23	27	31	35	39	43	47	51	55	59
8 point Univers 45	3.20	32	38	45	51	58	64	70	77	83	90	96
9 point Univers 45	2.90	29	35	41	46	52	58	64	70	75	81	87
10 point Univers 45	2.60	26	31	36	42	47	52	57	62	68	73	78
12 point Univers 45	2.25	23	27	32	36	41	45	50	54	59	63	68
8 point Univers 55	2.90	29	35	41	46	52	58	64	70	75	81	87
9 point Univers 55	2.60	26	31	36	42	47	52	57	62	68	73	78
10 point Univers 55	2.40	24	29	34	38	43	48	53	58	62	67	72
12 point Univers 55	2.10	21	25	29	34	38	42	46	50	55	59	63
8 point Univers 65	2.60	26	31	36	42	47	52	57	62	68	73	78
9 point Univers 65	2.40	24	29	34	38	43	48	53	58	62	67	72
10 point Univers 65	2.20	22	26	31	35	40	44	48	53	57	62	66
12 point Univers 65	1.90	19	23	27	30	34	38	42	46	49	53	57

Display Typography

1. Carefully examine the copy. Consider its meaning and its relationship to other elements on the page. Study the visual aspects of display copy: word lengths, number of words, word structure (presence and location of ascenders and descenders), and interletter relationships (see Fig. **8**, Syntax and Communication).

2. Select typefaces for exploration, considering their relationship to content, legibility factors, typesetting and printing methods.

3. Begin a series of small preliminary sketches, exploring alternative design possibilities. Consider type size and weight, division of the copy into lines, line arrangements (justified, unjustified, centered) and overall spatial organization. If a grid is being used, each sketch should reflect its structure.

4. Evaluate the sketches, and select one or more for further development. Criteria should be based on an overview of visual syntax, message, and legibility.

5. Prepare actual-size rough sketches of the page, working freely. Once again, select a sketch or sketches for further development.

6. Study type specimens to select the exact style, size, and weight to be used. Often, designers make tracings of the specimens to explore subtle visual characteristics of the type and to determine the desired interletter, interword, and interline spacing.

7. After these design decisions are made, the final layout can be prepared. It becomes the basis for type specification, client approval, and preparation of reproduction art. The degree of refinement may vary from a rough sketch to a tight comprehensive with set type, depending on the nature of the project.

Text typography

1. In the small preliminary sketches, text areas should be treated as rectangles or other simple shapes.

2. An initial character count of the typewritten manuscript (see Appendices A and B) should be made to determine its length.

3. Select a type style, considering its appropriateness to content and its relationship to the display type. Carefully study the type specimens to evaluate legibility, texture, and tone.

4. Working on tracing paper or at a computer terminal, plan a specific format, establishing line length, vertical column depth, and margins.

5. Select the desired type size and interline spacing. Then, copyfitting, as described in Appendix A, should be used to determine the specific area occupied by the text type.

6. Adjustments are now made in the format or the type specifications if the copyfitting procedure indicates that the type will not fit the allocated space.

7. Attention should be given to details: paragraph indication, interletter and interword spacing, and treatment of headings, folios, captions, and other supporting text material.

8. The designer can now prepare final layouts and mark specifications on the manuscript with assurance that the set type will conform to this plan.

Reviewing type proofs.

After proofs are received from the typesetter, the designer should carefully examine them while the proofreader is checking for editorial accuracy.

1. Compare the set type with the layouts for proper fit. Determine what, if any, adjustments are necessary.

2. Check the type proofs to insure that specifications were followed. Font selection, line lengths, and interline spacing should conform to the instructions.

3. Make sure that details were handled correctly. For example, did the typesetters overlook words set in italic or bold?

4. Use a T-square and triangle to check the horizontal and vertical alignment of columns.

5. Examine the interline and interword intervals, particularly in display type, to make sure that they conform to the specifications. Often, designers make subtle optical adjustments by cutting apart the proofs.

6. Look for awkward text settings, such as rivers, widows, and undesirable line breaks in unjustified typography. The editor or writer may be able to make small editorial changes to correct these problems.

7. Inspect proof quality. Common problems include rounded terminals due to inaccurate exposure, poor image sharpness, uneven or gray tone from incorrect processing, "dancing" characters that don't align properly on the baseline, poor kerning between misfit letters, and inconsistent proof tone within a long text.

8. Standard proofreaders' marks, listed in Appendix D, should be used to specify corrections.

Proofreader's marks

Instruction	Notation in margin	Notation in type	Corrected type
Delete	ℐ	the ~~type~~ font	the font
Insert	type	the ⌃font	the type font
Let it stand	stet	the ~~type~~ font	the type font
Reset in capitals	cap	the type font	THE TYPE FONT
Reset in lowercase	lc	THE TYPE FONT	the type font
Reset in italics	ital	the type font	the *type* font
Reset in small capitals	sc	See type font.	See TYPE FONT.
Reset in roman	rom	the (type) font	the type font
Reset in boldface	bf	the type font	**the type font**
Reset in lightface	lf	the type (font)	the type font
Transpose	tr	the font type	the type font
Close up space	◡	the ty pe	the type
Delete and close space	ℐ̂	the type foont	the type font
Move left	⊏	⊏ the type font	the type font
Move right	⊐	the type font	the type font
Run in	run in	The type font is Univers. It is not Garamond.	The type font is Univers. It is not Garamond.
Align	‖	the type font the type font the type font	the type font the type font the type font
Spell out	sp	③ type fonts	Three type fonts
Insert space	#	the type font	the type font
Insert period	⊙	The type font⌃	The type font.
Insert comma	⌄	One⌃two, three	One, two, three
Insert hyphen	⌒=⌒	Ten⌃point type	Ten-point type
Insert colon	⊙	Old Style types⌃	Old Style types:
Insert semicolon	⌃;	Select the font⌃ spec the type.	Select the font; spec the type.
Insert apostrophe	⌄	Baskervilles type	Baskerville's type
Insert quotation marks	⌄/⌄	the word type	the word "type"
Insert parenthesis	(/)/	The word type is in parenthesis.	The word (type) is in parenthesis.
Insert en dash	ⅼ/N	Flush left	Flush–left
Insert em dash	ⅼ/M/ⅼ/M	Garamond⌃an Old Style face is used today.	Garamond— an Old Style face— is used today.
Start paragraph	¶	⌃The type font is Univers 55.	The type font is Univers 55.
No paragraph indent	no ¶	⊏ The type font is Univers 55.	The type font is Univers 55.

c. 1450: First Textura-style type, Johann Gutenberg
1467: First roman-style type, Sweynheym and Pannartz
1470: Jenson, Nicolas Jenson
1495: Bembo, Francesco Griffo
1499: Poliphilus, Francesco Griffo
1501: First italic type, Francesco Griffo
1514: Fraktur, Hans Schoensperger
1532: Garamond, Claude Garamond
1557: Civilité, Robert Granjon
c. 1570: Plantin, Anonymous
c. 1570: Canon d'Espagne, The Plantin Office
c. 1582: Flemish bold roman, The Plantin Office
1616: Typi Academiae, Jean Jannon
c. 1670: Fell Roman, Peter Walpergen
1690: Janson, Nicholas Kis
1702: Romain du Roi, Philippe Grandjean
1722: Caslon Old Style, William Caslon
c. 1743: Early transitional types, Pierre Simon Fournier le
Jeune
c. 1746: Fournier decorated letters,
Pierre Simon Fournier le Jeune
1757: Baskerville, John Baskerville
c. 1764: Italique Moderne and Ancienne,
Pierre Simon Fournier le Jeune
1768: Fry's Baskerville, Isaac Moore
c. 1780: Bodoni, Giambattista Bodoni
1784: Didot, Firmin Didot
c. 1795: Bulmer, William Martin
1796: Fry's Ornamented, Richard Austin
c. 1800: Walbaum, J. E. Walbaum
c. 1810: Scotch Roman, Richard Austin
1815: Two Lines Pica, Antique (first Egyptian style),
Vincent Figgins
1815: Five Lines Pica, In Shade (first perspective font),
Vincent Figgins
1816: Two-line English Egyptian (first sans serif),
William Caslon IV
1820: Lettres Ornees, Fonds de Gille
1828: Roman, Darius Wells
1830: Two-line great primer sans serif, Vincent Figgins
1832: Grotesque, William Thorowgood
1838: Sans serryphs ornamented, Blake and Stephenson
1844: Ionic, Henry Caslon
1845: Clarendon, Robert Besley and Company
1845: Rustic, V. and J. Figgins
1845: Zig-Zag, V. and J. Figgins
1850: Scroll, Henry Caslon
1859: Antique Tuscan Outlined, William Page
1856: National, Philadelphia Type Foundry
c. 1860: P. T. Barnum, Barnhart Brothers and Spindler
c. 1865: French Antique (later called Playbill),
Miller and Richard
c. 1865: Old Style Antique, (called Bookman in the U.S.),
Miller and Richard
c. 1869: Runic, Reed and Fox
c. 1870: Figgins Condensed No. 2, Stevens Shanks
c. 1870: Bank Gothic, Bardhart Brothers and Spindler
1878: Circlet, Barnhart Brothers and Spindler
1878: Glyphic, MacKellar, Smiths and Jordan
c. 1885: Geometric, Central Type Foundry
c. 1890: Ringlet, Marr Typefounding
c. 1890: Gothic Outline No. 61, American Typefounders
c. 1890: Rubens, Marr Typefounding
c. 1890: Karnac, Marr Typefounding
1890: Century, L. B. Benton
1890: Golden, William Morris

1892: Troy, William Morris
1893: Chaucer, William Morris
1894: Bradley, Will Bradley
1895: Merrymount Type, Bertram Goodhue
1895: Century Roman, Theodore Low DeVinne and
L. B. Benton
1896: Cheltenham, Bertram Goodhue
1896: Vale Type, Charles Ricketts
1898: Grasset, Eugene Grasset
c. 1898: Paris Metro Lettering, Hector Guimard
1898–1906: Akzidenz Grotesque (Standard), Berthold
Foundry
1900: Eckmann-Schrift, Otto Eckmann
1900: Century Expanded, Morris F. Benton
1900: Doves Roman, T. J. Cobden-Sanderson and
Emery Walker
1901: Endeavor, Charles R. Ashbee
1901: Copperplate Gothic, Frederic W. Goudy
1901–04: Auriol, Georges Auriol
1902: Behrens-Schrift, Peter Behrens
1902: Subiaco, C. H. St. John Hornby
1903: Brook Type, Lucien Pissarro
1904: Korinna, H. Berthold
1904: Franklin Gothic, Morris F. Benton
1907: Behrens-Kursiv, Peter Behrens
1907: Clearface Bold, Morris F. Benton
1907–13: Venus, Bauer Foundry
1908: Behrens-Antiqua, Peter Behrens
1908: News Gothic, Morris F. Benton
1909: Aurora, Wagner and Schmidt Foundry
1910: Kochschrift, Rudolf Koch
1910–15: Hobo, Morris F. Benton
1911: Kennerly Old Style, Frederic W. Goudy
1912: Nicolas Cochin, G. Peignot
1913: Belwe, Georg Belwe
1914: Souvenir, Morris F. Benton
1914: Cloister Old Style, Morris F. Benton
1915: Century Schoolbook, Morris F. Benton
1915–16: Goudy Old Style, Frederic W. Goudy
1916: Centaur, Bruce Rogers
1919–24: Cooper Old Style, Oswald Cooper
1921: Cooper Black, Oswald Cooper
1923: Windsor, Stephenson Blake Foundry
1923: Tiemann, Walter Tiemann
1923: Neuland, Rudolf Koch
1926: Weiss Roman, E. R. Weiss
1927–29: Futura, Paul Renner
1927–29: Kabel, Rudolf Koch
1928: Ultra Bodoni, American Typefounders
1928–30: Gill Sans, Eric Gill
1928: Modernique, Morris F. Benton
1929: Zeppelin, Rudolf Koch
1929: Golden Cockerel, Eric Gill
1929–30: Metro, William A. Dwiggins
1929: Bernhard Fashion, Lucien Bernhard
1929: Bifur, A. M. Cassandre
1929: Broadway, Morris F. Benton
1929: Novel Gothic, H. Becker
1929: Lux, J. Erbar
1929–30: Perpetua, Eric Gill
1929–34: Corvinus, Imre Reiner
1930: Joanna, Eric Gill
1930: Dynamo, Ludwig and Mayer Foundry
1931: Prisma, Rudolf Koch
1931: Times New Roman, Stanley Morison
1931: Stymie, Morris F. Benton

1931–36: Beton, Heinrich Jost

1932–40: Albertus, Berthold Wolpe

1933: Agency Gothic, Morris F. Benton

1933: Atlas, K. H. Schaefer

1935: Huxley Vertical, Walter Huxley

1936: Acier Noir, A. M. Cassandre

1937: Peignot, A. M. Cassandre

1937: Onyx, Gerry Powell

1938: Caledonia, William A. Dwiggins

1938: Libra, S. H. De Roos

1938: Lydian, Warren Chappell

1938: Empire, American Typefounders

1939: Chisel, Stephenson Blake Foundry

1940: Trajanus, Warren Chappell

1945: Stradivarius, Imre Reiner

1946: Profil, Eugen and Max Lenz

1948: Trade Gothic, Mergenthaler Linotype

c. 1950: Brush, Harold Brodersen

1950: Michelangelo, Hermann Zapf

1950: Palatino, Hermann Zapf

1951: Sistina, Hermann Zapf

1952: Horizon, K. F. Bauer and Walter Baum

1952: Melior, Hermann Zapf

1952: Microgramma, A. Butti

1953: Mistral, Roger Excoffon

1954: Trump Mediaeval, Georg Trump

1955: Columna, Max Caflisch

1955–56: Egyptienne, Adrian Frutiger

1956: Craw Clarendon, Freeman Craw

1956: Murry Hill, E. J. Klumpp

1957: Meridien, Adrian Frutiger

1957: Univers, Adrian Frutiger

c. 1957: Helvetica, Max Miedinger

1960: Aurora, Jackson Burke

1961: Octavian, Will Carter and David Kindersley

1962: Eurostile, Aldo Novarese

1962–66: Antique Olive, Roger Excoffon

1964: Sabon, Jan Tschichold

1965: Americana, Richard Isbell

1965: Snell Roundhand, Matthew Carter

1965: Friz Quadrata, Ernest Friz

1966: Egyptian 505, André Gürtler

1966: Vladimir, Vladimir Andrich

1967: Serifa, Adrian Frutiger

1967: Americana, Richard Isbell

1967: Cartier, Carl Dair

1967: Avant Garde Gothic, Herb Lubalin
        and Tom Carnase

1967: Poppl-Antiqua, Friedrich Poppl

1968: Syntax, Hans E. Meier

1969: Aachen, Colin Brignall

1970: Olympian, Matthew Carter

1970: Machine, Tom Carnase and Ron Bonder

1970: ITC Souvenir, Edward Benguiat

1972: Iridium, Adrian Frutiger

1972: Times Europa, Walter Tracy

1972: University, Mike Daines

1974: American Typewriter, Joel Kadan

1974: ITC Tiffany, Edward Benguiat

1974: Newtext, Ray Baker

1974: Korinna, Ed Benguiat and Vic Caruso

1974: Serif Gothic, Herb Lubalin and Tony DiSpigna

1974: Lubalin Graph, Herb Lubalin, Tony DiSpigna,
        and Joe Sundwall

1975: ITC Bauhaus, based on Bayer's universal alphabet

1975: ITC Bookman, Ed Benguiat

1975: ITC Century, Tony Stan

1975: ITC Cheltenham, Tony Stan

1975: Concorde Nova, Gunter Gerhard Lange

1975: ITC Garamond, Tony Stan

1975: Marconi, Hermann Zapf

1976: Eras, Albert Hollenstein and Albert Boton

1976: Poppl-Pontiflex, Friedrich Poppl

1976: Zapf Book, Hermann Zapf

1977: Quorum, Ray Baker

1977: Korinna Kursiv, Edward Benguiat

1977: Italia, Colin Brignall

1977: Benguiat, Edward Benguiat

1977: Zapf International, Hermann Zapf

1978: Basilia, André Gürtler

1978: Bell Centennial, Matthew Carter

1978: Galliard, Matthew Carter

1979: Benguiat Gothic, Edward Benguiat

1979: Glypha, Adrian Frutiger

1979: Zapf Chancery, Hermann Zapf

1980: Fenice, Aldo Novarese

1980: Novarese, Aldo Novarese

1980: Icone, Adrian Frutiger

1980: Marconi, Hermann Zapf

1980: Edison, Hermann Zapf

1981: Adroit, Phil Martin

1981: Barcelonia, Edward Benguiat

1981: Isbell, Dick Isbell and Jerry Campbell

1982: Cushing, Vincent Pacella

1983: ITC Berkeley Old Style, Tony Stan

1983: Weidemann, Kurt Weidemann and Kurt Strecker

1983: Neue Helvetica, Linotype (Stempel)
        staff designers

1984: Macintosh screen fonts, Susan Kare

1984: Osiris, Gustav Jaeger

1984: Usherwood, Les Usherwood

1984: Veljovic, Jovica Veljovic

1985: Aurelia, Hermann Zapf

1985: Elan, Albert Boton

1985: Emigre, Zuzana Licko

1985: Kis-Janson, Autologic staff designers

1985: Lucida, Charles Bigelow and Kris Holmes

1985: Mixage, Aldo Novarese

1985: Oakland, Zuzana Licko

1986: Linotype Centennial, Matthew Carter

1987: Amerigo, Gerard Unger

1987: Charter, Matthew Carter

1987: Gerstner Original, Karl Gerstner

1987: Neufont, David Weinz

1987: Stone Informal, Sans, and Serif,
        Sumner Stone

1987: Charlemagne, Carol Twombly

1987: Zapf Renaissance, Hermann Zapf

1988: Visigoth, Arthur Baker

1989: Adobe Garamond, Robert Slimbach

1989: Giovanni, Robert Slimbach

1989: Helicon, David Quay

1989: Lithos, Carol Twombly

1989: Rotis, Otl Aicher

1989: Trajan, Carol Twombly

1990: Journal, Zuzana Licko

1990: Quay, David Quay

1990: Tekton, David Siegel

1990: Template Gothic, Barry Deck

1991: Print, Sumner Stone

1992: EndsMeansMends, Sumner Stone

1992: Syndor, Hans Edward Meier

Bibliography

Allen, Wallace, and Carroll, Michael. *A Design for News.* Minneapolis, MN: The Minneapolis Star and Tribune Company, 1981.

Anderson, Donald M. *A Renaissance Alphabet.* Madison, WI: University of Wisconsin Press, 1971.

————. *The Art of Written Forms.* New York: Holt, Rinehart and Winston, 1969.

Arnheim, Rudolf. *The Power of the Center: A Study of Composition in the Visual Arts.* Berkeley, CA: University of California Press, 1982.

Bojko, Szymon. *New Graphic Design in Revolutionary Russia.* New York: Praeger, 1972.

Burns, Aaron. *Typography.* New York: Van Nostrand Reinhold, 1961.

Carter, Rob. *American Typography Today.* New York: Van Nostrand Reinhold, 1989.

Chang, Amos I. *The Tao of Architecture.* Princeton, NJ: Princeton University Press, 1981.

Dair, Carl. *Design with Type.* Toronto: University of Toronto Press, 1967.

Damase, Jacques. *Revolution Typographique.* Geneva: Galerie Mott, 1966.

Doczi, Gyorgy. *The Power of Limits. Proportional Harmonies in Nature, Art and Architecture.* Boulder, CO: Shambhala Publications, l981.

Drogin, Marc. *Medieval Calligraphy: Its History and Technique.* Montclair, NJ: Allanheld and Schram, 1980.

Elam, Kimberly. *Expressive Typography.* New York: Van Nostrand Reinhold, 1990.

Friedman, Mildred, ed. *De Stijl: 1917–1931, Visions of Utopia.* New York: Abbeville Press, 1982.

Gardner, William. *Alphabet at Work.* New York: St. Martins Press, 1982.

Gerstner, Karl. *Compendium for Literates: A System of Writing.* Translated by Dennis Q. Stephenson. Cambridge, MA: The MIT Press,1974.

Goines, David Lance. *A Constructed Roman Alphabet.* Boston: David R. Godine, 1981.

Goudy, Frederic W. *The Alphabet and Elements of Lettering.* New York: Dover, 1963.

————. *Typologia: Studies in Type Design and Type-making.* Berkeley, CA: University of California, 1940.

Gray, Nicolete. *Nineteenth-Century Ornamented Type Faces.* Berkeley, CA: University of California Press, 1977.

Haley, Allan. *Phototypography: A Guide for in-House Typesetting.* New York: Charles Scribner's Sons, 1980.

Harlan, Calvin. *Vision and Invention: A Course in Art Fundamentals.* New York: Prentice-Hall, 1969.

Hiebert, Kenneth J. *Graphic Design Processes: Universal to Unique.* New York: Van Nostrand Reinhold, 1992.

Hofmann, Armin. *Graphic Design Manual: Principles and Practice.* New York: Van Nostrand Reinhold, 1965

————. *His Work, Quest and Philosophy.* Basel: Birkhäuser Verlag, 1989.

Hurlburt, Allen. *The Grid System.* New York: Van Nostrand Reinhold, 1978.

————. *Layout: The Design of the Printed Page.* New York: Watson-Guptill, 1977.

————. *Publication Design.* New York: Van Nostrand Reinhold, 1976.

Jensen, Robert, and Conway, Patricia. *Ornamentalism: The New Decorativeness in Architecture and Design.* New York: Clarkson N. Potter, 1982.

Kelly, Rob Roy. *American Wood Type 1828–1900: Notes on the Evolution of Decorated and Large Type and Comments on Related Trades of the Period.* New York: Van Nostrand Reinhold, 1969.

Kepes, Gyorgy. *Sign, Image, Symbol.* New York: George Braziller, 1966.

Knobler, Nathan. *The Visual Dialogue.* New York: Holt, Rinehart and Winston, 1967.

Lobell, Frank. *Between Silence and Light: Spirit in the Architecture of Louis I. Kahn.* Boulder, CO: Shambhala Publications,1979.

Machlis, Joseph. *The Enjoyment of Music: An Introduction to Perceptive Listening.* New York: W. W. Norton, 1977.

McLean, Ruari. *Jan Tschichold: Typographer.* Boston: David R. Godine, 1975.

————. *The Thames and Hudson Manual of Typography.* London: Thames and Hudson, 1980.

Meggs, Philip B. *A History of Graphic Design.* Second Edition. New York: Van Nostrand Reinhold, 1992.

————. *Type and Image: The Language of Graphic Design.* New York: Van Nostrand Reinhold, 1989.

Morison, Stanley. *First Principles of Typography.* Cambridge: Cambridge University Press, 1936.

————, and Day, Kenneth. *The Typographic Book, 1450–1935.* Chicago: The University of Chicago Press, 1964.

Müller-Brockmann, Josef. *Grid Systems in Graphic Design: A Visual Communications Manual.* Niederteufen, Switzerland: Arthur Niggli Ltd., 1981.

Rehe, Rolf F. *Typography: How to Make it Most Legible.* Carmel, CA: Design Research Publications, 1974.

Roberts, Raymond. *Typographic Design: Handbooks to Printing.* London: Ernest Benn Limited, 1966.

Rogers, Bruce. *Paragraphs on Printing.* New York: Dover, 1980.

Rondthaler, Edward. *Life with Letters—As They Turned Photogenic.* New York: Hastings House, 1981.

Rosen, Ben. *Type and Typography.* New York: Van Nostrand Reinhold, 1963.

Ruder, Emil. *Typography: A Manual of Design.* New York: Hastings House, 1981.

Ruegg, Ruedi. *Basic Typography: Design with Letters.* New York: Van Nostrand Reinhold, 1989.

Schmid, Helmut. *Typography Today.* Tokyo: Seibundo Shinkosha, 1980.

Scott, Robert Gillam. *Design Fundamentals.* New York: McGraw-Hill, 1951.

Solt, Mary Ellen, ed. *Concrete Poetry.* Bloomington, IN: Indiana University Press, 1970.

Spencer, Herbert. *Pioneers of Modern Typography.* London: Lund Humphries, 1969.

————. *The Visible Word.* New York: Hastings House, 1969.

Sutnar, Ladislav. *Visual Design in Action—Principles, Purposes.* New York: Hastings House, 1961.

Swann, Cal. *Techniques of Typography.* New York: Watson-Guptill, 1969.

Updike, Daniel Berkeley. *Printing Types: Their History, Forms and Use.* Cambridge, MA: Harvard University Press, 1937.

Picture Credits

(Frontispiece) *St. Barbara,* 15th Century German or French polychromed walnut sculpture. (50"H x 23"W x 13" D) 127.0 cm x 58.4 cm x 33.0 cm. The Virginia Museum of Fine Arts, Richmond. The Williams Fund, 1968.

Chapter One.

1. Impressed tablet from Godin Tepe, Iran. West Asian Department, Royal Ontario Museum, Toronto.

2. Facsimile of the cuneiform impression on a clay tablet, after Hansard.

3. The Pyramids at Giza, from *The Iconographic Encyclopaedia of Science, Literature, and Art* by Johann Georg Heck, 1851.

4. Egyptian Old Kingdom *False Door Stele,* limestone. The Virginia Museum of Fine Arts, Richmond. Museum Purchase: The Williams Fund.

5. Cuneiform tablet. Sumero-Akkadian. The Metropolitan Museum of Art, New York. Acquired by exchange with J. Pierpont Morgan Library, 1911.

6. Photograph of Stonehenge; courtesy of the British Tourist Authority.

7. Egyptian Polychromed Wood Sculpture, XVIII–XIX Dynasty. Ushabti. The Virginia Museum of Fine Arts, Richmond. Museum Purchase: The Williams Fund, 1955.

8. *The Book of the Dead of Tuthmosis III.* Museum of Fine Arts, Boston. Gift of Horace L. Meyer.

10. Phoenician inscription. The Metropolitan Museum of Art, New York. The Cesnola Collection. Purchased by subscription, 1874–76.

12. Photograph of the Parthenon; courtesy of the Greek National Tourist Office.

13. Photograph of Greek record of sale; Agora Excavations, American School of Classical Studies, Athens.

15. Photograph of a wall in Pompeii, by James Mosley.

17. Photographer anonymous; c. 1895. Private collection.

18. *Funerary inscription of Lollia Genialis.* Marble. The Metropolitan Museum of Art, New York.

19. Photograher anonymous; c. 1895. Private collection.

20. Photograph; courtesy of the Italian Government Travel Office.

24. Detail, "Christ attended by angels," from *The Book of Kells,* fol. 32v; photograph; courtesy of the Irish Tourist Board.

25 and 26. Photographs; courtesy of the Irish Tourist Board.

28. Photograph; courtesy of the French Government Tourist Office.

30. Bronze and copper *Crucifix.* The Virginia Museum of Fine Art, Richmond. Museum Purchase: The Williams Fund, 1968.

32. *Madonna and Child on a Curved Throne.* Wood, 0.815 x 0.490m (32 1/8 x 19 3/8 in.) National Gallery of Art, Washington. Andrew W. Mellon Collection, 1937.

34. Lippo Memmi; Sienese, active 1317–47. *Saint John the Baptist.* Wood, 0.95 x 0.46m (37 1/4 x 18 in.). National Gallery of Art, Washington. Samuel H. Kress Collection, 1939.

35. Photograph courtesy of the Italian Government Tourist Office.

37. Fra Filippo Lippi; Florentine c. 1406–69. *Madonna and Child.* Wood, 0.80 x 0.51m (31 3/8 x 20 1/8 in.). National Gallery of Art, Washington. Samuel H. Kress Collection, l939.

38. The Rosenwald Collection; The Library of Congress, Washington, DC.

39. Woodcut illustration from *Standebuch* by Jost Amman, 1568.

40. Photographer anonymous; c. 1895. Private collection.

42. Typography from *Lactantu*. . . . Printed by Sweynheym and Pannartz; Rome, 1468. The Library of Congress Rare Book and Special Collections Division, Washington, DC.

43. From *De evangelica praeparatione* by Eusebius Pamphilii.

Printed by Nicolas Jenson; Venice, 1470.

44. From *The Recuyell of the Historyes of Troye* by Raoul Le Fevre. Printed by William Caxton and Colard Mansion; Burges, c. 1475.

45. Filippino Lippi; *Portrait of a Youth.* Wood, 0.510 x 0.355 m (20 x 13 7/8 in.). National Gallery of Art, Washington, DC. Andrew Mellon Collection, 1937.

46. Erhard Ratdolt, earliest extant type specimen sheet. Published April 1, 1486, in Augsburg, Germany. Bayerische Staatsbibliothek, Munich.

47. Woodcut portrait of Aldus Manutius. Published by Antoine Lafrery; Rome, 16th century.

48. From *De aetna* by Pietro Bembo. Published by Aldus Manutius, Venice, 1495.

49. Page from *Virgil.* Published by Aldus Manutius; Venice, 1501.

50. Photograph by Rommler and Jonas; 1892. Private collection.

53. From *Underweisung der Messung* by Albrecht Durer; Nuremburg, 1525.

54. From *Champ Fleury* by Geoffroy Tory; Paris, 1529.

55. Photograph; courtesy of the French Government Tourist Office.

57. Titian; Venetian c. 1477-1565. *Cardinal Pietro Bembo.* Canvas, 0.945 x 0.765m (37 1/8 x 30 1/8 in.). National Gallery of Art, Washington, DC. Samuel H. Kress Collection, 1952.

58. Title page for *Elementary Geometry* by Oronce Fine. Printed by Simone de Colines; Paris, l544.

59. From *Hypnerotomachia Poliphili* by Fra Francesco Colonna. Printed by Jacque Kerver; Paris, 1546.

60. El Greco; Spanish 1541-1614. *Saint Martin and the Beggar.* Canvas, 1.935 x 1.030m (76 1/8 x 40 1/2 in.). National Gallery of Art, Washington, DC. Widener Collection, 1942.

61. From *Nejw Kunstliches Alphabet* by Johann Theodor de Bry; Germany, 1595.

62. Photographer anonymous; c. 1895. Private collection.

63. Detail, typographic specimens of Jean Jannon; Sedan, 1621.

64. Page from *Stamperia Vaticana Specimen;* Rome, 1628.

65. Photograph; courtesy of the Government of India Tourist Office.

66. Sir Anthony van Dyck; Flemish 1599-1641. *Henri II de Lorraine, Duc de Guise.* Canvas, 2.046 x 1.238m (80 5/8 x 48 5/8 in.). National Gallery of Art, Washington, DC. Gift of Cornelius Vanderbilt Whitney, 1947.

67. Jan Vermeer; Dutch 1632-75. *Woman Holding a Balance,* c. 1664. Canvas, 0.425 x 0.380m (16 3/4 x 15 in.). National Gallery of Art, Washington, DC. Widener Collection, 1942.

69. Photograph; courtesy of the British Tourist Authority.

71. Photographer anonymous; 1896. Private collection.

72. From the 1764 specimen book of W. Caslon and Son, London.

73. Photograph; courtesy of the Irish Tourist Board.

74. Title page for *Cato Major, or His Discourse on Old Age* by M. T. Cicero. Printed by Benjamin Franklin; Philadelphia, 1744.

75. Francois Boucher; French 1703-70. *The Love Letter,* 1750. Canvas, 0.813 x 0.741m (32 x 29 1/8 in.). National Gallery of Art, Washington, DC. Timken Collection, l959.

76. Anonymous; engraved portrait of John Baskerville.

77. From the specimen book of Thomas Cottrell, English typefounder; London, c. 1765.

78. Detail, title page of *Historie de Louis de Bourbon*. . . , using types and ornaments designed by Pierre Simon Fournier le Jeune. Published by Lottin; Paris, 1768.

79. Johann David Steingruber, 1702–1787. Engraved letter A from *Architectonishes Alphabet,* Schwabach, 1773. The Metropolitan Museum of Art. The Elisha Whittelsey Collection,

1955. The Elisha Whittelsey Fund.

80. Photograph; courtesy of the Library of Congress, Washington, DC.

82. Detail, title page using type designed by Bodoni. Dante's *Divine Commedy;* Pisa, 1804.

83. From Thorowgood's *New Specimen of Printing Types, late R. Thorne's, No. 2;* London, 1821.

84. Jacque-Louis David; French 1748-1825. *Napoleon in his Study,* 1812. Canvas, 2.039 x 1.251m (80 1/4 x 49 1/4 in.). National Gallery of Art, Washington, DC. Samuel H. Kress Collection, 1961.

85–6. From *Specimen of Printing Types* by Vincent Figgins; London, 1815.

87. From *Specimen of Printing Types* by William Caslon IV; London, 1816.

88. From *Manuale Typographico.* Published by Signora Bodoni and Luigi Orsi; Parma, Italy, 1818.

89. From Thorowgood's *New Specimen of Printing Types, late R. Thorne's, No. 2;* London, 1821.

90. Photograph; courtesy of the Virginia State Travel Service.

91. From *Bower, Bacon & Bower's Specimen of Printing Types;* Sheffield, c. 1825.

92. Wood engraving of Darius Wells, from *The Inland Printer;* Chicago, July 1888.

93. From *Specimen of Printing Types* by Vincent Figgins; London, 1833.

94. Poster by the Davy & Berry Printing Office; Albion, England, 1836.

95. From *Specimen of Printing Types by V. & J. Figgins, successors to Vincent Figgins, Letter-Founder;* London, 1836.

96. Courtesy of the Library of Congress Rare Book and Special Collections Division, Washington, DC.

97. Photograph; courtesy of The British Tourist Authority.

98. From *The Specimen Book of Types cast at the Austin Foundry by Wood & Sharwoods;* London, c. 1841.

99. From *A General Specimen of Printing Types.* Published by W. Thorowgood and Company; London, 1848.

100. Photograph; The Library of Congress Rare Book and Special Collections Division, Washington, DC.

101. Photograph; The Library of Congress Rare Book and Special Collections Division, Washington, DC.

102. From the wood type specimen book of William H. Page & Company; Greenville, Connecticut, 1859.

103. Private collection.

104. Honoré Daumier; French 1808-79. *The Third-Class Carriage.* Oil on canvas, 65.4 x 90.2m (25 3/4 x 35 1/2 in.). The Metropolitan Museum of Art, New York. Bequest of Mrs. H. O. Havemeyer, 1929. The H. O. Havemeyer Collection.

105. Private collection.

106. Private collection.

107. Courtesy of The New York Convention and Visitors Bureau.

108. Private collection.

109. Private collection.

110. Wood engraving from *The Inland Printer;* Chicago, December, 1889.

112. Courtesy of The French Government Tourist Office.

113. Photograph; courtesy of the Archives: The Coca-Cola Company.

114. Paul Gauguin; French 1848-1903. *Fatata Te Miti (By the Sea),* 1892. Canvas, 0.679 x 0.915m (26 3/4 x 36 in.). National Gallery of Art, Washington, DC. The Chester Dale Collection, 1962.

117. William Morris. *News from Nowhere.* Published by Kelmscott Press; London, 1892.

118. Title page from *Van nu en Straks.* Designed by Henri van de Velde, 1893.

119. Title page from *Limbes de Lumieres* by Gustave Kahn; Brussels, 1897.

120. From *The Inland Printer;* Chicago, June, 1900.

121. Title page from *A Lady of Quality* by Francis Hodgson Burnett. Published by Charles Scribner's Sons; New York, 1897.

122. Cover for Vienna Secession Catalog No. 5; Vienna, 1899.

123. Photograph; courtesy of the French Government Tourist Office.

124. Dedication page from *Feste des Lebens und der Kunst: Ein Betrachtung des Theaters als hochsten Kultursymbols (Celebrations of Life and Art: A Consideration of the Theater as the Highest Cultural Symbol)* by Peter Behrens; Darmstadt, 1900.

125. Filippo Marinetti, Futurist poem, S.T.F., 1914.

126. Cover, *Delikatessen Haus Erich Fromm, Haupt-List 2;* Cologne, c. 1910.

127. Wassily Kandinsky. *Improvisation 31 (Sea Battle),* 1913. National Gallery of Art, Washington, DC. Ailsa Mellon Bruce Fund.

128. War Bond Fund Drive poster for the British government by Bert Thomas, c. 1916.

129. Advertisement for the *Kleine Grosz Mappe (Small Grosz Portfolio)* from *Die Neue Jugend.* Designed by John Heartfield. Published by Der Malik-Verlag, Berlin, June 1917.

130. First cover for *De Stijl,* the journal of the de Stijl movement. Designed by Vilmos Huszar. Published/Edited by Theo van Doesburg, The Netherlands; October 1917.

131. Raoul Hausmann. *Poeme Phonetique,* 1919.

132. Piet Mondrian; Dutch 1872–1944. *Diamond Painting in Red, Yellow, and Blue.* Oil on canvas, 40 x 40 in. National Gallery of Art, Washington, DC. Gift of Herbert and Nannette Rothschild, 1971.

133. Poster announcing availability of books, by Alexander Rodchenko; Moscow, c. 1923. Private collection.

134. Illustration by Mike Fanizza.

135. Title page from *Die Kunstismen* by El Lissitzky and Hans Arp. Published by Eugen Rentsch Verlag; Zurich, 1925.

136. Proposed universal alphabet. Designed by Herbert Bayer as a student at the Bauhaus.

137. Constantin Brancusi; Rumanian 1876–1957. *Bird in Space.* Marble, stone, and wood, hgt. 3.446m (136 1/2 in.). National Gallery of Art, Washington, DC. Gift of Eugene and Agnes Meyer, 1967.

138. Title page for special insert, "Elementare Typographie" from *Typographische Mitteilungen;* Leipzig, October 1925.

139–40. Advertisements by Piet Zwart; courtesy of N. V. Nederlandsche Kabelfabriek, Delft.

141. Trial setting using Futura. Designed by Paul Renner. Published by Bauersche Giesserei; Frankfurt am Main, 1930.

142. Photograph; courtesy of New York Convention and Visitors Bureau.

143. Max Bill. Poster for an exhibition of African Art at the Kunstgewerbemuseum, Zurich.

144. Alexey Brodovitch. Poster for an industrial design exhibition at the Philadelphia Museum of Art.

145. Walker Evans. Photograph, "Fields family, sharecroppers," Hale County, Alabama. The Library of Congress, Washington, DC.

146. Jean Carlu. Advertisement for Container Corporation of America, December 21, 1942.

147. Max Bill. Poster for an exhibition of Art Concrete at the Kunsthalle, Basle.

148. Paul Rand. Title page for *On My Way* by Hans Arp. Published by Wittenborn, Schultz, Inc; New York, 1948.

149. Willem de Kooning. *Painting,* 1948. Enamel and oil on canvas, 42 5/8 x 56 1/8 in. Collection; Museum of Modern Art, New York. Purchase.

150. Ladislav Sutnar. Cover for *Catalog Design Progress* by K. Lonberg-Holm and Ladislav Sutnar. Published by Sweet's Catalog Service; New York, 1950.

151. Illustration by Stephen Chovanec.

152. Henri Matisse; French 1869-1954. *Woman with Amphora and Pomegranates.* Paper on canvas (collage), 2.436 x 0.963m (96 x 37 7/8 in.). National Gallery of Art, Washington, DC. Ailsa Mellon Bruce Fund, l973.

153. Josef Müller-Brockmann. Poster for a musical concert; Zurich, Switzerland, January, 1955.

154. Saul Bass. Advertisement from the Great Ideas of Western Man series, Container Corporation of America.

155. Willem Sandberg. Back and front covers for *Experimenta Typopgraphica.* Published by Verlag Galerie der Spiegel; Cologne, 1956.

156. Saul Bass. Film title for *Anatomy of a Murder.* Produced and directed by Otto Preminger, 1959.

157. Photograph; courtesy of the New York Convention and Visitors Bureau.

158. Carlo L. Vivarelli. Cover for *Neue Grafik.* Published by Verlag Otto Walter AG; Olten, Switzerland, 1959.

159. Henry Wolf. Cover for *Harper's Bazaar* magazine, December, 1959.

160. Gerald Holton. Symbol for the Campaign for Nuclear Disarmament; Great Britain, c. 1959.

161. Otto Storch. Typography from *McCall's* magazine; July 1959.

162. Karl Gerstner. Poster for the newspaper *National Zeitung;* Zurich, 1960.

163. Herb Lubalin. Advertisement for Sudler and Hennessey Advertising, Inc.; New York.

164. George Lois. Advertisement for A. H. Robins Company, Incorporated.

165. Photograph; courtesy of the Virginia State Travel Service.

166. Seymour Chwast and Milton Glaser, Push Pin Studios, Inc. Poster for the Lincoln Center for the Performing Arts, New York.

167. George Lois. Cover for *Esquire* magazine, October 1966.

168. Seymour Chwast and Milton Glaser, Push Pin Studios, Inc. Poster for Filmsense, New York.

169. Photograph; courtesy of the Public Relations Department, City of Montreal, Canada.

170. Designer not known. Symbol widely used in the environmental movement.

171. Photograph; courtesy of the National Aeronautics and Space Administration.

172. Wolfgang Weingart. Experimental interpretation of a poem by Elsbeth Bornoz; Basle, Switzerland.

173. Herb Lubalin. Volume 1, Number 1, of *U&lc.* Published by the International Typeface Corporation, New York.

174. Cook and Shanosky, commissioned by the American Institute of Graphic Arts under contract to the U. S. Department of Transportation. From *Symbol Signs,* a series of thirty-four passenger-oriented symbols for use in transportation facilities.

175. Bruce Blackburn, then of Chermayeff and Geismar Associates. Symbol for the U. S. Bicentennial Commission and stamp for the U.S.Postal Service, first released in 1971.

176. Photograph; courtesy of the French Government Tourist Office.

177. Trademark reproduced by permission of Frederic Ryder Company; Chicago, Illinois.

178. Willi Kuntz. Poster for an exhibition of photographs by Fredrich Cantor, FOTO Gallery, New York.

179. Title film for *All That Jazz,* Twentieth Century-Fox. Director/Designer Richard Greenberg, R/Greenberg Associates, Inc., New York, NY.

180. Photograph; courtesy of the Office of the Mayor, Portland, Oregon.

181. Warren Lehrer, designer. Published by ear/say, Purchase, NY, and Visual Studies Workshop, Rochester, NY.

182. Designed by Ted Mader and Tom Draper; Ted Mader + Associates, Seattle, WA. Published by Peachpit Press, Inc., Berkeley, CA.

Chapter Three

3. Designed by Frank Armstrong, Armstrong Design Consultants, New Canaan, CT.

4. Willi Kunz. Poster; 14 x 16 1/2 in.

6. Designed by Frank Armstrong, Armstrong Design Consultants, New Canaan, CT.

30. Designed by Frank Armstrong, Armstrong Design Consultants, New Canaan, CT. Photograph by Sally Anderson-Bruce.

32. Designer: Philip Meggs.

35. Designer: Ben Day.

54. Designed by Frank Armstrong, Armstrong Design Consultants, New Canaan, CT.

62. Designer: Ben Day.

75-77. Designed by Keith Jones.

78. Eugen Gomringer. "ping pong," from *Concrete Poetry: A World View.* Edited by Mary Ellen Solt, Indiana University Press, 1970.

92. Designer: Herb Lubalin; courtesy of *The Reader's Digest.*

97. Photograph; courtesy of Olivetti.

102. Gerrit Rietveld. Red/blue chair, 1918. Collection Stedelijk Museum, Amsterdam.

103. Reprinted with permission of *Minneapolis Star and Tribune,* Minneapolis, MN.

106. Designer: Rob Carter; courtesy of Best Products Company.

108. Photograph; courtesy of Daniel Friedman.

109. Photograph; courtesy of Best Products Co., Inc.

110. Eugene Gaillard. French marquetry cabinet, late nineteenth century. Carved mahogany. Collection of Sydney and Frances Lewis.

Chapter Five

4, 5, 6, and 10. Photographs; courtesy of Mergenthaler Linotype Company.

14. Photograph; courtesy of Visual Graphics Corporation.

16. Courtesy of Visual Graphics Corporation.

18. Courtesy of Autologic, Inc., Newbury Park, CA.

22. Courtesy of Serif & Sans, Inc., Boston, MA.

24. Reprinted courtesy of Macworld Communications, 501 Second Street, San Francisco, CA 94107.

34. Microphotographs courtesy of Mike Cody, Virginia Commonwealth University, Richmond, VA.

Chapter Seven

1-8. Courtesy of the National Aeronautics and Space Administration, Washington, DC.

Chapter Eight

5. From *American Advertising Posters of the Nineteenth Century* by Mary Black; courtesy of Dover Publications, Inc., New York, NY.

Sources for specimen quotations

Pages i, 180 -185, 212-217, 224-225, 232-233, and 240-241. From *The Book Beautiful* by Thomas James Cobden-Sanderson. Hammersmith: Hammersmith Publishing Society, 1902.

Pages 111, 252-255. From *The Alphabet and Elements of Lettering* by Frederic W. Goudy, courtesy of Dover Publications, Inc., New York, NY.

Type Specimen Index

Printing: Courier-Westford, Westford, Massachusetts

Binding: Courier-Westford, Westford, Massachusetts

Typography: 9/11 Univers 55 with 7/11 Univers 55 captions and
                       9/11 Univers 65 headings output by The Graphics
                       Gallery, Richmond, Virginia
                       Phototypositor display specimens by Riddick
                       Advertising Art, Richmond, Virginia

Design: First edition: Rob Carter, Stephen Chovanec, Ben
                       Day, and Philip Meggs; Second edition: Rob Carter
                       and Philip Meggs

Design assistance: First edition: Tina Brubaker Chovanec, Justin Deister,
                       John Demao, Akira Ouchi, Tim Priddy, Anne Riker,
                       Joel Sadagursky, and Jennifer Mugford Weiland;
                       Second edition: Linda Johnson, Jeff Price, and Brenda
                       Zaczek

Photography: George Nan

                       The authors wish to thank the following people for
                       their contributions to this book. At Van Nostrand
                       Reinhold, design editor Amanda Miller, production
                       editor Ron McClendon, and production manager Kurt
                       Andrews guided this book through the editorial and
                       production phases. Steve Samuel, Sean Sykes, and
                       Mike Carosi of The Graphics Gallery contributed
                       immeasurably to the typesetting process. Jerry Bates,
                       Margaret Bates, Tina Brubaker Chovanec, Diana
                       Lively, and Harriet Turner provided logistical support.
                       At Virginia Commonwealth University, John Demao
                       and Dr. Murry N. DePillars offered encouragement.